Trips and Trails, 1

Family Camps, Short Hikes and View Roads Around the North Cascades

Third Edition

Text: E. M. Sterling
Photographs: Bob and Ira Spring
Maps: Marge Mueller and Helen Sherman

THE MOUNTAINEERS
Seattle

The Mountaineers: Organized 1906 "...to explore, study, preserve and enjoy the natural beauty of the Northwest..."

Published by The Mountaineers, 306 2nd Avenue West
Seattle, Washington 98119

Published simultaneously in Canada by
Douglas & McIntyre Ltd., 1615 Venables Street
Vancouver, British Columbia V5L 2H1

Manufactured in the United States of America
Second edition, April 1978; second printing June 1980;
third printing October 1981; fourth printing October 1983
Third edition, December 1985

Copyedited by Sharon Bryan
Designed by Marge Mueller
Cover: Mount Baker from Artist Point, Mount Baker National Forest.

Library of Congress Cataloging in Publication Data

Sterling, E. M.
Trips and trails.

Includes bibliographical references.
Contents: v. 1. Family camps, short hikes, and view roads around the North Cascades — v. 2. Family camps, short hikes, and view roads in the Olympics, Mt. Rainier, and South Cascades.
1. Hiking — Washington (State) — Guide-books. 2. Camp sites, facilities, etc. — Washington (State) — Guide-books. 3. Family recreation — Washington (State) — Guide-books. 4. Washington (State) — Description and travel — 1981- — Guide-books. I. Spring, Bob, 1918- . II. Spring, Ira. III. Title.
GV199.42.W2S75 1983 917.97′5 83-2253
ISBN 0-89886-115-2 (vol. 1)
ISBN 0-89886-069-5 (vol. 2)

CONTENTS

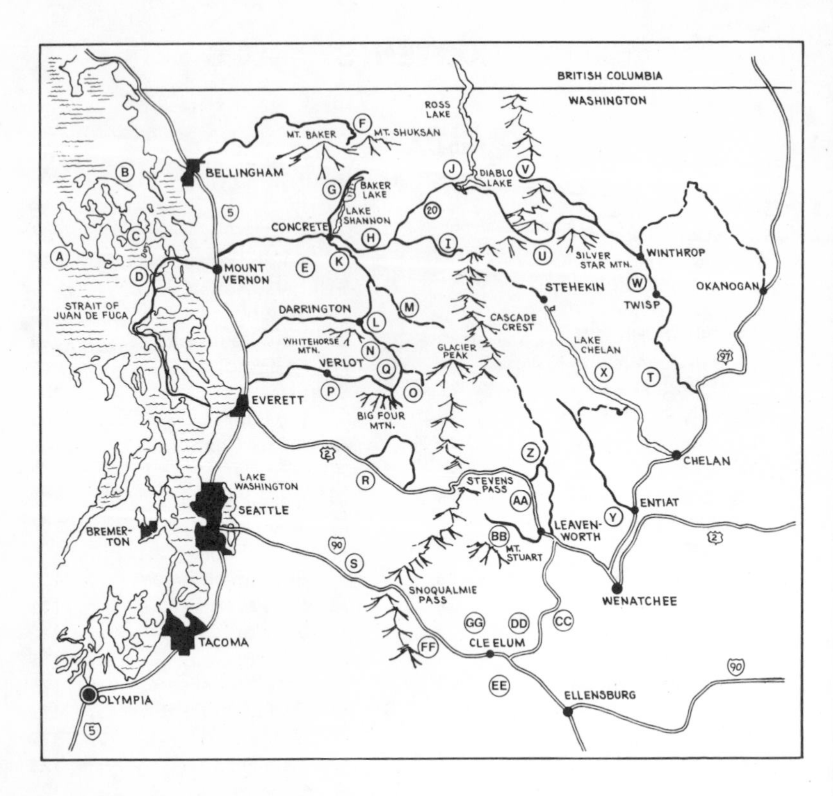
BRITISH COLUMBIA
WASHINGTON
ROSS LAKE
MT. BAKER
MT. SHUKSAN
BELLINGHAM
BAKER LAKE
DIABLO LAKE
LAKE SHANNON
CONCRETE
MOUNT VERNON
SILVER STAR MTN.
WINTHROP
STEHEKIN
TWISP
OKANOGAN
STRAIT OF JUAN DE FUCA
DARRINGTON
CASCADE CREST
WHITEHORSE MTN.
GLACIER PEAK
LAKE CHELAN
VERLOT
EVERETT
BIG FOUR MTN.
CHELAN
LAKE WASHINGTON
STEVENS PASS
ENTIAT
SEATTLE
BREMER-TON
LEAVEN-WORTH
MT. STUART
WENATCHEE
SNOQUALMIE PASS
TACOMA
CLE ELUM
OLYMPIA
ELLENSBURG

EXPLANATION OF SYMBOLS

Trails suitable for children up to 8. Easy and safe walking for all ages.

Difficult trails. Safe if walked sanely and knowledgeably. But no place for uncontrolled youngsters (of any age) or persons who tire easily. Hike only in lug-soled shoes.

Sunday-driver-type roads. Mostly paved or well-graded gravel. Roads that can be driven easily by the most nervous driver—young or old. Easy on new cars.

Rough roads. Often extremely dusty on hot days and slick after rains. But none are unsafe (see introduction), providing they are driven with constant care. On some, 10 miles an hour is speeding.

ROAD CHANGES: The U.S. Forest Service is in the process of changing the numbers on forest roads. Therefore, some of the numbers listed in this book may not be the same as those found on forest road signs.

Individual forests are publishing lists which show all of the changes, as they are made. Inquire at forest headquarters or district ranger offices.

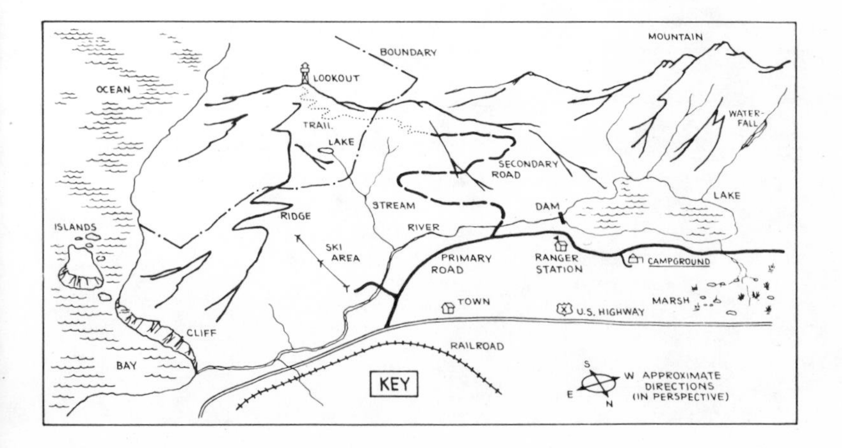

Mount Baker from Dock Butte

FOREWORD

Among the titles proposed for this book was **Lazy Camper's Guide to Mountain Recreation,** to suggest that one need not be a daring climber or steel-muscled backwoodsman to enjoy the North Cascades and San Juans. The idea was rejected because it conjured up the tourist who rarely gets out of the car and when he does keeps one hand on the door, and the camper who stakes out a homestead in a campground and for the whole weekend never leaves the quadrilateral bounded by trailer, or motorhome, picnic table, water faucet, and privy.

The implied emphasis in the title finally chosen is on trips and trails **from** campgrounds (though many can equally well be done in a day from the city). The book is designed to lead **away** from the camp and into the woods, along the trails, and beside the rivers and saltwater shores, and up from well-traveled main roads onto lonesome roads with views and walks and things to do. Campgrounds are described, and the author surveys the theory and practice of "light camping" (as opposed to the expensive, equipment-over-burdened, mechanized variety), but the theme of the book is that while camping is good fun, it's even more fun to go snooping around.

The country covered is for everyone. Lack of outdoor experience is no barrier. Fresh from the sidewalks of New York or the tall corn of Iowa, one can enjoy these trips and trails to mountains and beaches. Nor is age a barrier. Often one hears a mother or father with small children say, "We'd like to get out, and we will when the kids are older." In fact, the average child of 2 or 3 can manage several miles a day under his own power—more with an occasional piggyback ride—and have a grand time splashing in puddles, peering at beetles.

Looked at another way, this book is an introduction. References at the end of this volume lead the more experienced traveler deeper into valleys, higher on peaks, and farther along beaches. Beyond, for those who feel the call, lie mountain climbing, kayaking, bicycling, ski touring and snowshoeing, and what you will.

The Philosophy of Anti-City

Cities are necessary devices, but conveniences and pleasures fitting in a city may be nuisances or even crudities in the outback. Unfortunately, too many people fail to distinguish between city and non-city. Attracted to mountains and beaches precisely by the elemental simplicity, they insist on burdening themselves with luxuries and paraphernalia and gadgetry and noisemakers and impedimenta of the subdivision and freeway.

A refinement of taste is needed. People who like both city and back country should not carry the city into the wilds. Let them shed the noise, the clutter, and the hullabaloo as they would a sweater on a hot day. Let them—let us all!—approach the green of forest and meadow, the white of glacier and snowbank, and the blue of the Inland Sea unfettered by the pastimes and preoccupations of urban life.

Camper trucks and even trailers and motorhomes have their place. But people who seal themselves into portable subdivisions come evening or a sprinkle of rain miss the sound of the river, the brush of the wind, the smell of the trees. They may leave at home the telephone and TV, but the radio they have along, turned on loud to drown out the owls.

The motorcycle is no worse than the automobile, and in truth is not as bad by far—two wheels less, two tons less. Cities will be better off when more people move about with a minimum of metal and fossil-fuel consumption. Motorcycles are also excellent for back roads, including (in Washington State) thousands of miles of tracks impassable or uncomfortable for automobiles. Motorcycles should be encouraged on roads and rough tracks (as well as on city streets) as a partial solution to the automobile problem.

However, it is an article of faith here that machines are inappropriate and anti-social—and above all, in **bad taste**—on traditional foot trails. The National Park Service agrees and bans motorized vehicles absolutely from paths. The U.S. Forest Service by law must ban motorcycles from wilderness areas, but it complacently accepts them on most trails outside wilderness areas, and, indeed, rebuilds many to allow wheeled travel.

The philosophy of anti-city dictates that all traditional foot trails, everywhere, be closed to machinery of every kind. As the gasoline lantern pollutes night, the infernal combustion engine pollutes quiet.

North Cascades

The creation in 1968 of the North Cascades National Park, the Ross Lake and Lake Chelan National Recreation Areas, and the Pasayten Wilderness was an important Act by Congress to retain some of the nation's wild heritage in this corner of the country.

Another milestone occurred in 1984 with the passage of the Washington Wilderness Act, which created new wilderness areas and expanded a number of existing ones. In the North Cascades the act created the Henry M. Jackson Wilderness, the Mt. Baker Wilderness, the Boulder River Wilderness, and the Sawtooth Wilderness. The bill added lands to the Glacier Peak Wilderness. Despite this notable triumph, the job of wilderness preservation is not yet complete in the North Cascades. For example, although the High Ross Dam controversy was resolved in favor of the land (see Section J, 19), applications for so-called "low head" hydroelectric projects are on file for numerous streams in the region. One example is the dam proposed for Twin Falls State Park, along I-90 a few miles east of North Bend (see Section S, 20).

And then there's logging.

Despite what you may have heard about Washington's timber industry, the bulldozer and the chainsaw have continued to chew deeper and higher into the last old-growth forests. Most of the logging done under Forest Service auspices on public land is unquestioned by even the devoutest friend of trees. Some forests can reasonably be considered "surplus" to the recreation needs of this and the next generation. In some others, policies of minimum-sized, naturally shaped patch cuts, with buffers of old-growth trees left around camps and other recreational sites, provide some justification for the doctrine of "multiple-use." In many places, logging and recreation can live together—or at least the realities of political economics force a shotgun wedding. But for multiple use to be a reality rather than an empty slogan, logging operations must be so conducted that they do not, through negligence or ignorance, foreclose on subsequent recreational uses of the land. First, the Forest Service should refrain from opening new tracts of land to logging until cutting has been completed along already existing logging roads. Then, as soon as a cut is complete, the Forest Service should close the road and allow the land to return to its wild state.

Moreover, The Mountaineers disagree that wilderness and scenery must invariably come second to lumber, plywood, and pulp. Certain of the heartland valleys and gentler slopes have a value only the sacrilegious would measure in dollars. Preserving the relatively few stands of low-elevation old growth forest is especially important. Research conducted on old-growth forests here in the Northwest has demonstrated their importance as unique habitats for a variety of plants and animals. They also help maintain clear streams capable of supporting healthy fisheries and thirsty critters (including those of the two-legged persuasion). Old-growth forests also serve as irreplaceable reservoirs of genetic diversity,which we will allow to diminish only at our own great peril. The nation as a whole (which owns—as a whole—the public lands in and around the North Cascades) can easily afford to forego exploitation of the timber in these last remnants of the great lowland forest of the Pacific Northwest.

Campground Changes

Although recreational use on national forests has been increasing year after year, and is projected to keep on increasing into the future, the Mt. Baker-Snoqualmie National Forest has been cutting its campground services drastically.

In 1985 the Forest eliminated more than a third—35 percent—of its campsites and ceased operating more than half—56 percent—of its formal campgrounds. The number of maintained campgrounds dropped from 64 to 28 in the single year. And the total number of campsites was cut to 723 units from 1,118 units in 1984. (Oddly, other forests—the Wenatchee and Okanogan among them—have not instituted such reductions.)

Mt. Baker-Snoqualmie officials contend that all of the cuts were made necessary by reductions in the forest's budget. Yet the level of the campground and camp site reduction far exceeded cuts in the amount of money budgeted by the forest for the support of those programs. While the level of campground operations was cut in half, the amount budgeted for developed recreation, including campgrounds, dropped only about 8 percent, sliding from $711,000 in 1984 to $656,000 in 1985.

Further, while the amount budgeted for developed recreation, including campgrounds, was cut 8 percent from 1984 to 1985, the total agency budget remained about the same.

In addition, the Mt. Baker-Snoqualmie National Forest significantly changed its method of "managing" the campground system.

In some instances the Forest left camping areas, many of them riverside sites, open to public use after having removed not only tables and fire rings but also toilet facilities. These camps were "abandoned" to provide what agency officials call a "take-care-of-yourself" experience, but without addressing the environmental/pollution problems likely to be caused by such uncontrolled use.

In other instances, particularly in the extremely popular Verlot area, Forest managers gated many camps converting them to "rent-a-campground" sites which can be reserved by large groups for fees ranging from $15 to $50 a night. Individual families who may have camped at these small sites before must now either camp in the larger, busier, noisier fee camps, or seek out undesignated places in the forest without sanitation facilities thus, again, adding to forest environmental/pollution problems.

The amount of management responsibility that rests with local officials is not entirely clear. Spokesmen for the Forest say that budget constraints were placed on them by regional officials. Decisions on how budgets restraints were to be met, however, appear to have been made locally. People interested in commenting on Forest Service budgets may contact the Forest Supervisors' offices, the regional office in Portland, or their Congressman.

San Juan Islands

Until recently, this unique archipelago seemed outside the turbulent 20th-century continuum, permanently safe.

Today, Fidalgo Island, largely a "farm" of oil refinery tanks and stacks, is the destination of ever more and ever larger tankers full of oil, threading their way through the narrow passages of the San Juans—with the constant threat of even just one spill, a spill that can smother with oil the beaches, the inter-tidal starfish, anemones, and other tidal pool life, as well as the unsuspecting fish and waterbirds.

Guemes Island barely escaped instant industrialization, and other islands are coming under the gun for industrial development, real estate promotion, and other contributors to the Gross National Product.

Some land has been set aside by the state and federal governments for recreation and scenic protection. The Mountaineers take special pride in Moran State Park, established a half-century ago through the efforts of its members. More recent are the San Juan National Historical Park and the San Juan Wilderness, the latter encompassing "bird" rocks scattered offshore from the major islands. However, not enough of the San Juans have legal protection sufficient to guarantee perpetuation of their special charm, even if Cypress Island does make it as a State Natural Area Preserve.

About The Mountaineers

The Mountaineers, with groups based in Seattle, Everett, Tacoma, Bellingham, and Olympia, invite the membership of all lovers of outdoor life who sympathize with the purposes of the organization and wish to share in its activities.

The above brief and partial summary of Mountaineer concerns in the North Cascades and San Juans (in other areas are other concerns) suggests the importance of the club role in conservation education and action. If you share these concerns, your membership is particularly desired and needed.

Preservation, though, is only one side of the coin; the other is using and enjoying the back country.

The Mountaineers sponsor a year-round program of climbing, hiking, camping, ski-touring, and snowshoeing. Hundreds of outings are scheduled each year, ranging from single-day walks to trips lasting 2 weeks or more. On a typical weekend as many as 20 or 30 excursions may be offered, from ocean beaches to the summit of Mt. Rainier. In addition, members engage in countless privately-organized trips of all kinds; perhaps a major value in belonging to an outdoor organization (The Mountaineers or any other) is the opportunity to meet other people with similar interests, to make new friends.

For further information on club activities and how to join, write The Mountaineers, 300 Third Ave. West, Seattle, Washington 98119.

THE MOUNTAINEERS

Safety Considerations

The reason the Ten Essentials are advised is that hiking in the backcountry entails unavoidable risk that every hiker assumes and must be aware of and respect. The fact that a trail is described in this book is not a representation that it will be safe for you. Trails vary greatly in difficulty and in the degree of conditioning and agility one needs to enjoy them safely. On some hikes routes may have changed or conditions may have deteriorated since the descriptions were written. Also, trail conditions can change even from day to day, owing to weather and other factors. A trail that is safe on a dry day or for a highly conditioned, agile, properly equipped hiker may be completely unsafe for someone else or unsafe under adverse weather conditions.

You can minimize your risks on the trail by being knowledgeable, prepared and alert. There is not space in this book for a general treatise on safety in the mountains, but there are a number of good books and public courses on the subject and you should take advantage of them to increase your knowledge. Just as important, you should always be aware of your own limitations and of conditions existing when and where you are hiking. If conditions are dangerous, or if you are not prepared to deal with them safely, choose a different hike! It's better to have a wasted drive than to be the subject of a mountain rescue.

These warnings are not intended to scare you off the trails. Hundreds of thousands of people have safe and enjoyable hikes every year. However, one element of the beauty, freedom and excitement of the wilderness is the presence of risks that do not confront us at home. When you hike you assume those risks. They can be met safely, but only if you exercise your own independent judgment and common sense.

INTRODUCTION

If the following pages have any single message, it's this: camping has very little to do with campgrounds. Not that campgrounds aren't important. They are. Camping starts there and campgrounds in every mountain, park, and seashore area are described here. But the essence of camping lies completely outside the campground and has nothing to do with erecting tents, washing dishes, chopping wood, or lugging water from creeks.

Fun is the keynote of camping. And it's to be found along trails and logging roads in flowers, stars, waterfalls, vistas, seashells, and beautiful rocks. It's in the thrill of seeing, touching, and hearing the surprises of nature.

We make no pretense of having listed everything of interest or beauty near campgrounds in the areas covered here. It would be impossible to do so. Every trail and logging road holds some secret. We offer, rather, an introduction—a sampling of what's to be found.

We hope, simply, that readers who have not camped before may find reason here to start, that those who have camped but confined their camping to campgrounds will be encouraged to explore around them, and that longtime campers who have already savored the secrets of the area's wildness will find a few flavors still missed.

Many of the pleasures here must be walked for. A few lie at the edge of a car door. But the majority can be enjoyed only on trails that wind along rivers, through deep forests, and across high, alpine meadows.

Almost all of the hikes are confined to 2 miles or less, one way, and at 2 miles an hour—an average rate for mountain travel—should be completed in 2 to 3 hours. Add time, of course, to enjoy what is hiked in to see. Readers new to wildland walking should allow even more time. It's always better to have an extra hour left than to force a family into a grinding effort to keep ahead of a clock.

All the trails described should normally be easy to find and stay on. Most are clearly marked and signed. Rock cairns and blazes must be followed on only a few. No goal here demands cross-country hiking. Novices, however, should turn back any time they feel the route is unsafe or obscure.

Footwear is important, but most families need not buy any new equipment for most of the hiking trips listed here. Sturdy shoes make walking more enjoyable. Forest trails are often a constant repetition of mud, roots, and rocks, interlaced with patches of snow, creeks without bridges, windfalls, and rain-sopped brush. (And that's the way they should be. Sidewalks belong in cities.) Tennis shoes, however, will suffice for test trips, if nothing better is available. But once a family has decided on hiking as a camping way-of-life, hiking boots with rubber-lug soles purchased from a mountaineering equipment store are a wise investment. Often such shoes, particularly for children, can be purchased used.

Hikers should always carry what The Mountaineers consider the "Ten Essentials"—sunglasses, knife, matches, firestarter, first aid kit, flashlight, compass, a map, extra clothing (particularly if you start out in shorts and T-shirt and head for high altitudes), and extra food—all carried in a rucksack "just in case."

Some of the short trails offer opportunities for "test" backpacks. Families can shake down equipment and practice the required packing discipline without risking the cost of failure on a longer trip.

Trails listed in books like these have a tendency to come and go at the whim of whatever agency manages the land. The Forest Service, for instance, which manages most of the areas listed here, seems to have few qualms about logging over long-established paths.

Loggers, you may be told, are the ones to blame for not replacing trails destroyed in logging. But remember, it is the Forest Service that is responsible for making certain that the loggers do the work—and do it correctly.

We note some of the places where trails have been destroyed. But if you come across such a place, don't stand mute in your anger and disappointment. Write the district ranger if you like. Better yet, write to your congressman or senator. Congress has never been able to change much. But it does control the dollars and change may occur most quickly if Congress attacks an agency's source of dollars.

Logging roads are exactly what the name implies: roads designed, built, and used for logging operation. They are often rough, steep, muddy, narrow, and dusty. Many switchback endlessly. Some seem penciled on cliffs. Occasionally one may be blocked by snow, slides, or fallen trees. (And this, too, is the way it should be. Highways also are for cities.) But most can be driven safely, with care and caution, albeit in low gear, by a passenger car. Providing, of course, drivers realize they may be forced to turn back by conditions no one can control.

You should always drive roads identified in the text as hazardous with extra care, staying alert for any danger that might suddenly appear in front of you.

A blocked road, however, need not ruin a trip. You can always park and walk. A short hike often can salvage a tremendous view that would otherwise be missed.

High-altitude roads may remain closed by snow until late summer. When planning high trips through early July, you should telephone ranger stations in advance for a road report.

Campsites here range from those in highly developed—and over-crowded—campgrounds on main thoroughfares to primitive, undeveloped, and uncrowded spots along remote logging roads.

In 1985, campgrounds in some forests were being abandoned because the Forest Service said it didn't have enough money to maintain them. Usually the campground equipment—tables and stoves—was left in place, but pit toilets were sometimes removed. Here too it may pay to complain to rangers or your congressman. In many cases it's not a true lack of money—there's often lots to spend on new logging highways—but a failure (unwillingness?) to budget any of it for recreation purposes. And remember that it's your tax money that's being spent, and nobody else's.

All formal campgrounds offer the camping basics of a parking space, tables, firepits, toilet facilities, and water from a well, creek, or lake. Fee camps provide piped water and restrooms, as extras. The fee, however, also buys crowds.

In the National Forests—and in National Forests **only**—one may pitch camp anyplace. The practice is starting to cause concern as the number of people and sanitation problems grow. But it's still allowed providing the camper carries ax, shovel, and bucket for fire control.

Firewood is provided in some National Forest camps. Otherwise it must be rustled alongside mountain roads—away from camp. More sensibly, use a gas stove.

Again: A warning! You may find some of the National Forest Service campgrounds listed here closed as the result of agency budget-cutting efforts. You may even find that a few of the campgrounds have been "eliminated". However, you can still camp at abandoned, ungated sites, under present agency rules, even though tables, fire rings, and even pit toilets may have been removed.

Equipment

A weekend camping trip takes very little equipment. A few pots and pans, a stove, sleeping bags, and a shelter of some sort will more than get the job done. Many novices, however, so overwhelm themselves with elaborate tents, chairs, lanterns, cushions, cots, mattresses, tables, ice chests, jugs, heaters, and even sinks they spend most of their time doing nothing but loading and unloading gear.

A new camper should buy nothing until he is certain he needs it—and probably not then. Avoid mistakes by borrowing or renting to start, buying only after you've either tried out equipment or seen others use it under campground conditions.

There are no secrets to acquiring good equipment. Deal with a reputable store—preferably one dealing in mountaineering equipment. Buy standard brands at standard prices, avoiding big promotions and "sales" unless you **know** the gear is good. When in doubt, talk to other campers.

Sleeping bags filled with 3 to 4 pounds of synthetic fiber seem most popular at present. Durability of the outer covering appears to pose the biggest choice factor. Down-filled bags are favored by many, but unless a family expects to do extensive backpacking the lighter weight is seldom worth the much higher price.

Mattresses range from lightweight plastic- or rubber-foam pads to conventional air mattresses. The pads range in thickness from an inch or less to 4 to 6 inches, with the thinner ones favored by all except comfort-demanding car campers. Fabric air mattresses are more durable than the purely plastic ones.

A **camp stove** has become virtually indispensable as the supply of firewood in and around campgrounds diminishes. Never base meal plans on a campfire alone. The two-burner pump-type stoves are popular. But the compact backpacker-types offered at mountaineer, alpine, and recreational equipment stores are much preferred by many.

The **tent** is the most expensive item in a camping outfit and perhaps the least essential. Actually, all the average camper does there is sleep. Many campers find plastic tarps sufficient protection and use nothing else. Most campers, however, eventually end up with a tent for the sake of privacy in crowded areas, and as protection from wind in higher camps.

Tents come in all shapes and sizes. Again, buy what you want from a reputable equipment store after considering such matters as ease in setting it up, size, stability in the wind, weight, bulk, and, of course, price.

Other equipment such as tarps, lanterns, ice chests, gas and water cans, ovens, chairs, axes and saws, etc., should be purchased only after the need arises—if then. All campers carry some extras. But the competency of the camper and the amount of time spent away from equipment enjoying "camping" invariably can be measured by how few extras there are.

Pots, Pans, and Menus

Cooks face the most difficult equipment-paring job of all. City-type cooking takes all sorts of equipment, as any household kitchen proves. Obviously, it can't all be hauled to camp. Picking the right items can certainly be difficult. But the cook who wants to partake in the pleasures of camping—and cooking and dishwashing do not qualify—will get the job done. Experienced camping cooks have done it. A novice will find a way.

First of all, families have no right to expect fancy meals in the woods—even if they may get them. Whims of the city should be left there. Finicky children should be ignored. The desires of the cook come first. And no family should go camping just to eat, anyway.

Simple menus, preplanned and packaged, can reduce cookery and equipment to a minimum. Many cooks serve the same camp meals trip in and trip out—and on paper plates too. After all, weekend camping involves only 4 meals out of the week's total of 21. The family can complain while it's home.

Select pots and pans to fit menu needs, leaving home those not needed. Camping cooks generally prefer a separate set of utensils, primarily because it's impossible to keep camping pots scoured to kitchen standards. Cooking kits are popular, but many campers use home discards and let it go at that.

Cooking aids and staple stocks should also be chosen carefully and pared relentlessly. Brass scouring pads, cheesecloth dish towels (they dry rapidly), firestarters, mitten potholders, can openers, a jackknife, tongs, and a couple of spoons are included in most cooking sets. Food staples should be transferred to plastic containers to save space and provide some control over items carried. Cardboard boxes get wet and glass breaks.

Clothing

Weekend trips demand very few clothes. In most instances, the ones worn from home will do. Except for rain gear, swim suits, and sweaters for chill evenings, many families carry just one set of extra clothing hoping that only one child falls in the creek.

Exceptions, of course, must be made for those who suffer from the cold and who should be permitted to take all sorts of warm extras for the privilege of having them along in the first place.

There are no camping style standards—yet. Comfort's the only rule.

Packing

A firm plan for packing and loading equipment can save time and soothe nerves on any camping trip. Each piece of equipment should be stored in the same container in the same place and loaded into the same spot in the car on each trip.

Campers use every type of container from wicker baskets through packboards to cardboard boxes (not preferred). Checklists help.

Courtesy

There was a time when people could do as they wanted in the campgrounds and on the mountain trails of the Pacific Northwest. But not anymore. There are too many people now. Each person must bend a little to the needs of those around him. Courtesy is no longer a nicety. It's imperative.

Radios. Music is lovely and news is interesting but served secondhand in a crowded campground both are a plague. If radio owners have a universal failing beside their choice of music (I like mine, but hate yours) it's their complete indifference to how far their sound penetrates a campground at night. No radio should be played after 10 p.m., a traditional camp bedtime. And the sound at other hours should not exude beyond the radio owner's own campsite.

Lanterns. Light your own world but not that of others in the campground. Remember, the lantern that hisses and glares over your camp table also glares and hisses through the walls of **every** nearby tent. Lanterns are completely unnecessary on long, late summer evenings. But if you feel you must use one, shield its glare.

Trail bikes. Trail bikes have a place...somewhere. But it most certainly is **not** in a campground. And campers should have no qualms about seeking their ouster whenever they appear. Bikes are banned by regulation in **all** campgrounds. But it's up to campers to see the rules are enforced. Therefore, anytime—ANYTIME—they appear, report them promptly to rangers. Rangers can't control them without your help. They will welcome your complaint.

Garbage. Not too long ago, campers and hikers were advised to bury or burn their garbage. Some publications still advise it. But don't. Garbage nowadays either should be put in a garbage can or else lugged home and disposed of there. Even in remote trail areas, campers must not drop, hide, bury, or burn their trash. **Haul all trash back.**

Trees. If firewood is not supplied in a campground, do **not** chop your own. Many campgrounds look as if they had undergone an artillery barrage, with every tree and shrub splintered and mangled by hatchets and saws. If you must have firewood, seek it amid the windfallen limbs and snags of logging roads. Some campers haul dry wood from home.

Vandals. There is little use in urging campers to refrain from destroying campground facilities and equipment. Those who perform such acts are beyond urging. Report any vandalism you witness to authorities. Let them impose whatever punishment the law affords.

Fire. Every year rangers battle blazes caused by campers who simply fail to think. In formal campgrounds, confine fire to established firepits. In primitive areas, douse all fires until the coals **feel** cool, and carry a shovel, ax, and bucket at all times.

E. M. STERLING

ACKNOWLEDGMENTS

Anyone who compiles a book like this must first be grateful for the overwhelming beneficence of Washington State's vast outdoors. Material here needed only to be found; its creation was already complete.

But one still owes huge obligations to people. The book could never have been completed without the encouragement and continual assistance of our families. Gratitude must also be extended to the officials of the national parks, national forests, and state parks with special appreciation to rangers and members of their staffs. All contributed generously of their time and knowledge.

And finally, thanks must be extended again to those at The Mountaineers who have been so gracious with their help, encouragement, and suggestions. Particular appreciation must be extended to Helen Sherman for her revisions of the maps and to Todd Sterling for his assistance in reviewing many of the trails.

Nor do we limit our thanks only to these. Every person who ever roamed the mountains and beaches of the state in search of recreation also had a hand. For it is because of them that many of the wild spectacles of our area still exist today. As it will have been because of all of you—our readers—if they exist tomorrow.

E. M. STERLING
BOB AND IRA SPRING

Ferry in Wasp Passage

A SAN JUAN ISLAND

Inland forest trails, shoreline strolls, spectacular panoramas, and a bit of history—all within public lands on largely private islands.

Open all year.

Take the Washington State ferry to San Juan Island. All tickets are round trip. On your return trip to Anacortes, you can, if you like, get off the ferry at Orcas (see B) or Lopez islands and get back on another eastbound ferry at no extra charge. You cannot make intermediate stops on westbound runs.

By auto, bike, or afoot.

Remembering always that in summer, late auto arrivals—coming or going—may be left ashore. Bicyclists and walkers face no such problem.

1 SAN JUAN ISLAND NATIONAL HISTORICAL PARK

History was the original reason for these parks on the shores of San Juan Island. But the best reasons for visiting them now are their scenery, wildlife, and rich meadows and seashores.

The parks were established, primarily through the efforts of the late Senator Henry M. Jackson, as a memorial to the peaceful solution of a war-threatening border dispute between the U.S. and Britain which arose out of the shooting of a pig.

In June of 1859, an American settler on the island shot an Englishman's pig because it was rooting in his garden. When Canadian authorities tried to arrest the American (the national border then wasn't all that clear), the U.S. military responded with a 66-man army. The British, in return, called up their fleet.

For the next 12 years the British stood ready at their fort on the north end of the island and the U.S. waited in its fort on the south end while a German kaiser settled the argument by establishing what's still the border between the U.S. and Canada through the Haro Strait.

Don't think for a moment, though, that these squabbles were the first signs of human activity here. Archaeologists, digging in middens in the old camps, have found evidence that Indians lived on the shores of the island 1,500 years ago.

ENGLISH CAMP

Pleasant and easy forested trails here wind along the shore to secret coves or climb to a "mountain" view at 650 feet.

Drive northwesterly from Friday Harbor on the Roche Harbor Road, turning south at the "T" fork. Watch for signs.

From a paved parking area, cross the meadows in the fort complex with its blockhouse, barracks, hospital, commissary, and farmhouse and follow a beach trail .5 mile through madrona and Douglas fir forest to a pleasant picnic and rest spot at Bell Point. Lots of seabirds in season.

For a vista that stretches to Mount Baker and over all of the San Juan islands, take a

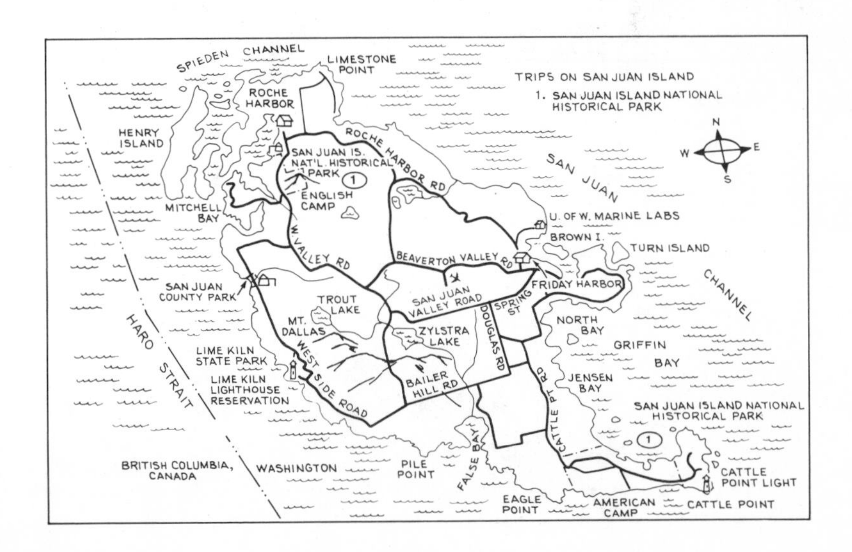

trail uphill from the fort complex, through forest, across the highway, and on to the English cemetery. Follow the path to the top of Young Hill for the first and only open vista. A mile walk.

AMERICAN CAMP

A rare gem of coastline this, on the most southeasterly point of the island where Cattle Point juts out into San Juan Channel between the Strait of Juan de Fuca and Griffin Bay.

Hike miles of open beach, stroll through forests, and, on state land, explore the rocky home of the Cattle Point lighthouse.

From Friday Harbor drive out of town on Spring Street following signs to American Camp.

To wander **the beach strip** both east and west, drive about 1.5 miles east of the American Camp park headquarters to a junction. Turn south here, on Pickett's Lane, to a parking area near the beach. Driftwood here. Rocky headlands. Birds, seals, sometimes whales. And a grassy shore slope constantly swept by hawks and eagles, with paths beckoning everywhere.

The public beach extends west to Eagle Cove and east to the Cattle Point lighthouse. Explore all 4 miles.

To walk **through forest** to secretive Jakle's Lagoon, turn north off the main park road at the beach road junction (see above). Park at the end of the road in a few hundred yards.

Follow old moss- and needle-covered logging paths (no crested rock and gravel roads here!) generally downhill, bearing left, to the lagoon with its gravel bars, driftwood, and bird-filled pools. No signs. Or, just wander across the meadow down to any of the other small beaches of your choice.

To visit **the lighthouse,** drive first to the Cattle Point park of the State Department of Natural Resources, and then return up the road, a short quarter-mile, beyond a woods to a gated, overgrown path on the water side of the road. Tidepools. Vistas. Small dunes. Lots of birds. And rabbits, of course. The lighthouse in less than .25 mile.

LIME KILN LIGHTHOUSE

A short walk through a madrona grove leads to a lighthouse that still marks the channel up Haro Strait.

Drive south from San Juan County Park (see below), turning right in about 2 miles in the middle of a sharp switchback to a gated parking lot at state park property.

Make your way to unmarked, overgrown roads generally downhill toward the water and the lighthouse. A few hundred yards. Or hike straight ahead on the abandoned road through more madronas to the park boundary and a view of the abandoned lime kiln (private property).

CAMPGROUND

San Juan County Park—16 sites on a grassy bluff above Haro Strait. Open year round. Restroom. Boat launch. Fee.

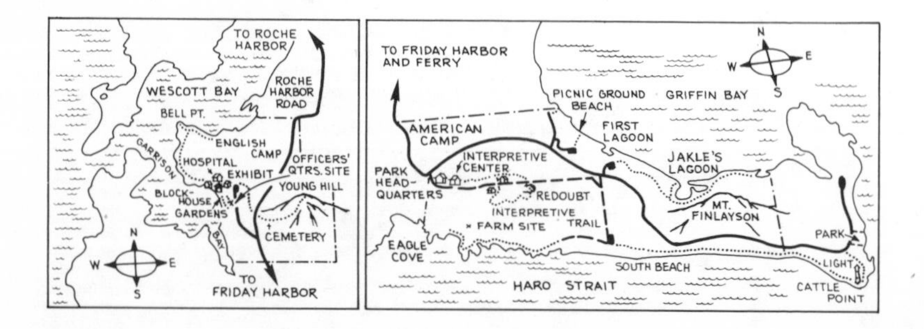

Picnic area at Cascade Lake, Moran State Park

B MORAN STATE PARK

Sweeping marine views and freshwater lakes on Orcas Island in the middle of the spectacular San Juans. But, oddly, no saltwater facilities at all.

Take a Washington State ferry from Anacortes to Orcas Island. (If you also wish to visit San Juan Island, see section A for additional ferry information.) The park is open all year round. Busiest on weekends but seldom crowded except on holidays. Most campers stay several days because of the ferry costs.

Park offerings include four mountain lakes, viewpoints atop Mount Constitution (2,409) and from the Little Summit Lookout (2,039)—both reached by road—miles of pleasant forest trails, waterfalls, and deer around almost every corner. (No poisonous snakes and no bears.) Supervised swimming on Cascade Lake.

B MORAN STATE PARK

MOUNT CONSTITUTION

Views to almost everywhere from the highest point in one of the most scenic island areas in the world.

Climb to the top of the fortlike tower or simply stand on ground-level viewpoints to see a vista that sweeps from Vancouver Island to Garibaldi in British Columbia, past Baker to Rainier and over all of the islands in the San Juan group to the Olympics, Victoria, and beyond.

Road closed at dusk each evening near Mountain Lake and sometimes during the day in winter if snow is reported on the road near the summit. (No notice of road closures is posted. You won't know about it until you reach a gate.)

CAMPGROUNDS

North End—50 sites above the road on a wooded slope. Beach area and recreation center across the road on Cascade Lake. A pleasant shaded area. Restroom. Piped water. State fee.

Midway—57 sites on both sides of the road beyond the recreation center area. About 17 sites near the lake. Some on the lake. Others on wooded loops above the road. Two restrooms. Piped water. Fee.

South End—17 sites in an open wooded area near the water on the south end of Cascade Lake. The oldest site on the lake and one of the most popular. Generally full. Restroom. Piped water. Cooking shelter. Fee.

Mountain Lake—18 sites on a small peninsula on Mountain Lake. Primarily used by fishermen, but a quiet camp away from highway noise. No swimming in the reservoir lake. Restroom and pit toilets. Piped water. Fee.

Cold Springs—A picnic spot in an isolated timber area. Capped spring in a rustic pavilion. Pit toilets. Spring water. Cooking shelter.

Note: Campgrounds are often full during peak summer periods. If "campground full" warnings are posted at the Anacortes ferry terminal, campers are urged to turn back. Some campers on some weekends have had to return home because no spaces were available.

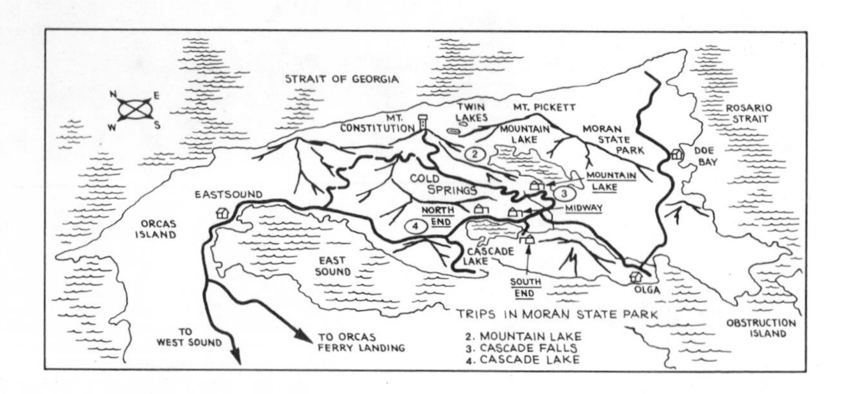

Sunrise from Mount Constitution

2 MOUNTAIN LAKE

MOUNTAIN LAKE TRAIL

Hike from the top of Mount Constitution through forest, along a rocky ledge, and past Twin Lakes to the Mountain Lake Campground, 3.6 miles.

The trail drops sharply off the far side of the turnaround loop below the tower area along ledges of lichen- and moss-covered rock with occasional views. At the first trail junction, 1.1 miles, keep right.

At the second junction, keep right and downhill again.

From Twin Lakes (see Twin Lakes Trail) continue downhill another 2.1 miles to Mountain Lake Campground.

LITTLE SUMMIT LOOKOUT TRAIL

From viewpoint to viewpoint with even more views in between.

Hike 2.2 miles from the tower area on Mount Constitution down to Little Summit Lookout (2,039). Find trail along the left side of the TV transmitter building, dropping at the start through timber, to a series of view ledges. Timber along the trail has been attacked by blister rust.

You can, of course, drive to the lookout. Turn off the road to Mount Constitution at a signed spur.

Junction in 1 mile with Cold Springs trail. Keep left. A few more views in the last .5 mile. Watch for trail marker in the last .2 mile, making sure to turn uphill, to the right, at a junction with a trail that leads sharply downhill.

Trail ends near the road. Turn back uphill to the 40-foot lookout tower. Views, however, only from the ground. The tower, owned by the Department of Natural Resources, is usually closed.

TWIN LAKES TRAIL

An easy trail wanders along Mountain Lake and then up a cool, shallow valley to two much smaller mountain lakes, 2.1 miles.

Hike north out of the Mountain Lake Campground about 1.3 miles, turning away from the lake at the junction beyond the second creek. Trail follows a small stream through alder brakes in an old homestead area—watch for signs of tumbledown cabins—to a second junction only a few yards from the first lake.

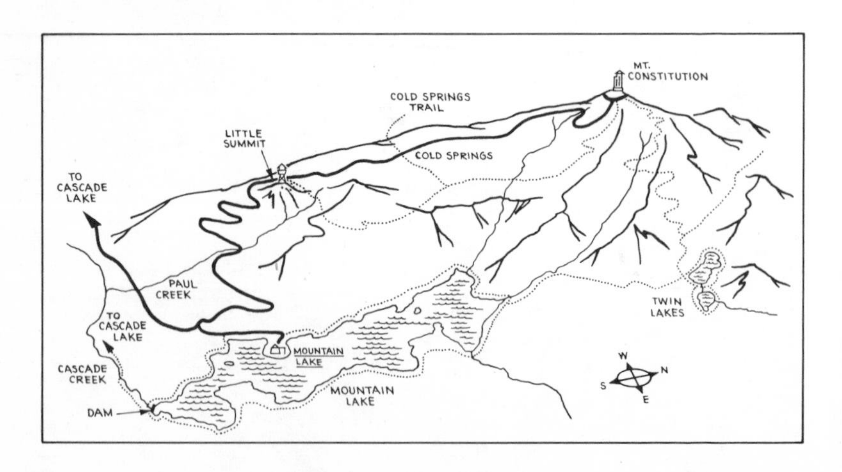

Mountain Lake and Rosario Strait from Mount Constitution

Cascade Falls

AROUND-THE-LAKE TRAIL

A pleasant water-grade trail all the way around Mountain Lake. About 4 miles, round-trip.

For a clockwise hike, take the trail north out of the Mountain Lake Campground, keeping right at the junction with the Twin Lakes trail. Trail drops below a dam to a footbridge at the south end of the lake. Turn right beyond the bridge to return to camp.

3 CASCADE FALLS

MOUNTAIN LAKE TO CASCADE LAKE

Hike along Cascade Creek past Rustic and Cascade waterfalls to Cascade Lake. 2.7 miles.

Take the Cascade Lake trail south out of Mountain Lake Campground, continuing downstream beyond the dam. Watch for sections of old wooden flume used in the original water system near the trail.

Waterfalls in the last half of the trail. Watch for signs. When the trail crosses the highway, head up the road to the right to find trail on the other side.

Last stretch follows an aluminum flume built to stabilize the level of Cascade Lake. To avoid a useless climb over a ridge in back of the South End Campground, watch for view of the lake down a draw below the flume sections, picking up a way-trail down an old road to camp.

CASCADE FALLS

A wispy 100-foot skein of water in a cool green canyon, .25 mile by trail.

Watch for sign off the main park road about 1 mile beyond the recreation center. Trail drops gradually to a marked overlook.

For a much smaller waterfall, take a trail upriver to the left. Rustic Falls in less than .25 mile.

4 CASCADE LAKE

SOUTH END TRAIL

An easy, pleasant walk along Cascade Lake from the South End Campground to the recreation center with a wooden bridge, flowers, and modest views along the way.

Find the trail at the far end of the South End Campground near the lake shore. Leaving the camp, it wends across a rocky slope above the lake, dropping through an alder grove to a bridge across the inlet to the smaller, southern section of the lake. Keep to the

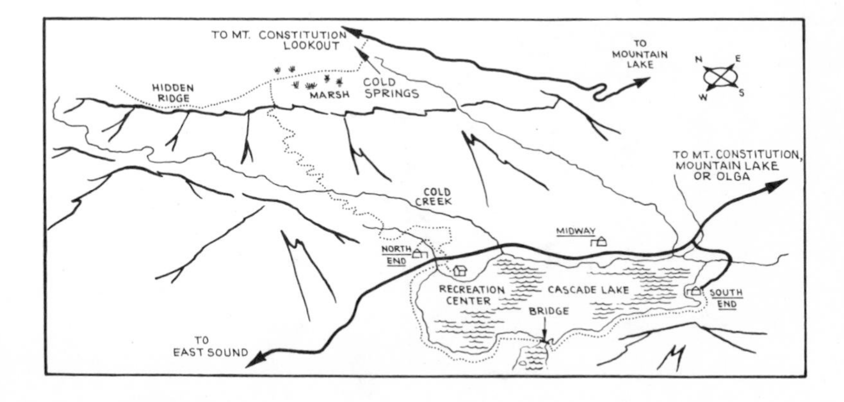

Picnic area at Cascade Lake

right on trails that climb along a rocky bluff. Sedum and tiger lilies in season.

At the upper end of the lake the trail drops across a muddy area near the shore, crossing in front of the park ranger's house to the picnic and recreation center.

COLD SPRINGS TRAIL

Another drive-up and walk-back trail. This one from Cold Springs picnic area down a series of switchbacks with occasional views to the recreation center at Cascade Lake.

Take the trail out of Cold Springs picnic area through a wet but open creek bottom, turning downhill in about .3 mile at junction with a trail that leads around the mountain to Twin Lakes and the Mount Constitution tower.

About 2 miles to the lake.

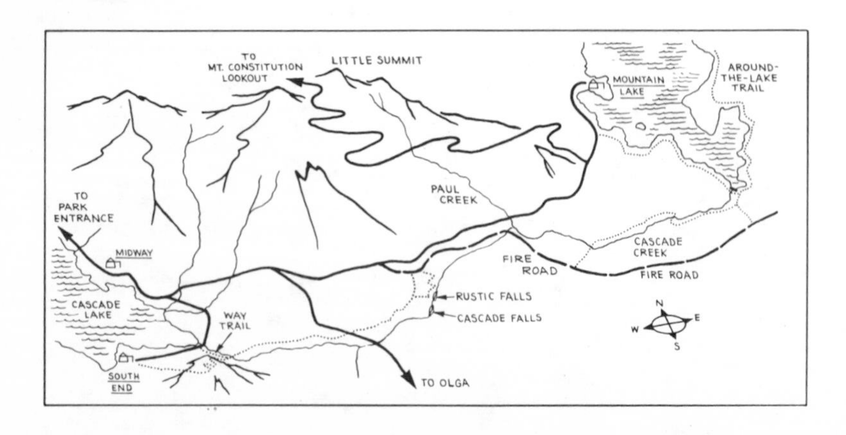

Deception Pass Bridge from Pass Island

C DECEPTION PASS STATE PARK

Salt water, fresh water, forests, and beaches—all overshadowed by a rushing tidal river beneath a spectacular bridge.

On both sides of Deception Pass between Fidalgo and Whidbey islands, 18 miles from Mount Vernon. Or take the ferry from Mukilteo and drive up Whidbey Island from the south.

One of the most popular parks in the state. Over 2.5 million visitors a year. And no wonder! Two freshwater lakes, forest trails to beaches and scenic overlooks, tidepools full of sea life, a marsh with a wildlife of its own, and the tidal river that changes directions about every 6 hours.

The park is busy most summer weekends and packed on holidays. Some parts of it are open all year round.

Supervised swimming, playground facilities, and tidepool displays add to the attraction. And no motors are allowed on the lakes. Ideal for canoes.

One warning: jet fighters from the nearby naval air installation often splinter any chances of peace here. If you camp you may find the noise—particularly at night—

unbearable, even in the presence of so much beauty. Planes swooping down over the park to land sound as if they're going to fly right through your tent.

CAMPGROUNDS

Bowman Bay—24 sites on Bowman Bay north of the pass. A wooded area overlooking the bay. The campground is often crowded and heavily used by trailers. All too little separation between units. Restrooms. Piped water. Playground equipment. Open summer only. State fee.

Cranberry Lake—Picnic sites in an open parklike area on the east end of Cranberry Lake. Restroom. Piped water. Playground. Dock. Boat rental concession. State fee.

Forest Camp—230 sites. No special trailer sites. On wooded loops in pleasant forest area north of Cranberry Lake. All sites except those at the older east end are well separated. Sites at west end are closest to the beach and lake. Restrooms. Piped water. Some sites open all year. State fee.

5 BOWMAN BAY

ROSARIO TRAIL

Hike along a bluff above Bowman Bay to sweeping views from Rosario Head.

Find trail off the northwest corner of Bowman Bay Campground. Trail winds along the side of the steep bank above the bay ending near the boat dock on the west side of Rosario Head.

Climb onto grass alpinelike meadows above Rosario Bay for best views in all directions—from the bridge to the San Juans.

SEA LIFE

Tidepools and clams.

For best natural pools and low tide, drive to the Rosario Bay picnic area on the north side of the bridge. Divers prowl the rock pools around Rosario Head. Starfish and sea urchins at the lowest tides.

Look but don't take. If every one of the 2.5 million who visit this park every year took just one small creature home, there soon would be none left for anyone to see.

For clams—fewer and fewer each year—drive to Hoypus Point beyond the Cornet Bay boat-launching area. Park land extends south and west of the point. Butter clams on minus tides. Check for red tide first.

LIGHTHOUSE POINT

Camus flowers in May against green slopes and the dark blue of the sound on a trail that leads across a series of open bluffs to an unmanned Coast Guard light, a series of

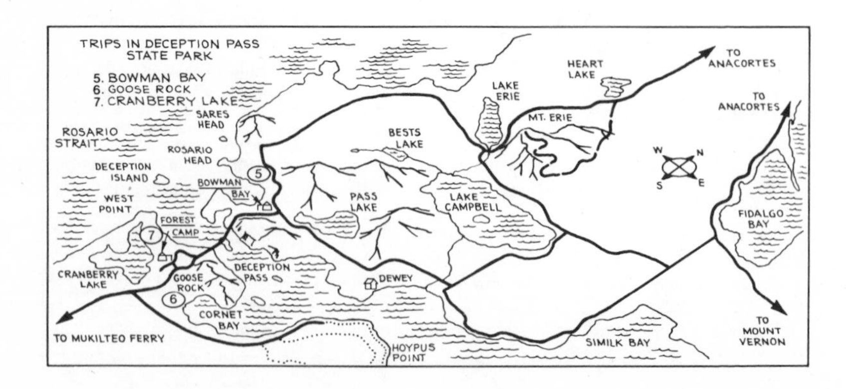

Tidal pool

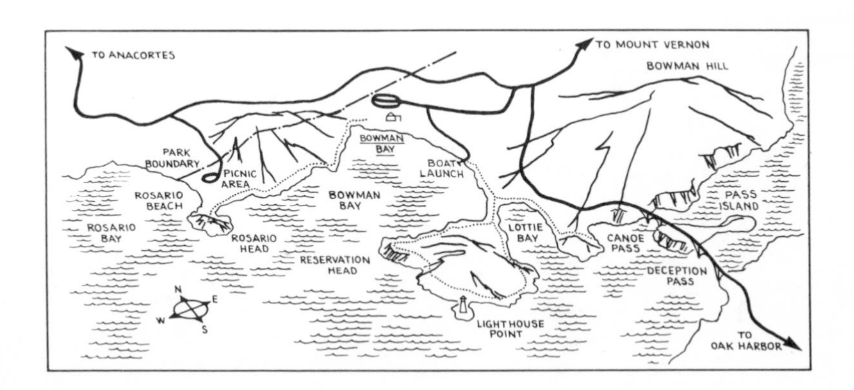
TO ANACORTES
TO MOUNT VERNON
BOWMAN HILL
PARK BOUNDARY
PICNIC AREA
BOWMAN BAY
BOAT LAUNCH
ROSARIO BEACH
BOWMAN BAY
PASS ISLAND
ROSARIO BAY
ROSARIO HEAD
LOTTIE BAY
CANOE PASS
RESERVATION HEAD
DECEPTION PASS
N
E
W
S
LIGHTHOUSE POINT
TO OAK HARBOR

rock coves, and high views of Bowman Bay.

Follow the trail along the bay south of the boat launch, taking a fork to the right (west) beyond the first headland. Or walk around the headland at low tide to a flat spit of land between Bowman and Lottie bays.

Trail continues west along the pass with small sand coves, rest spots, and viewpoints sprinkled along the way. Don't be tempted to climb on the automated Coast Guard light at the far end of the peninsula. It can be dangerous, and you can see as much from the trail.

To return, follow way-trails along the north side of the peninsula. Spurs lead out on headland rocks. Look for a small arch carved by tidal action in one.

Best views of Bowman Bay and the campground from the highest point on the peninsula in the northeast corner.

CANOE PASS

Look up at the high Deception Pass bridge from a small cove almost beneath the structure.

Find a trail south, along the shore of Bowman Bay beyond the boat launch ramp, toward a saddle to Lottie Bay.

Take a fork to the left at the saddle hiking to an overlook point and then down to a cove with its view up at the bridge.

6 GOOSE ROCK

Look down on most of the park. Cornet and Skagit bays, east to the Cascades, and west to the Olympics from flower-covered rocky slopes east of the bridge.

Find the trail at the south end of the bridge, heading east. Trail leaves either side of the highway. Follow the broad trail above the pass, taking almost any spur trail uphill, following unmarked paths to the highest point.

To return, follow the ridge crest east, taking a broad trail downhill.

Continue on the trail near the water and walk all the way around to Cornet Bay and around the park's group camp. Occasional spur trails lead down to rocky ledges close to the water.

PASS ISLAND

Paths lead from small parking area on the east side of the road to an historic marker and open grass meadows.

A plaque erected by the Daughters of the American Revolution tells how Vancouver discovered Deception Pass on June 10, 1792, thinking at first he had found a river.

Paths lead down the slopes of the island to pleasant resting places above the swift water of the pass.

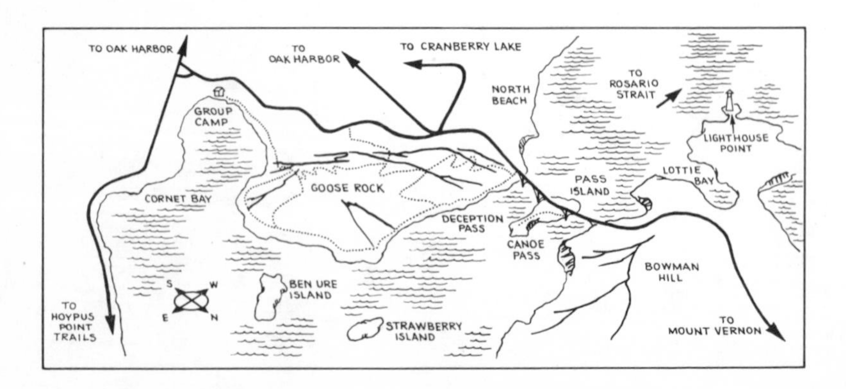

Air view of Deception Pass and Cranberry Lake

HOYPUS POINT

Forest and beach walks here in what may be the least used corner of the park.

From the main park entrance, drive south on the state highway, turning left (east) onto the Cornet Bay Road, continuing past the group camp and marina and on to the end of the road on the east side of the bay.

Stop at any of several roads or trailheads and wander as long and as far as you like. Peaceful surprises where you find them. Lush, open Douglas fir forest carpeted with sword fern.

At the end of the road, stroll the gravel beach at low tide. Hoypus Point in .25 mile. A sliding shoreline tilts old trees, some festooned with licorice ferns, in grand arches over the beach. Views here toward the inland islands of Skagit and Similk bays.

7 CRANBERRY LAKE

Marshes and beaver houses in addition to swimming and fishing.

Canoe into the marshy area on the south side of the lake to search for beaver houses hidden in the high weeds. Beaver, muskrat, and mink inhabit the marsh.

A paved .25-mile loop trail leads south from the bathhouse at West Beach through a small dune area to a swamp and lake-viewing platform. Picnic tables en route.

Or hike into the bogs from the south end of the Cranberry Lake picnic area. No trails. Hop from log to log and bog to bog into a swampy world of frogs, lily pads, polliwogs, redwing blackbirds, canaries, purple honeysuckle, skunk cabbage, and bugs. A short walk leads into an entirely new ecological world. Beaver houses, however, cannot be reached on foot.

CRANBERRY LAKE TRAIL

From the Cranberry Lake picnic area across a soggy corner of the lake to Forest Campground.

A spur trail leads from the picnic area, north of the picnic area, around the lake, to the main road and the campground. Just far enough from the campgrounds and road to forget—for an instant, at least—that they are there.

BEACH WALKS

From the bridge to West Point and from West Point south along sand and gravel beaches looking out on the pass and Puget Sound.

From the bridge westward along the south side of the pass either walk along the beach—at low tide—or along the shore trail. Find the shore trail off the west end of the

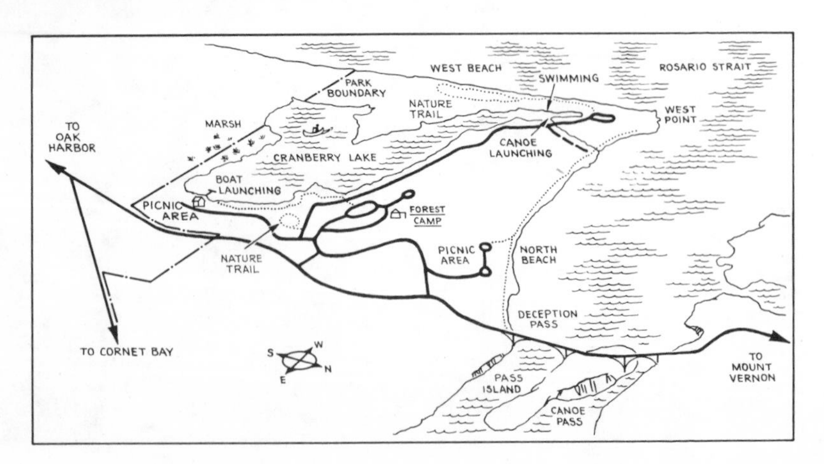

Bowman Bay

picnic road loop below the bridge. Pick your own way along the beach.

From West Point south follow the beach to the park boundary, 1 mile. Continue farther at low tide, remembering that the beach is private property.

No clams on either beach. Agates are sometimes found on both, with best picking on the west beach whenever the gravel is exposed by action of the waves.

NATURE TRAIL

Stop for a moment and introduce yourself to the plants you're likely to meet as you stroll through the forests of this park.

Find the short trail across from the park office at the intersection of the road to Cranberry beach and the picnic area.

An easy .25-mile walk.

Campbell Lake and Skagit Bay from Mount Erie

D ANACORTES

It certainly won't seem as if you are in a city. But the features listed here are all owned—and were developed—by that community.

Wild place. Panorama places. Campgrounds. Lakes. Beaver ponds. Even the seashore. In a complex of sites that any city would have a right to be proud of. Fantastic. Really.

MOUNT ERIE

The well-known capstone to some 2,200 acres of forest, wetlands, and mountaintops—almost within walking distance of the city—now managed by the Anacortes Community Forest Lands Advisory Board.

From Anacortes, drive west out of the city on 32nd Street to I Avenue and then south to H Avenue, turning east beyond Heart Lake onto Mount Erie Road, following it uphill to the end.

From Deception Pass State Park, drive north about 4 miles beyond Pass Lake, taking a paved road sharply west along the north side of Lake Campbell. Turn right near the end of the lake onto a road to Anacortes and then right and uphill again on a paved road to Mount Erie just as the Anacortes Road crests and drops toward Heart Lake.

Pick your own high rock for a favorite vista or follow trails to two established viewpoints—one to the south over Lake Campbell, Deception Pass, and on to Mount Rainier. Or the other to the east with Mount Baker, the Skagit delta, and the oil refinery.

Hang-glider enthusiasts leap from these rocks to soar over the valley, and climbers sometimes practice on the faces of rock.

WHISTLE LAKE

Hike off the road to Mount Erie on trails to and around Whistle Lake, with its small island just east of the mountain. (Look down on it from Mount Erie's eastern viewpoint.)

A 3.5-mile hike-and-scramble over trails and old, old logging roads will take you around Whistle Lake and past Toot Swamp through old forests of Douglas fir and cedar. With birds in several habitats.

Lots of peace and quiet, although trail bikes may interrupt your pleasures.

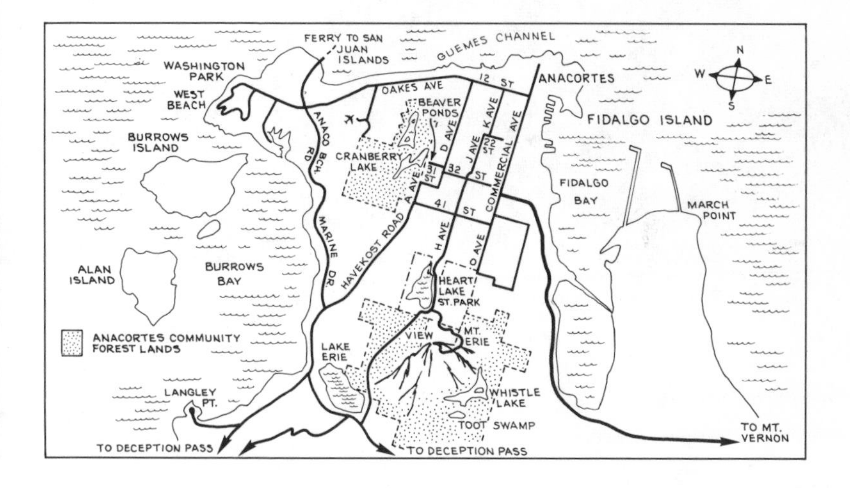

Burrows Pass from Washington Park. Mount Erie in distance

8 WASHINGTON PARK

A place to explore first, and to camp second. With sneaky, beautiful scenes out over the waters of Puget Sound in almost every direction from both trails and roads.

A self-sustaining park (from fees) operated by the Anacortes Parks and Recreation Department.

To find this 220-acre campground and scenic wonder, drive west out of Anacortes toward the San Juan ferry dock and then keep right on going to the end of the road.

You can drive past most of the prime scenic spots, parking at appropriate pull-outs for picnics along the way. Or for the sheer pleasure of it, prowl the 3.2 miles of signed footpaths that lead to places like Burrows Bay, Green Point, Fidalgo Head. Many of the paths wind through forest, but all of them end up at startling panorama points.

CAMPGROUND

Washington Park—49 sites with water and electrical hookup. Twenty-six sites without. All in a forested area in the center of the complex. Restrooms. Water. Picnic area. Boat launching. Fee.

BEAVER PONDS

Two short walks lead to several beaver ponds—almost in the middle of the city.

In 1.5 miles explore ponds bordering the 32nd Street swamp on trails off the end of 31st Street beyond D Avenue. Park at the end of the street.

The path (107) heads west then turns south (108) to a dam between two beaver ponds. You'll probably miss the beavers; they prefer to work at night. But you can at least admire their work.

Return as you came or continue on around to D Avenue, walking north back to your car.

For the second pond, turn south off Oakes Avenue just beyond the road to the Anacortes ferry dock, following the Anaco Beach Road–Marine Drive south to Bryce (in about 1 mile), winding easterly on Bryce to Clyde Way, parking at the end of the street.

A 2-mile easy walk takes you through wetlands, past beaver ponds, and on to drier forests of old-growth cedar and Douglas fir. Pack your lunch.

Note: For up-to-date details on all of these city trails, buy maps and a trail guide at an Anacortes bookstore. These forest-trail projects are supported by timber sales from the community lands.

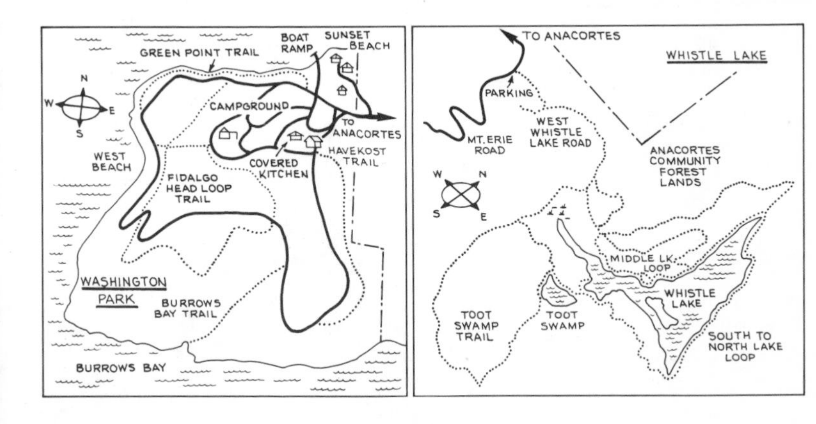

E THE WEST SLOPE

Catalog all of the great things about Washington State and you'll find them here—on the west slope of the North Cascades.

In the long section between Snoqualmie Pass and the Canadian border, find almost everything you could order:

Around Mount Baker, high flower-meadow vistas of the grand volcano with all its protecting peaks.

Up the Skagit River and its tributaries, deep forests, eagles, hot springs, and waterfalls.

On the loop highway between the drainages of the Stillaguamish, all of that with rushing rivers too.

And, finally, in off-highway crannies of Snoqualmie and Stevens passes, lookouts, still more waterfalls, and scenic vista points.

Highway I-5 leads to all of the gateway roads out of Bellingham, Mount Vernon, Arlington, Everett, and Seattle. Paved state roads lead up the major valleys with Forest Service logging roads taking the visitor to the most choice recreation points.

And you can travel here by foot or car. Follow spring up into the mountains and follow autumn all the way back down with the exact time of each season subject to the whims of weather, year to year.

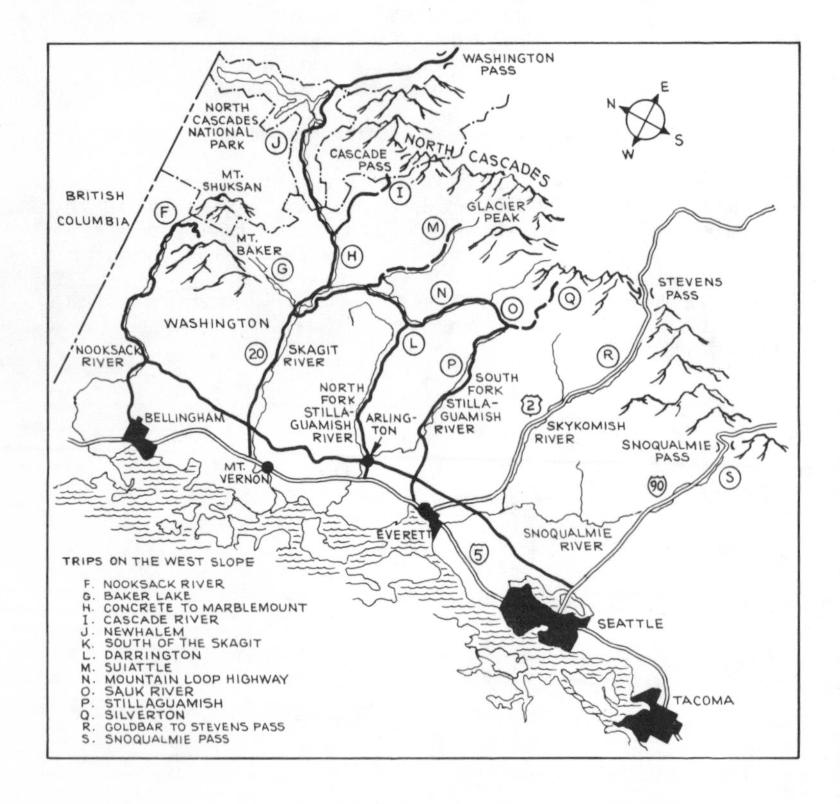

Foot bridge over the Suiattle River near the end of Suiattle River Road

Picture Lake and Mount Shuksan

F NOOKSACK RIVER

From shaded river trails to blazing mountain views. Mount Baker and Mount Shuksan dominate the valley. But leaf-imprint rocks, waterfalls, big trees, alpine flower meadows, and teeming salmon runs give it greater dimension.

From the freeway through Bellingham (watch for the Mount Baker Exit No. 255), drive east on Highway 542. The pavement ends at Mount Baker Lodge. A gravel road continues to Austin Pass and Kulshan Ridge.

GLACIER CREEK ROAD

Mount Baker often hides some of its better views around corners or over ridges. But not so on Glacier Creek Road. Here the mountain booms out a full view with no obstructions at all.

Drive about .5 mile east from the Glacier Ranger Station on Highway 542, turning south on Glacier Creek Road No. 39 for another 8 miles. The road climbs steadily over easy switchbacks with views much of the way. Just beyond the Kulshan Cabin trail parking area (7.5 miles), the road ducks into timber and then leaps out on the edge of the mountain again, up a single, steep pitch, to a turnaround viewpoint (4,000).

The view spreads north down the Glacier Creek Valley and eastward to Baker, taking in Roosevelt and Coleman glaciers, Black Buttes (Colfax, Lincoln, and Seward Peaks). Pretty even on a misty day. Good sunsets too. Huckleberries along the upper sections of the road.

THOMPSON CREEK SALMON RUN

Thompson Creek receives the biggest run of spawning salmon on the Nooksack River system. At its peak, the lower mile of the small stream literally boils with struggling fish. However, the salmon only run heavily every other year. Odd-numbered years offer the biggest displays. Best time is in late August and September.

The easiest viewpoint is from the Thompson Creek bridge. From Highway 542, drive south on the Glacier Creek Road about a mile. The run can also be observed in Gallop Creek in the town of Glacier. But the run there nowhere equals the Thompson Creek show.

CAMPGROUNDS

Douglas Fir—2 miles easterly from Glacier, 30 sites, some near the river, others on a shaded forest loop. Pit toilets. Pump. Community kitchen. Closed during week.

Nooksack—4 miles from Glacier, 19 units, most away from the river in heavy undergrowth. Pit toilets. Piped water. Fee camp.

Excelsior—Group camp by reservation only, 7 miles from Glacier.

Silver Fir—13 miles from Glacier, 19 tent and 12 trailer units with most sites on the river. Others back on forest loops. Sandbar at upper end of campground provides wading for children. Pit toilets. Piped water. Kitchen. Fee camp.

Hannegan—Trailhead camp at the end of the Hannegan Road No. 32 about 5 miles from the paved highway. Used largely by hikers and packers heading into the North Cascades, 6 sites.

Bridge—6 unmaintained sites in a forest area on the Nooksack River. Drive east of the Glacier Ranger Station, turning south on Glacier Creek Road and then east on Deadhorse Road No. 37. Campground in about 4.5 miles, just west of the closed old bridge.

Canyon—6 sites off Canyon Creek Road. Turn north on Canyon Creek Road just east of Douglas Fir Campground. Camp in little more than 6 miles.

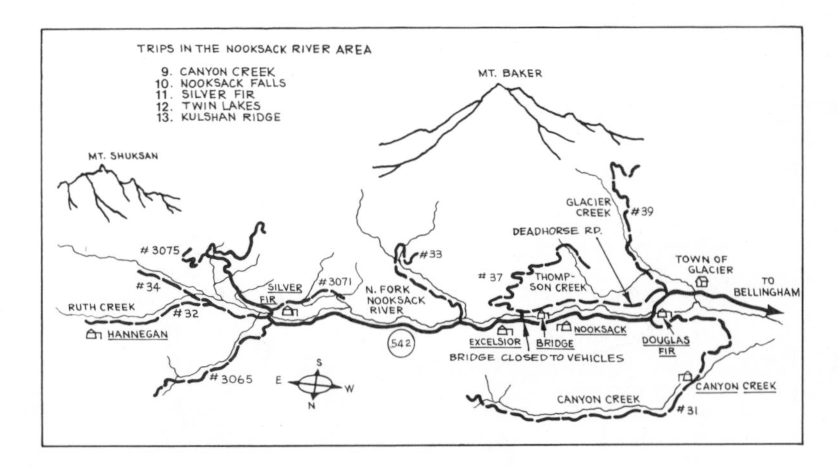

9 CANYON CREEK

HORSESHOE BEND TRAIL

A very pleasant 2-mile stroll along an interpretive trail to absolutely no place at all. The trail leaves the highway end of the Douglas Fir Campground beneath the concrete bridge (or from the highway at the southeast corner of the bridge). It wanders along the Nooksack through lush, river-bottom vine maple, past an old log seat carved out of a stump, over a bridge, and up a stairway.

The first part ends next to a noisy river rapids. The trail then climbs quickly to a ledge and stays above the river until it ends at water level again.

The trail does exactly what it's designed to do: provide a relaxing end to a busy day. Time? Just as long as you want to spend.

EXCELSIOR RIDGE TRAIL

Hike past two pretty tarnlike lakes, through forest and across meadows to a high ridge that overlooks the best of everything. Less than 2.5 miles.

About 2 miles east of Glacier, turn north off the Mount Baker Highway onto Canyon Creek Road No. 31, driving to the trailhead at the end of the road in about 15 miles.

The path starts out in a clear-cut, quickly enters forest, and soon skirts the two Damfino lakes. Trail bikes are supposed to turn left here for other trails. You turn right and follow the trail uphill through more forest and then across several meadows, dropping slightly before climbing to Excelsior Pass (5,300) with explosive views of Baker, Church, and Bearpaw peaks, and the endless clear-cut blotches of Canyon Creek basin. Explore ridges and mountaintops as the spirit moves you.

Trails drop down the mountain to the highway (4.5 miles) or wander along the ridge to Welcome Pass (5 miles) and, again, down to the highway.

LEAF-IMPRINT ROCKS

Imprints of leaves and fossilized plants, millions of years old, in uplifted rock deposits right beside the road.

To find two fossil sites, take the first logging road north beyond the Douglas Fir Campground—Canyon Creek Road No. 31.

For the first location, drive just short of the 4-mile marker post on the right—and just beyond as well—watching for layered, vertical formations in the road cuts to the right.

For the second (2.5 miles from highway), turn right on Spur Road No. 3120. Find imprints in a cliff about 300 feet before the next road junction.

Black, crumbly rock contains matted fossils of stems and stalks. Flat sandstone sections often bear imprints of leaves. Seek samples in broken material on the lower side of the road.

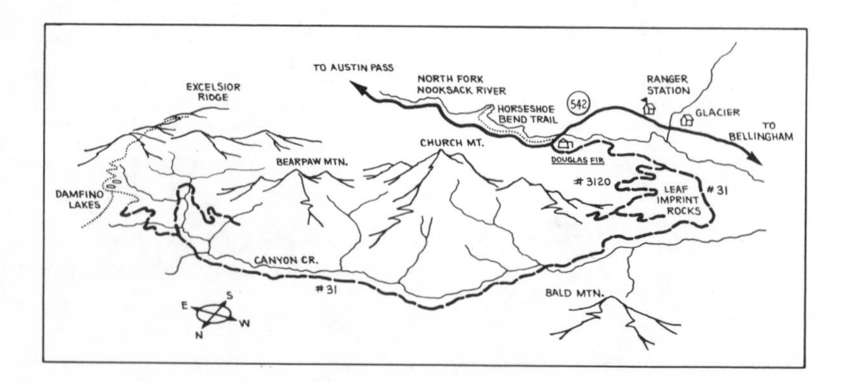

Leaf fossils found alongside Road No. 3120

10 NOOKSACK FALLS

One of the largest volume waterfalls in the forests of northwestern Washington. The full Nooksack River plunges 170 feet into a tight gorge with a thundering, earth-shaking roar.

Watch for a sign indicating the falls about 7 miles from the Glacier Ranger Station on Highway 542. Drive .5 mile on Forest Road No. 33 to the bridge. The falls are on the right.

A steel fence rims the steep cliffs around the falls, but still approach the edge with caution. Full views of the torrent come in peeks and glimpses between clefts in the rock along the high trail downstream. The falls are on property owned by Puget Sound Power and Light Company. Observe warnings. Can be dangerous.

SKYLINE DIVIDE TRAIL

A hike of about 2 miles brings tremendous views of Mount Baker, Mount Shuksan, and Excelsior Ridge from the high alpine meadows of the Skyline Divide (5,800).

Drive about .5 mile east from the Glacier Ranger Station, turning south on the Glacier Creek Road No. 39. Then, in about 300 feet, turn east on Deadhorse Road No. 37. Follow the logging road 14 miles as it makes its way first east and then back to the west,

Mount Baker from Skyline Ridge

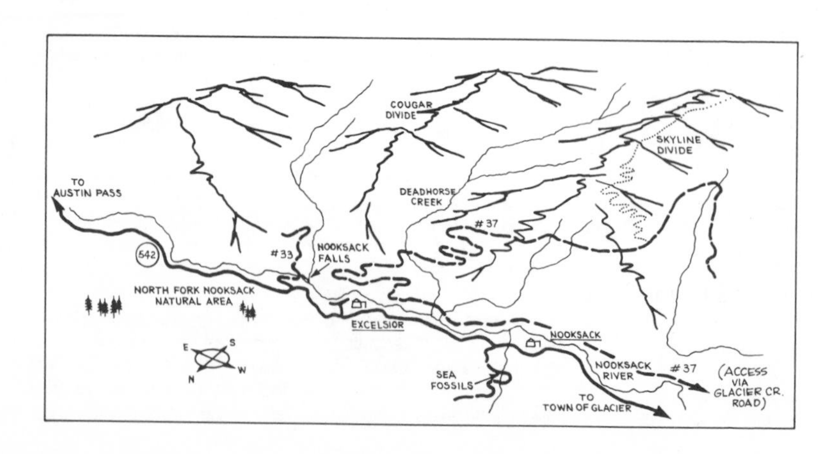

climbing in a series of switchbacks over the river valley with views toward the ridge, Church, and Bearpaw peaks. Trail signs and parking area on the right side of the road.

Trail, on the left, climbs sharply 2 miles (first views within a mile) before breaking out into alpine meadows, continuing on south 3 miles more along the ridge with no particular ending. Big, long views of Baker most of the way.

BIG FIR AREA

A 4-mile stretch of forest beginning about 10 miles east of the Glacier Ranger Station containing prime examples of original-growth Douglas fir, hemlock, and cedar, and the natural forest undergrowth common to such stands.

The trees are in the North Fork Nooksack Natural Area—a formal preserve a mile deep, which is supposed to be kept in its natural state—along the north side of the highway. (Some of the Douglas firs here are more than 600 years old and measure nearly 6 feet in diameter. Some of the largest trees near the highway, however, have already fallen to the chainsaw, having been deemed a hazard.)

11 SILVER FIR

Three logging roads lead to easy and grand views of Mount Shuksan from the Silver Fir Campground.

For the quickest view, drive east on the Hannegan Road No. 32 less than .25 mile, after turning off the paved highway just before the bridge at the Silver Fir Campground. For even fuller views, continue on Road No. 32 less than 2 miles, taking the first spur road to the right. Continuous views of the mountain clear to the end of the spur, about 3 miles.

For the third viewpoint, drive up the main highway toward Mount Baker Lodge and Heather Meadows, taking Road No. 3075 spur to the left on a sharp switchback about 5 miles from the Silver Fir Campground. Drive less than 1 mile until road rounds a razorlike ridge. Views of the mountain looking up White Salmon Creek. The vertical end of Hanging Glacier is about 700 feet high.

RUTH MOUNTAIN VIEW

An easy 2-mile hike in late summer leads to flower meadows and views of snow-topped Ruth Mountain (7,105). The trail leaves Hannegan Camp at the end of the Hannegan Road No. 32, about 5 miles from the main highway at Shuksan.

Ruth Mountain comes into view within the first mile. Brush gives way to meadows in less than 2 miles. Views too of Mount Sefrit, Nooksack Ridge, and Granite Mountain. Trail eventually leads to Hannegan Pass, 4 miles.

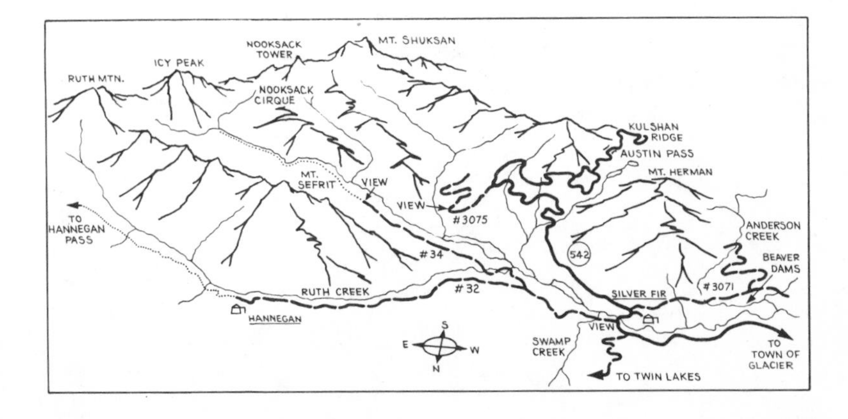

NOOKSACK CIRQUE

A trail through rich forest leads to gravel bars on the Nooksack and then, by hook or crook, along the river to increasing views of the Cirque. (Note: Closure of the bridge on Road No. 34 in late 1985 adds 2 miles to the trip.)

Turn east off the Mount Baker Highway beyond the highway garages—but before you cross the Nooksack River bridge—onto Hannegan Road No. 32 and then right again onto Road No. 34 up the North Fork of the Nooksack to the end.

Trail starts out on an old logging road for about 1 mile and then winds through a rich, almost rain forest for another mile before reaching the river, where the formal trail ends. Many stop here to sun on the gravel bar, eat lunch, and look up at Icy Peak and the top of Ruth Mountain. But others pick their way on up the riverbed, finding hints of unmaintained trails in the scrubby woods on the left. Boundary of the North Cascades National Park at about 3 miles. Views up at Shuksan in around 4 miles.

GOAT MOUNTAIN

It can be a struggle, but the high meadows at the end with the Ruth Creek Valley below, Mount Baker above, and glacier-silted Price Lake in the distance are the final reward.

Find the trail to the north, uphill, off the Hannegan Road No. 32 about 2.5 miles east of the Mount Baker Highway. The lower part of the trail climbs in forest and through brush. Few views. Soggy meadows and dry outcrops at the end of more than 2 miles.

Add less than a mile and climb to higher meadow views and the end of the trail (not to the top of Goat Mountain!).

12 TWIN LAKES

A spectacular alpine camping area. Two crystal lakes at 5,200 feet tucked into flower and heather meadows and surrounded by mountains.

But not an area to plan on. This county road, maintained by miners, is seldom open before mid-July and some years not at all. The last mile of the steep, narrow, very rough road is always difficult and occasionally impassable. And some years the road may be open while the lake basin is still packed with snow. If firm trip plans are required, check with the ranger in advance. And leave town prepared to backpack your gear at least the last 2 miles.

Camp at developed sites between the two lakes and on a bench above the lower lake. There are a few sites on the north side of the upper lake for those prepared to pack their equipment. Campers and hikers should treat the area with loving care. Its beauty is particularly fragile. Thoughtless visitors can add nothing, but destroy much.

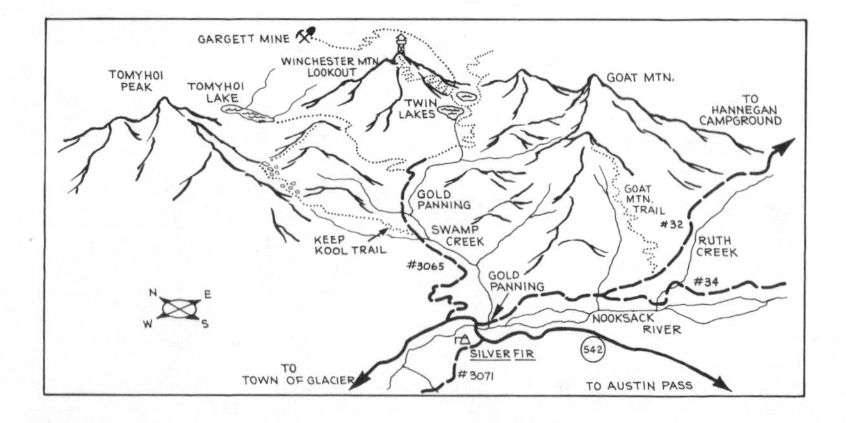

Nooksack Ridge from Ruth Creek Trail

Twin Lakes and Mount Baker

Drive 13.5 miles east of the Glacier Ranger Station, turning north on Road No. 3065 just beyond the highway maintenance barns at Shuksan. Seven miles to the lakes, or park at the creek crossing beyond the Tomyhoi Lake Trail and hike the rest of the way, 1.5 miles.

GARGETT MINE TRAIL

When the snow is gone, a pleasant walk of a mile or more over open alpine flower slopes. Some years the trail is blocked all summer by snowfields, tricky to cross even with an ice ax.

Trail starts north between the lakes. At .25 mile, keep right at the junction with the trail to Winchester Mountain Lookout.

The mine trail, little used but still easy to follow, skirts the northeast side of Winchester Mountain climbing toward Low Pass and then along the ridge crest to High Pass. Views of Canadian peaks, Mount Larrabee, the Pleiades, and Skagit Ridge. Trail eventually winds to Gargett Mine, 3 miles, on the slopes of Larrabee.

To reach the Winchester Mountain Lookout—1.5 miles—turn uphill at the junction. Again, the trail may be blocked, some years, by dangerous patches of snow. Trail switchbacks to the lookout, which is operated on an emergency basis only.

GOLD RUN PASS

A 2-mile walk leads to views north of peaks near the Canadian border and south of overpowering Mount Baker.

Take the Tomyhoi Lake Trail off the road toward Twin Lakes (see above) 4.5 miles from the main highway. The trail climbs alternately through meadows and forest to the top of the pass. Drop downhill another 2 miles to Tomyhoi Lake or explore ridges at the pass.

KEEP KOOL TRAIL

Not really! Only after you finally reach the meadows and surround yourself with a panorama of cool tarns and snowy peaks.

The trail starts to the left of the Road No. 3065, which heads north toward Twin Lakes (see above).

The trail starts on an overgrown old logging or mining road, climbing in fits and starts to its first meadow in 2.5 miles. Follow the trail through the flowers here or climb to the next plateau (another .5 mile) to more tarns and much better views from below Yellow Aster Butte. Baker, Goat, Winchester, Shuksan, and everything else.

13 KULSHAN RIDGE

Heaven knows how many visitors mistake the most obvious and spectacular peak in the Heather Meadows–Mount Baker Lodge area for Mount Baker. The big, rugged mountain, of course, is Shuksan, one of the most photographed in the U.S. And Baker, as usual, is hidden, reserving its views for those willing to drive a little bit farther or hike a little bit higher.

Artist Point parking lot on Kulshan Ridge, about 2 miles beyond the lodge at the end of the highway, offers the easiest views of the evasive Mount Baker. But the sometimes-road, as often walked as driven, is seldom clear of snow before the end of July and many years not until late August—if at all. So be sure to leave town prepared to walk at least part of the way in snow.

Drive as far as the road permits and then walk on to the parking area just beyond Austin Pass at 4,700 feet. Views of Baker, Shuksan, and Ptarmigan Ridge—all rising above snow-patched alpine flower meadows.

ARTIST POINT

A favorite spot for photographers seeking pictures of Mount Baker at her best. No formal trails. No signs. But an easy .5-mile walk along tourist paths to a series of viewpoints atop a ridge.

From the parking area, walk out the ridge extending off to the southeast. Along with Baker, more views of Shuksan, and the lesser ridges southeast above Baker Lake. Find

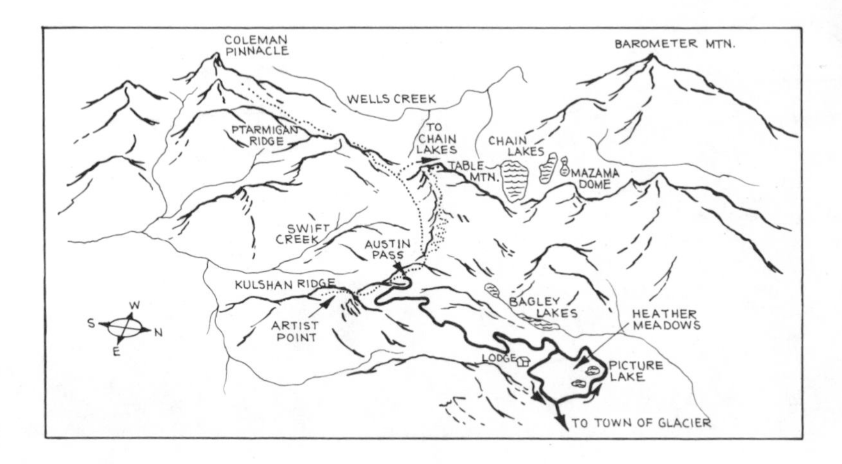

Mount Baker from Artist Point

a reflecting pool on the south side of the point. Either walk over the top and drop about 100 feet below or contour around the east side. For best pictures of Baker, get there before noon.

COLEMAN PINNACLE VIEW

A level 1-mile scenic walk with continuous views of Mount Baker plus occasional down-valley glimpses of Baker Lake. Take the Chain Lakes trail from the west end of the Artist Point parking area to the passlike alpine area at the far end of Table Mountain, stopping before the trail turns and drops down toward Chain Lakes.

Watch for marmots in the rocks both above and below the trail and for the modest magenta paintbrush among the more colorful alpine flowers alongside the trail.

Chain Lakes: Another mile, mostly downhill.

PTARMIGAN RIDGE

Add another mile or more to the easy walk (above) and pick up still more vistas of high meadows, deep valleys, and Mount Baker.

From the saddle where the Chain Lakes trail turns right, continue forward toward the mountain on a path that drops downhill slightly and then climbs again to Ptarmigan Ridge.

Snow sometimes covers the ridge all year. But the pathway, at least to the first ridge, is generally clear (observe it from the saddle). The trail continues on to Camp Kiser, an unmarked alpine area.

TABLE MOUNTAIN

A steep and, in spots, precipitous, .5-mile climb from the Artist Point parking area on Kulshan Ridge to the top of Table Mountain for unencumbered views of all surrounding peaks.

Take the Chain Lakes trail out of the far end of the parking lot, watching for an uphill trail in about .25 mile. Trail switchbacks very steeply to the plateau-top of the mountain. Definitely not for the queasy or those new to the ways of mountain trails.

At the top, the trail crosses a pretty alpine meadow dotted with cold pools to a steep snowfield, extremely dangerous to cross without proper mountaineering gear and training.

Mount Baker from Road No. 3725

G BAKER LAKE

A busy recreation area that seems to get busier every year.

The man-made lake is the biggest attraction. But the mountains on both sides offer a wide variety of view drives and hikes, hot springs, waterfalls, alpine scenes, and forest lookouts.

Take I-5 north to Mount Vernon, turning east on the North Cascades Highway (Exit No. 230). About 4 miles beyond the Hamilton–Lyman exit, take the Baker Lake–Grandy Lake Road to the north. Mount Baker National Forest boundary in about 12 miles.

CAMPGROUNDS

Horseshoe Cove—34 units in second-growth timber, long, sloping swimming area behind a log boom ideal for children. No lifeguard. Flush toilets. Piped water. Concession operated.

Bayview—Group camp. Primitive site. Reservations only.

Boulder Creek—10 units in wooded site along a glacial creek. Many who plan trips into mountain areas prefer it to the busy lakeshore camps. Pit toilets.

Panorama—16 units on an open, unshaded peninsula. All sites are near the water. But little beach. Views of Blum, Shuksan, and Baker from shore. Pit toilets. Boat launching. Concession operated.

Park Creek—12 units on Park Creek off Morovitz Creek Road No. 1144. About half the sites along the creek. All in pleasant, shaded forest area. Gets heavy use despite the fact it's away from the lake. Pit toilets.

Morovitz Creek—3 units. Secluded camp off the Morovitz Road No. 1144 in shaded, big timber with a small, pretty stream, pond, and bugs. Pit toilet.

Shannon Creek—20 units in wooded area near lake. Most sites on wooded loops away from the lake. Pit toilets.

Maple Grove—6 units on the east side of the lake about 1.5 miles northeast of Horseshoe Cove. Boat and trail camp. Sites back a little from the lake with views of Mount Baker. Not busy, usually. Pit toilets. Water from nearby streams.

Kulshan—40 sites west of Upper Baker Lake Dam. A Puget Power campground. Flush toilets. Piped water. No fee.

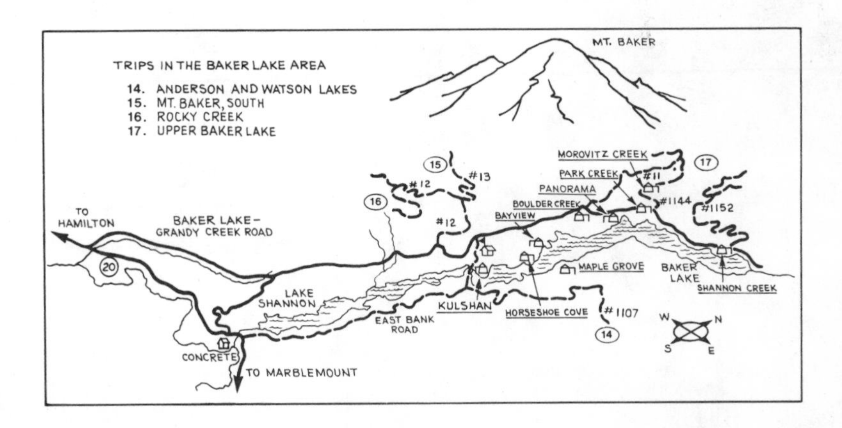

Watson Lake

14 ANDERSON AND WATSON LAKES

Two clusters of high alpine lakes in spectacular meadow country less than 3 miles from the end of a high and scenic but sometimes poorly maintained logging road.

Trail starts uphill sharply from a parking area and then climbs briskly up and down to the lakes trail junction in a short 2 miles. Trail uphill to the left climbs steeply over a ridge and then down to the two big Watson lakes (4,475 feet). Views over both from a steep meadow before you reach the lakes.

Trail to the right leads to the first of several smaller but more open Anderson lakes in less than .5 mile. Bear off to the right at the first lake for a breathtaking view of Mount Baker from a pretty meadow just across the creek. Other views, from both lakes, of Mount Watson and Bacon Peak.

(For high views of mountains in this area—but not of the lakes—hike to the site of a former lookout (5,420 feet) on Anderson Butte, 1 mile. The path climbs always persistently and sometimes steeply to a rocky outcrop with Baker and Shuksan and piles of peaks to the south.)

Camping at Watson lakes on the first lake or on open meadows between the lakes. Camping in the Anderson lakes area on meadows everywhere. Spend a day at either lake area or a weekend at both.

Drive across the Upper Baker Dam about 1.25 miles south of Horseshoe Cove Campground, bearing north (left) on Anderson Creek Road No. 1107. About 10.5 miles to the trailhead.

SHADOW OF THE SENTINELS

A .5-mile nature-loop trail through old-growth timber, some more than 500 years old. Prime examples of towering Douglas fir, silver fir, and hemlock are identified along the trail together with other forest plants common to the region.

Drive .5 mile north of the Koma Kulshan Guard Station, 11.5 miles north of Concrete. Watch for parking area and sign on the right side of the road.

EAST BANK TRAIL

Stroll from a dusty road through cool forest to a pleasant bay on Baker Lake.

Trail ends at Maple Grove Campground on the east side of the lake (4 miles), winding through pleasant timber above the lake with occasional views out at Mount Baker, dropping down to the small bay at the mouth of Anderson Creek in 2 miles.

Drive over Upper Baker Lake Dam (see Anderson–Watson Lakes), bearing north on Anderson Creek Road No. 1107. Trail on the west side of the road in 1 mile.

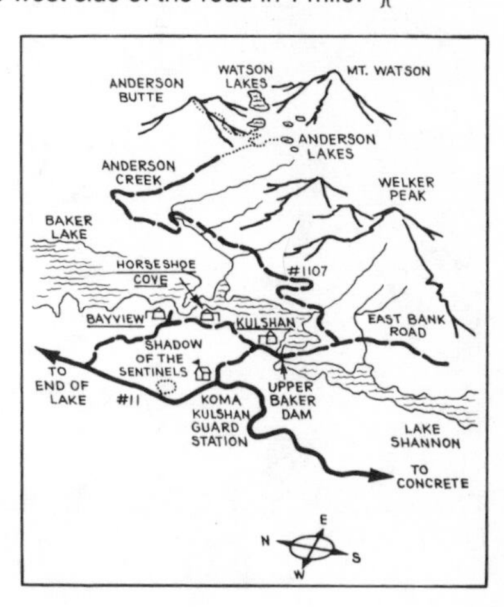

15 MOUNT BAKER, SOUTH

No matter how many times you prowl these meadows and ridges, each will always seem like the first.

Surprises everywhere. If it's not another family of marmots, it'll be a waving field of cotton grass. Or a crag you never noticed before. Or a meadow you should have explored there years ago.

Find the trail through Schriebers Meadow and on to Morovitz Meadow and the Railroad Grade at the end of Road No. 13 about 8.7 miles from the highway at Rocky Creek bridge. Look for a trail sign about 25 yards off the road on a parking spur to the south.

SCHRIEBERS MEADOW

An easy walk through open-timbered huckleberry and flower meadows about as long as you want to make it.

Follow the trail (see above) over Sulphur Creek and then wander through increasingly open timber past occasional small ponds, each with its own reflected glimpse of Mount Baker to the north.

In about 1 mile, the path passes a tumbling shelter and then three swift streams from the Easton Glacier.

But there's no real need to hurry on if you haven't the energy or the time. Clearings and small patches of trees and even hints of ponds and sinkholes beckon everywhere.

A damp area, infested with mosquitos through much of the summer. But bugless in the fall when the meadows turn rich with berries and color.

MOROVITZ MEADOW

The ultimate, really. A place you truly can't believe.

From Schriebers Meadow (above), hike another mile up switchbacks to lower Morovitz Meadow. More views and more places begging to be explored.

One ridge may look out over a barren moraine on one side and down on a whole city of marmots on the other. The next ridge may feature wind-bowed trees. Another, snarls of rock. And over all of them, your proud and stately host, Mount Baker.

Spur trails lead to Park Butte Lookout (5,450 feet) in another mile and Baker Pass in 1.2 miles. You'll most certainly decide to come back another time and spend—the rest of your life!

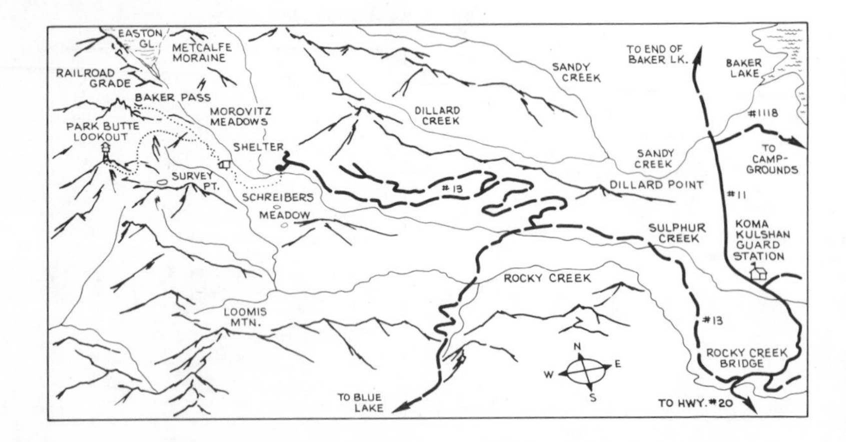

Mount Shuksan and fog-covered Baker Lake from Dillard Point

16 ROCKY CREEK

A scenic drive and scenic hike lead to a high ridge overlooking Baker Lake with still more scenic views of all the major peaks in the Mount Baker area.

Take the Rocky Creek Road No. 12 west at the Rocky Creek bridge less than .5 mile inside the Mount Baker National Forest boundary about 10 miles north of Concrete. After 7 miles turn left onto Road No. 1230, following the signs to Blue Lake and Dock Butte trails, another 4 miles. Good views of Baker, Shuksan, Blum, and other North Cascade peaks along the last 3 miles.

At the end of the road, trail to the Butte and Blue Lake (see below) climbs out of a clear-cut to a trail junction over a slight ridge. Dock Butte trail, to the right.

DOCK BUTTE

Salute the world from another of the dozens of former lookout sites that dotted ridgetops in this region.

Follow the Dock Butte trail (above) to the right, climbing steadily up a series of switchbacks with increasing views out toward Baker.

In less than 1 mile, an open meadow—flowers in summer, colors in fall—atop a beautiful alpine ridge. Views swing from the Twin Sisters to the east around through Baker and Shuksan, up the Baker River valley to the Pickets, and westward to Blum, Hagan, and Bacon.

Follow the ridge trail south past pleasant pools, grey outcrops of rock, overgrown mine prospects, weathered trees, and camping spots.

The trail, however, becomes increasingly difficult to follow the farther south it goes, disappearing completely in some places. Trails bearing to the left afford access to a cross-ridge with views of Glacier Peak, Whitehorse, and White Chuck.

Bear to the right along the rising ridge to the south to find Dock Butte in another mile. A very steep trail shoots up the west side of the pointed butte to a former lookout site where Mount Rainier is added to the vista. Probably not for novices or the queasy.

BLUE LAKE

Named precisely. A pretty, clear-blue lake tucked into the base of the Dock Butte ridge. A pleasant, easy trip. 1 mile.

Take the trail to the left at the junction about 100 yards from the end of Road No. 1230. The trail drops down through a timber area to the attractive 13-acre lake at 4,000 feet. Talus slopes rise at the far end. But subalpine meadows surround the rest.

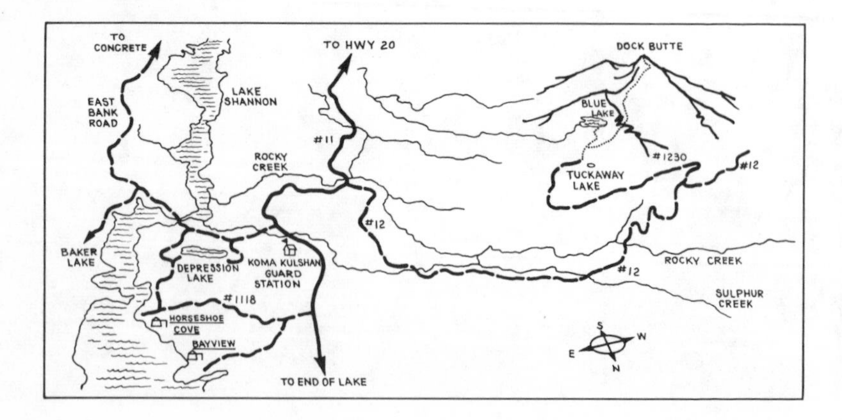

Air view of Dock Butte and Mount Baker

17 UPPER BAKER LAKE

BAKER HOT SPRINGS

The question here is simple: Can you turn back the clock?

Just a few years ago, after the Forest Service installed a fancy trail, big parking area, changing house, outhouse, and picnic tables, some 18,000 people poured into this place every year—and overwhelmed it.

Now the agency is trying to turn back the clock. The fancy entrance sign, changing house, picnic tables, and even the bathing tubs are gone. The agency has stopped maintaining the trail but hot springs devotees have been keeping it up.

But the springs remain, still bubbling from the earth at 110 degrees. You can soak your feet here and sprawl out in a gravel pool. But the "amenities" are gone—thank heavens—and so, it appears, are many of the people.

Take Road No. 1144 off the main highway at the Park Creek Campground. Watch for an unmarked parking area and trail on the left in about 3 miles. A quarter-mile to the springs.

RAINBOW FALLS

The highest waterfall in the Baker Lake area plunges 200 feet into a steep canyon. Two ways to see it. But no way to hike to it.

For a low-level but interesting view, drive 4.3 miles from the lake highway on Road No. 1144 (past the hot springs trail above), taking a sharp right turn at a junction in another .5 mile onto Road No. 1130. The falls—a solid rainbow if the sun is right—in another .5

mile. Walk a short path to the viewpoint. But use caution beyond that point. No trails. Cliffs.

For a higher view with background mountains too, turn left off the paved road beyond Boulder Creek onto Road No. 1130, turning left again in about 2 miles onto Road No. 1131 toward the Boulder Ridge trailhead.

Two big vistas **down** on the falls and out at the peaks in a little more than 3 miles.

BAKER RIVER TRAIL

Peace here in the twin pleasures of towering trees and a busy river. Stroll 1 mile or 3 in the solitude of a virgin forest broken only by the occasional surprise glimpses of the surrounding peaks—Mount Blum (view in .5 mile), Easy Ridge (in 2 miles), and Whatcom Peak (just a little farther).

Drive beyond the end of Baker Lake on the main Forest Road No. 11, turning north (left) at the four-way junction (watch for Griners Shelter sign), driving another .5 mile to a shelter cabin and the start of the trail. Trail leads into North Cascades National Park in about 1.5 miles.

MOUNT BAKER VIEWS

Mount Baker, difficult to see from highways near the lake, comes out of hiding completely on Road No. 1152. Turn north off the lake highway near the upper end of Baker Lake, about 3 miles beyond Baker Lake Resort. Either follow No. 1152 to the end, with views of Mount Baker most of the way, or take the Shuksan Lake Road Spur No. 1160 to the right for vistas of Mount Baker, Baker Lake, and Mount Blum. (The spur does not go to Shuksan Lake, however.) Poor views of Shuksan from either spur. Too close to the mountain.

SALMON-REARING PONDS

Large man-made gravel beds at the upper end of Baker Lake provide a nearly natural setting in which salmon spawn. Brood sockeye are trapped in pens below Baker Dam and trucked to the ponds in tanks. The spawn hatches naturally in the gravel beds and the young fish are eventually released downstream. Spawning fish can generally be seen in late September and October.

Drive beyond the end of Baker Lake on the main Forest Road No. 11. At the four-way junction beyond the lake, turn south. Main ponds are fenced but are often open to the public. Salmon can also be seen during the peak of the fall run in the unfenced, pondlike sections of Intake Creek at the end of short unmarked spur trails to the right (west) of the road to the main hatchery complex.

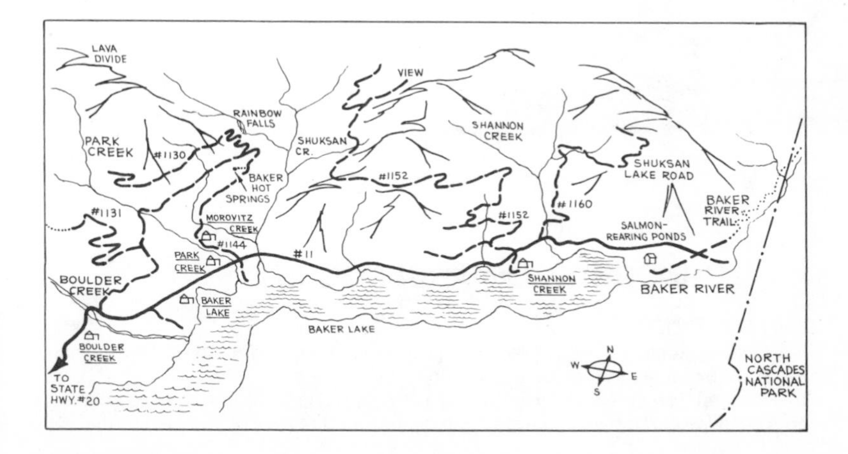

Shaggy mane (Coprinus comatus) *mushroom near Baker Lake*

Bald eagles on a tree overlooking Skagit River near Rockport

H CONCRETE TO MARBLEMOUNT

FISH ELEVATOR

Spawning salmon, trying to reach the upper Baker River, swim into tank traps below Baker Dam and are trucked to rearing ponds above the lake.

In Concrete, cross the old bridge just east of town and turn sharply right into a parking area below the bridge and near steel structures over the river. Tourist ramps lead out over trapping pens where salmon are caught in tanks that are lifted out of the river and emptied into trucks backed out on special ramps. Taped-message installation. Trucking operation takes place during the height of the fall salmon run.

EAGLE SANCTUARY

Hundreds of magnificent bald eagles winter here, feeding on salmon which have spawned and died in the Skagit River.

From December through February observe the birds—as many as 300 at a time—along both sides of the river between Rockport and Marblemount. Take your binoculars. Or take a guided trip by raft.

The birds are often most visible in the tops of trees. But if you're lucky you can see groups of them haggling over fish on sandbars or river banks. This is a Nature Conservancy sanctuary aimed at preserving an important wintering ground for these grand birds. Observe, but don't disturb!

SAUK MOUNTAIN

Great views of the Sauk, Skagit, and Cascade river valleys from the end of a zigzag road. But still greater ones from an abandoned lookout at the end of a trail.

Drive north on the gravel forest road just **west** of Rockport State Park off Highway 20. After about a mile the road starts a series of switchbacks to a junction in 7 miles. Turn right to a turnaround parking and overlook area in a few hundred yards.

Great vistas from the parking area, but follow the well-developed switchback trail across the steep flower meadow to reach the top of the ridge with its heather, snowfields, abandoned lookout, and fantastic vistas, with Glacier Peak, Mount Baker, Shuksan, Whitehorse, White Chuck, and Pugh towering over all the river valleys. A steep spur trail leads down to Sauk Lake visible below.

The trails here can be treacherous. So use care. Don't shortcut switchbacks, and warn those who do of the danger of knocking rocks down on those below.

ROCKPORT TRAIL

Even if you don't camp at the State Park, it's worth a stroll down the short wooded trails south of the highway, across from the campground.

One short loop trail—the Sauk Springs trail—wanders through a rich, rain-forestlike grove of big conifers and moss-draped maples, with forest flowers and berries in season.

The other trail—more like a lane—leads to a viewpoint overlooking the Skagit River. Easy, pleasant—and restful.

CAMPGROUNDS

Rockport State Park—50 trailer sites, 4 walk-in tent sites, 4 with walk-in shelters. Restrooms. Water. Nature trails. Vistas. On Highway 20 about 10 miles east of Concrete. State fee.

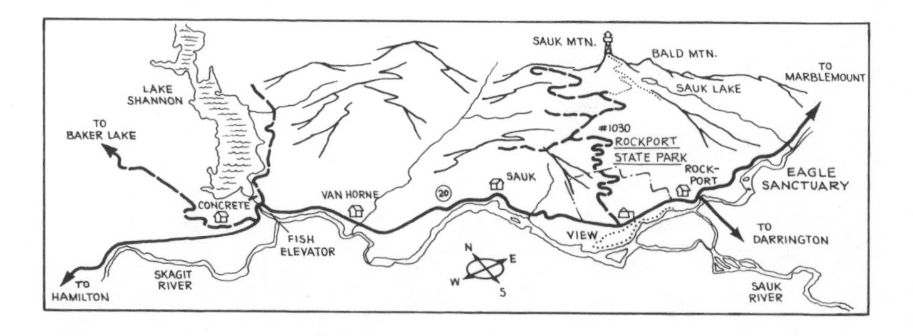

Small tarn at Cascade Pass. Eldorado Peak in distance

I CASCADE RIVER

CASCADE PASS

The queen of all the short Cascade mountain hikes. Longer than most in this book—3 miles, but easy—the trail leads to a spectacular alpine pass with views in every direction. In North Cascades National Park.

Follow the Cascade River Road 20 miles east from Marblemount to its end in a parking and picnic area. Views here of the hanging glaciers on Johannesburg Mountain to the south-southwest and of Cascade Pass to the east.

A trail switchbacks very gradually through timber, topping out at last on a long traverse toward the pass across open alpine meadows with long, constant views. Paintbrush, monkey flowers, penstemons, and whole hillsides of red columbine.

From the pass, hike north to the top of Sahale Arm for more spectacular views and higher heather meadows. This entire fragile high area is for day-use only. No camping at all. Pit toilets off the trail on both sides of the pass.

HIDDEN LAKE TRAIL

It's 4 miles to Hidden Lake lookout. But a 2-mile walk leads to heather-meadow views over open slopes below the higher ridges. Take your lunch and spend an hour here watching marmots and comparing the splendor of a small, high valley to the squalor of a city street.

Turn off the Cascade River Road 2 miles east of Marble Creek Campground onto Sibley Creek Road No. 1540. Road climbs to view of Snowking and Lookout Mountains. Trail, at end of road, climbs a mile through timber before breaking out on open slopes.

CAMPGROUNDS

Marble Creek—28 units, some along the Cascade River, others back on forest loops. Newer units nearest the highway. Others down narrow roads, difficult for trailers, at the far end of the camp, 9 miles from Marblemount. Pit toilets. Fee camp.

Mineral Park—22 units on both sides of the North Fork of the Cascade River, and along the main river. A few units oriented to the river but most in the big timber, 17 miles from Marblemount. Pit toilets.

Johannesburg—Backcountry camp for hikers at the head of trail to Cascade Pass. At the end of road, 23 miles from Marblemount. Backcountry use permit required.

Note: All backcountry camping within the park by permit. Camping is limited to designated sites along trails. Wilderness camps allowed at least a mile off trails—by permit also.

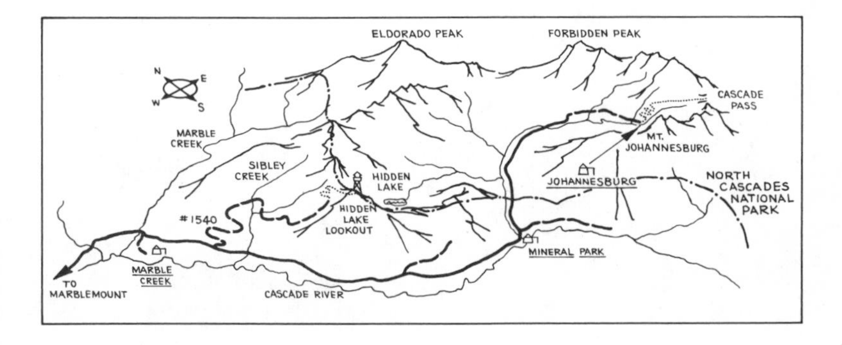

Davis Peak and Diablo Reservoir

J NEWHALEM

Seattle City Light's General Store seems to be the biggest attraction in Newhalem. But there is a lot more to see and do.

Powerhouse, falls, and garden—Walk through a series of flower-filled rock gardens to see a pretty waterfall and look down on the generators in Gorge Powerhouse.

Park across from the powerhouse, on the right, just beyond the townsite, and walk one of two bridges to the other side of the river.

Find the gardens on formal rock terraces behind the powerhouse. Blooming plants in season, with rhododendrons in the spring.

Ladder Creek Falls tumbles through rock gorges to the right of the powerhouse.

Displays in the powerhouse viewing gallery describe the workings of the 175,000 kilowatt generating system operated by the City of Seattle.

Trail of Cedars—A short walk over a suspension bridge and around a loop of forest trail offers a restful look at the abundance of the forests here.

Find the trail and the suspension bridge at the end of the road past the General Store. Signs mark the self-guiding nature stroll.

THORNTON CREEK VIEWS

A gravel road climbs sharply, hanging onto hillsides in places, to views of the Upper Skagit Valley, Marblemount, Teebone Ridge, and the snows of Snowfield and Colonial peaks.

Turn uphill onto the Thornton Lakes Road about 2.6 miles west of the Newhalem Creek Campground. At the end of the road in 5 miles, walk down the lakes trails another 2 miles for a higher viewpoint. Thornton Lakes 5 miles from the road end.

STETATTLE CREEK TRAIL

Walk here a few minutes or an hour to find your way back to nature again.

Find the trail, just beyond the bridge over Stetattle Creek, on the left side of the road entering the town of Diablo. The path starts in lush woods along the creek and then climbs gradually, with occasional views of Davis Peak. Trail ends in about 3 miles.

OAKES PEAK VIEWS

Select your own vistas of the Bacon Creek Valley from logging roads high on the side of Oakes Peak.

Turn north from the North Cascades Highway onto Road No. 1060 about 5 miles north of Marblemount, turning uphill to the right in about a mile on Road No. 1062. Best views near the top.

CAMPGROUNDS

Bacon Creek—Picnic sites near Bacon Creek around a gravel parking lot 5 miles north of Marblemount on the north, uphill side of the road.

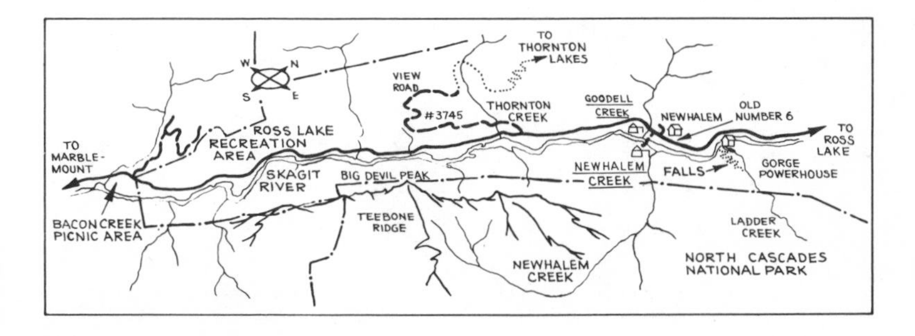

Goodell Creek—22 sites with two group camps. Just south of Newhalem in North Cascades National Park. Pit toilets. Piped water. Launch area for river rafts.

Newhalem Creek—129 sites with 13 walk-in sites. Flush toilets. Piped water. In pleasant forest 14 miles east of Marblemount on the edge of Newhalem.

18 DIABLO AND ROSS DAMS

THUNDER CREEK TRAIL

A pleasant stroll of about 1 mile (or more) along a level trail on the Thunder Arm of Diablo Lake. Find the trail near the water at the south end of Colonial Creek Campground. It follows the arm of Diablo Lake, which gradually dwindles into Thunder Creek at a bridge, 1 mile. The trail continues on up Thunder Creek. Walk as far as you like.

ROSS DAM TRAIL

Hike to Ross Dam from the North Cascades Highway and trails leading up Ross Lake to Big Beaver Creek and down to Diablo Dam.

Drive beyond Colonial Creek Campground 4 miles to a trailhead on the left side of the road. Trail switchbacks .8 mile down to the dam and a resort. An easy walk down but a short, stiff hike back up.

Cross the top of the dam to reach the Big Beaver trail. Take the spur road down to Diablo Lake to find the head of the trail (see below) that leads back to Diablo Dam.

DIABLO LAKE TRAIL

If you can plan your trip right, take a boat one way and walk the other to see Diablo Lake from every point of view.

Start and end your trip at a parking area near the Seattle City Light dock on Diablo Lake. The road, off Highway 20, crosses the top of Diablo Dam.

Take a Seattle City Light tug up Diablo Lake from the dock near the top of Diablo Dam to the base of Ross Dam and then walk back on the trail from the suspension bridge below Ross Dam.

The trail wanders 3.8 miles, with the best vistas of the lake and mountains in the middle section as it climbs out on a rocky bluff high above the water.

RUBY CREEK TRAIL

For a respite along a mountain stream with very little struggle and lots of peace, park and walk as far as you like up Ruby Creek, well out of hearing of the North Cascades Highway.

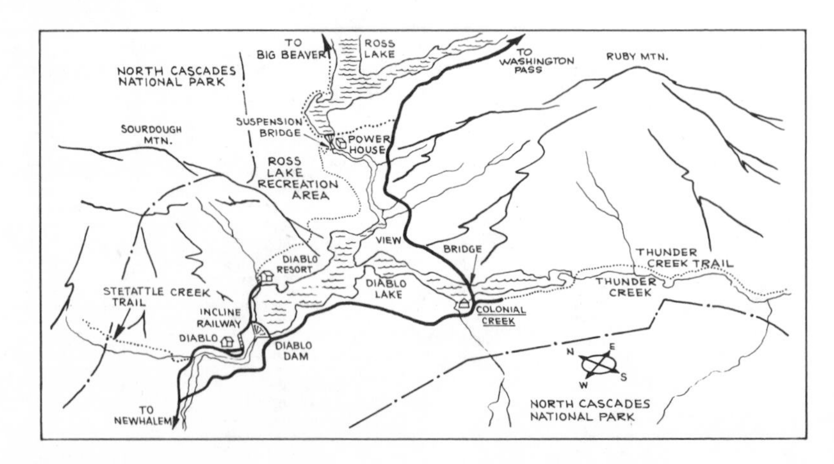

Thunder Arm and Colonial Peak

Drive east on the highway about 6.5 miles from the Diablo Lake overlook to a parking area for the Panther Creek and East Bank trails—on the creek side of the road.

From the parking lot, cross the bridge below the parking lot and walk to your right for a brushy trail that leads past what used to be Ruby Camp and then up along the side of Ruby Creek past occasional places to lunch, cool your feet, or just relax. Not for uncontrollable children. The river here is swift and the water is bone cold.

The trail to the left—the East Bank trail—is better maintained, but it climbs away from the river and offers little in the first two miles.

Note: The National Park Service has proposed spending $500,000 on new view and parking points along the North Cascades Highway from Copper Creek to Ross Lake. No money is expected to be available for the projects before 1986 or 1987—if then.

CAMPGROUND

Colonial Creek—165 sites on both sides of the North Cascades Highway on Thunder Arm of Diablo Lake, 23 miles northeast of Marblemount, 65 units north of the highway, 100 units south, including a new 5-trailer loop. No units oriented to the lake. All on pleasant wooded loops. Some walk-in sites. Restrooms. Piped water. Boat launching. Charge camp.

19 ROSS LAKE

It will probably take historians as long to define all the skirmishes and combat groups that took part in the 40-year battle over raising Ross Dam as it did to fight it.

Since construction began on the dam in 1938, and particularly after an international joint commission approved raising it 122 feet in 1942, conservation groups and others on both sides of the border fought to stop it.

But today, the big battle is over and the recreation features that everyone wanted to save seem safe.

British Columbia and the City of Seattle in 1984 agreed not to raise the dam after the prolonged dispute was resolved, finally, in a treaty signed by the U.S. and Canada.

Skymo Creek Falls and Ross Reservoir

In a nutshell (if that's possible), City Light abandoned plans to raise the dam any higher in return for electricity from British Columbia at a price generally equivalent to what it would have cost City Light to raise the dam.

Under the accord, City Light is expected to pay about $22 million a year to British Columbia for additional power for at least the next 35 years, under an agreement that extends until 2066.

But much more significantly, City Light and British Columbia agreed to kick in some $1,250,000 a year for the next four years for environmental, wildlife, and wilderness opportunities along the lake and in the Skagit watershed. The two agencies will also make contributions to the fund based on power purchases each year.

The environmental projects, to be authorized by a special joint commission, are expected to include work on trails—including one linking Manning Park in Canada with North Cascades National Park—trail bridges, the removal of stumps along the lake,

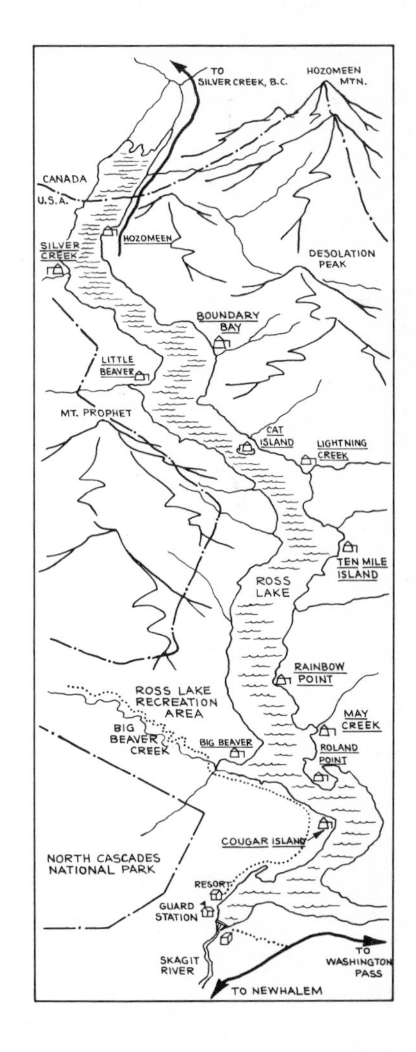

shoreline improvements, and the purchase of private timber and mineral rights in the area.

So—rent a boat, paddle your canoe, or hike in this newly stabilized recreation area and remember all of the organizations such as The Mountaineers, government agencies, and even political parties on both sides of the border which made your trip possible. And more, which saved places like Big Beaver Valley from flooding and destruction.

CAMPGROUNDS (boats only)

Roland Point—2 units, 4 miles north of the dam. Undeveloped.
Rainbow Point—4 units, 5 miles north of dam.
Big Beaver—7 units, 5 miles north of dam.
Lightning Creek—6 units, 12 miles from dam.
Cat Island Camp—7 units, 12 miles, with big view of Jack Mountain glaciers.
Little Beaver—7 units, 16 miles from dam, views of Hozomeen Mountain to the northeast.
Other camps at **Silver Creek, Boundary Bay, Ten Mile Island, May Creek,** and **Cougar Island.**
Hozomeen—122 units. Largest campground on the lake. Access by boat or by road (40 miles) from Hope, B.C. Piped water. Restrooms.

Mount Baker from side of Finney Peak

K SOUTH OF THE SKAGIT

Two former lookout sites with fine vistas, but....

And a pretty lake now thankfully protected by the Glacier Park Wilderness.

To explore the **lookouts,** drive south across the Skagit River out of Concrete, turning left. Turn right in about 10 miles on Forest Road No. 17. Lots of logging traffic in midweek.

To reach the **lake,** drive south out of Rockport on the highway to Darrington, turning east onto Road No. 16 a little more than 2 miles beyond the bridge.

Drive almost to the end of the road and then stroll, most peacefully, and tenderly, to Slide Lake.

(The Forest Service, for the past decade or two, has publicly concentrated all of its efforts in these valleys on logging. We, who worked on this book, were told that 20 years ago. As a result, the agency not only hasn't developed any new recreation features, it has done nothing to save what was there.)

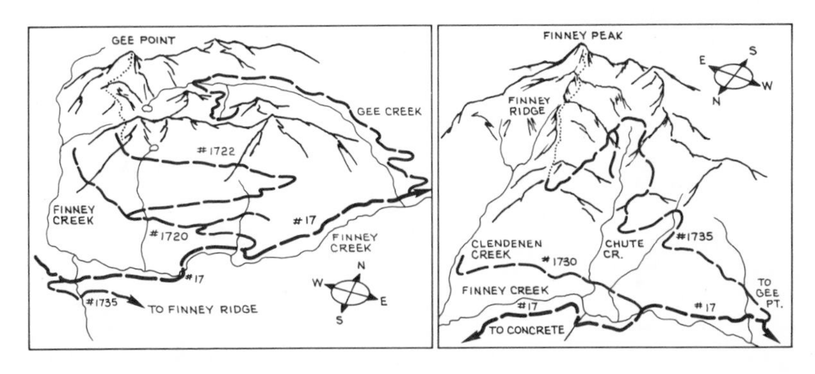

So go here and look at the results of that commitment and effort. Then wonder. Just wonder.

GEE POINT

A former lookout site with grand views out at mountains north, east, and south. **But....**

Start hunting for the trail to the lookout at the end of Road No. 1722. (Turn north off No. 17 in 10.3 miles onto No. 1720 and right off 1720 onto No. 1722 in 2 miles.) The high roads can be rough in places, and most of the heavily logged valleys look like strip mines.

Park just beyond the small lake, walk to the end of the road, and look for a hint of an unsigned path uphill at the very end. Pick your way over logs and rocks to the top of the clear-cut and the old trail. The Forest Service lists the logged-over trail, which was "rebuilt" by loggers and accepted by the agency under a contract to "restore" it, as open to horses and trail bikes. But judge, when you scramble up it, if it was even "restored" for hikers.

Follow blazes and the old trail about a mile to a burned cabin in a meadow just below the point, picking your way through the rocks to the top. No trail markings here at all. Vistas only at the top.

FINNEY RIDGE

The views here still exist: all the big peaks around Darrington to the south, and Baker and Shuksan to the north. And now only .25 mile from the road.

Turn off Valley Road No. 17 about 12 miles from the state highway, following Road No. 1735 to the end. Climb up the ridge through the clear-cut (no trail at all) hoping to find the ancient path still atop the ridge in the—as yet—unlogged trees.

This trail (?) is also listed as open to trail bikes and horses. Spare the horses. But don't worry about the trail bikes.

SLIDE LAKE

A spectacular triple lake, lying in a mountain bowl, at the end of a short trail filled with moss-covered boulders and other surprises.

From Rockport, drive south on the Rockport–Darrington Road, turning east (left) in 1.9 miles onto the Illabot Creek Road No. 16 and driving to the Otter Creek trailhead in 20 miles.

The trail wanders through a cool, shady tumble of old boulders topped with huge, ancient hemlocks. Don't hurry. Nature worked a long, long time to create this scene, so soak up all of the visual surprises as you go. Forest flowers, huckleberries, salmonberries, gooseberries in season.

The trail reaches the lake, just inside the Glacier Peak Wilderness, in an easy mile, but continues another .5 mile before reaching the main lake and the best vistas.

Camp and picnic places at the end of the trail along with views up at Snowking Mountain. Permits needed for camping. And treat the area with care. It could so easily be destroyed.

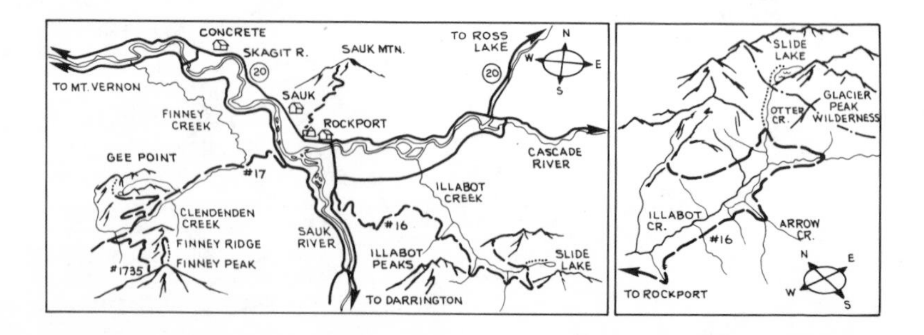

White Chuck Mountain from Helena Ridge Road

L DARRINGTON

Three logging roads lead to sweeping vistas of the river valleys and snow-covered peaks in the Darrington area.

NORTH MOUNTAIN LOOKOUT

A 14-mile drive out of Darrington to expansive views of the Sauk and Suiattle river valleys extending, on clear days, from Puget Sound to Glacier Peak with Mount Baker, Shuksan, White Chuck, Whitehorse, Bedal, Pugh, and Sloan peaks thrown in.

Driving out of Darrington, toward Rockport, pass the ranger station and turn 45 degrees left at the swimming pool down a road that runs diagonally through piles of lumber. Follow signs on Roads No. 28 and No. 2810 to the lookout at 3,956 feet.

SEGELSEN CREEK ROAD

Swiss-type views of the farms in the Stillaguamish Valley near Darrington, climbing to vistas that include Glacier, White Chuck, Whitehorse, Pugh, Sloan, and Bedal Peaks.

Turn north on 187th N.E. (Swede Heaven Road) about 5 miles west of Darrington on Highway 530. Drive about .5 mile after crossing the North Fork of the Stillaguamish River and take a dirt road (Forest Service Road No. 18), which angles up the hillside. First views in 10 miles. Higher drives bring better views of the nearby peaks. Road continues over ridge to Concrete.

OLD MOUNTAIN LOOP

Start your mountain loop trip out of Darrington on the old highway and still enjoy some of the pleasures of the forest and the Sauk. Cross the river in downtown Darrington and then head south on the old road just across the bridge. Nothing exceptional, really. But at least you'll know you left town. Joins the "official" highway at the confluence of the White Chuck and Sauk.

CAMPGROUNDS

French Creek—30 units in heavy, damp undergrowth of an alder stand. No longer maintained.

Clear Creek—10 units with 8 designated as trailer units. Sites near the river. But the campground, only 9 miles from Darrington, tends to get heavy town visitor use—night and day. Follow the main street in Darrington (Darrington Street) to the end, turning right along the river to the south.

20 FRENCH CREEK

First of the National Forest camping areas down the North Fork of the Stillaguamish River. From Arlington, take Highway 530 east. Turn south at sign about 8 miles west of Darrington or 2 miles east of the community of Hazel.

BOULDER CREEK AND FALLS

A level-grade hike of 1 mile through a rich, greenery-draped gorge to a wisp of waterfall pluming from a high cliff into a raging creek.

Drive beyond French Creek Campground on Road No. 2010 about 2.5 miles, watch-

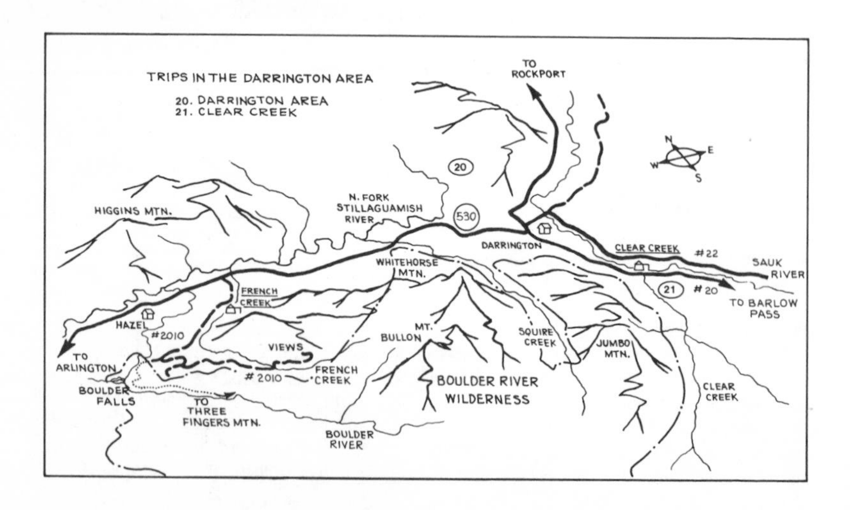

Whitehorse Mountain and North Fork Stillaguamish River Valley

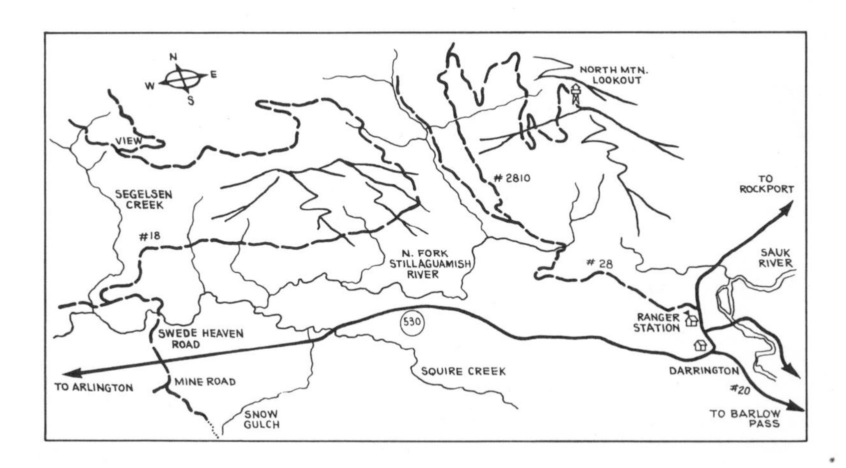

ing for a trail sign on the right. Drive a short way down the trail road to park.

Trail follows an old, grown-over road above Boulder Creek. Pass above the first shelter in about .5 mile. Follow the trail above the river to a shelter, nested near huge boulder pools on the creek. The falls lie 200 yards beyond the shelter, draping off the cliff Enchantment Valley-style, varying in size with the season. Maintained trail continues 4 miles to the Boulder Ford Camp. A pretty walk as far as you want to go. Huge salmonberries along the trail in season. Trail open some winters. Now in the Boulder River Wilderness.

FRENCH CREEK VIEWS

Look at the valley of the North Fork of the Stillaguamish River and tilted strata of Higgins Mountain on the other side. Follow French Creek Road No. 2010 beyond the French Creek Campground up a series of switchbacks. Twisty and steep at first, the road gets better and worse as logging starts and stops.

21 CLEAR CREEK

CLEAR CREEK TRAIL

A pleasant .75-mile path climbs through stately timber high over a Clear Creek gorge.

Find this often unmarked trail across the road from the turnaround loop at the end of the Clear Creek Campground. The path drops off the side of the road and then climbs sharply upward, winding along the edge of the canyon, higher and higher above the creek.

The path ends at a logging road. (An old trail continues to Frog Lake, but it is seldom maintained and sometimes impossible to follow.)

Allow enough time for daydreaming and soaking up the beauty of the view into the gorge.

OLD SAUK TRAIL

Hike a gentle 3 miles along the Sauk River past big old cedar stumps, remnants of what was once an ancient old-growth forest. Open most of the year.

Find the trail off the river side of the Loop Highway No. 20 about .7 mile south of Clear Creek Campground. Trail ends at the highway, about 3.5 miles from the campground.

Spawning steelhead and salmon in the fall.

ASBESTOS CREEK FALLS

Waterfalls from the sky down as Asbestos Creek pours off Jumbo Mountain in a continuous series of cascades.

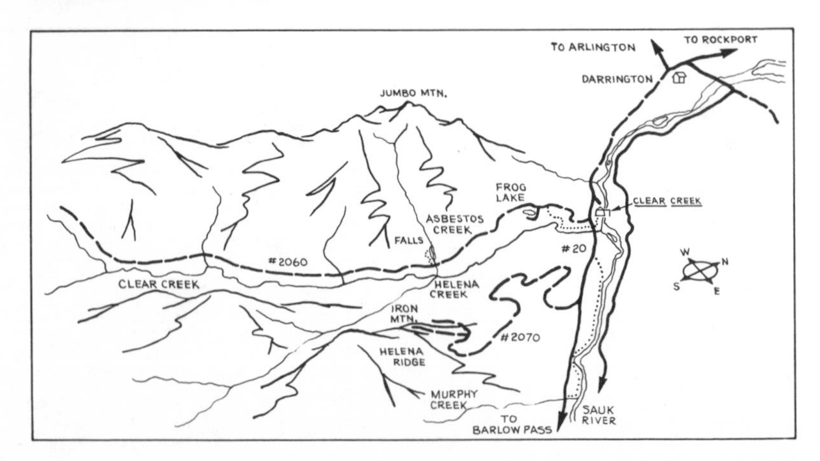

Take Clear Creek Road No. 2060 to the right at the entrance to Clear Creek Campground. The road fords Asbestos Creek in 2 miles. Falls to the right. For better views, scramble up the left side of the canyon. Watch for slippery rock.

Stop at Frog Lake on the way back. It's the little pond below the logging road. Entrance road at the lower end. Great place for polliwogs.

HELENA RIDGE ROAD

At 3,000 feet, see Mount Baker, Darrington, White Chuck Valley, Glacier Peak, Pugh, Bedal, and White Chuck.

Follow Road No. 20 past the Clear Creek Campground south of Darrington, turning right on Road No. 2070 in about a mile. Take the second spur right, up Helena Ridge toward Iron Mountain.

From the Helena Ridge Road

Unnamed waterfall beside the Suiattle River Road

M SUIATTLE RIVER

A popular access to the Glacier Peak Wilderness. But offering several recreation diversions of its own. Take the paved County Road north out of Darrington toward Rockport, turning east in about 6.5 miles onto the Suiattle River Road. Road ends at the trailhead into the wilderness area, 26 miles. Pronounced "Soo-attle."

BIG CREEK CASCADE

Big Creek plunges down a steep, narrow canyon that many visitors drive over without realizing it even exists. Stop at the first concrete bridge on the Suiattle River Road No. 26, at about 7 miles. The bridge spans the gorge. Signs of an old washed-out road in the gorge. No trail to the bottom.

CAMPGROUNDS

Buck Creek—29 units in one of the prettiest campgrounds in the state. Some sites near the creek, others back on timbered loops. All well separated in a grand stand of timber. (But there are fewer trees each year. Some of the older ones are being cut because they are believed to be dangerous (?)). Pit toilets, 24 miles from Darrington. **Note:** Loops on the east side of the river have been closed.

Downey Creek—Generally undeveloped. Sites on both sides of the creek. Older, primitive area, 30 miles from Darrington. Pit toilets.

Sulphur Creek—20 units. Sulphur Creek splits the campground, with most sites near either the creek or the Suiattle River, 32 miles from Darrington. Pit toilets.

22 SUIATTLE ROADS

Pleasant drives here, but even better places for picnics near creeks and the tumbling Suiattle River, now officially part of the national Wild Scenic River system.

To explore the south side of the river, turn south over the river about 6 miles west of Buck Creek Campground onto Road No. 25. Watch for dolomite mining claims along the way—white rock similar to marble. Uphill spur roads lead to views over the valley and into Glacier Peak Wilderness.

For more forest (perhaps), but still passing glimpses of the river, drive to the end.

BUCK CREEK TRAIL

A shady, easy walk through lush timber past rolling big-boulder rapids and deep pools along an unmarked trail north of the Buck Creek Campground.

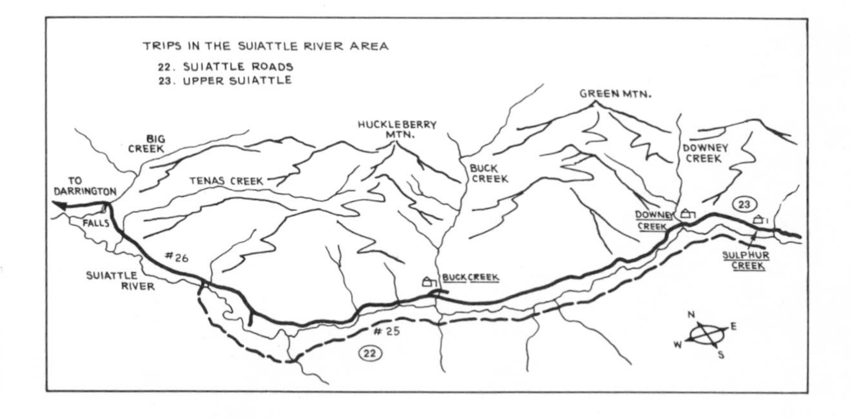

Find the path on the west side of the creek just beyond the uppermost campsite.

The trail enters the Glacier Peak Wilderness, following Buck Creek for about .75 mile before climbing up a lush ridge then dropping back to the creek. Once it crosses the creek, the trail ends in forest.

The path once went on to Horse Creek in about 5 miles.

To hike down to the Suiattle River, find a fisherman's trail on the west side of the creek south of the road. Lots of windfalls to clamber over and under. But the noisy creek will listen to all your complaints.

GREEN MOUNTAIN TRAIL

A steep trail through a mossy forest to one of the largest meadow systems in this area. Overlook the Suiattle River and Downey Creek valleys with Glacier Peak, Box Meadow, and Circle Peaks in the background. Trail enters the Glacier Peak Wilderness in about .25 mile, reaching meadows at 1.5 miles, continuing another 2.5 miles to Green Mountain Lookout.

Turn up the Green Mountain Road No. 2680 2 miles east of the Buck Creek Campground—the first road beyond the Green Mountain pasture area. The road starts with views, but then winds back through a series of blackened clear-cuts.

Clear-day views of Glacier Peak near the end of the road. Find the trail at the end of a spur road which turns to the left off Road No. 2680 shortly before it ends. And don't be fooled by any old trail mileage markers. They were posted before the roads were built.

23 UPPER SUIATTLE

SULPHUR CREEK TRAIL

An arboretum of wild greenery along a creek of pools, waterfalls, rocks, and gravel bars.

Find the trail on the left of the Suiattle River road near the Sulphur Creek Campground entrance. It climbs steeply at the start but soon drops down to the creek. Go as far as you like. Trail ends in 2 miles. But all of it is worth a walk. Lots of good picnic spots.

For a side trip, take a spur trail to a sulphur spring. Turn right down a well-worn path at a wilderness sign about .7 miles from the road. The path crosses the creek on a system of flattened footlogs which can be treacherously slippery when wet. Turn upstream, finding the sulphur spring seep, out of a rockslide, in less than 25 yards.

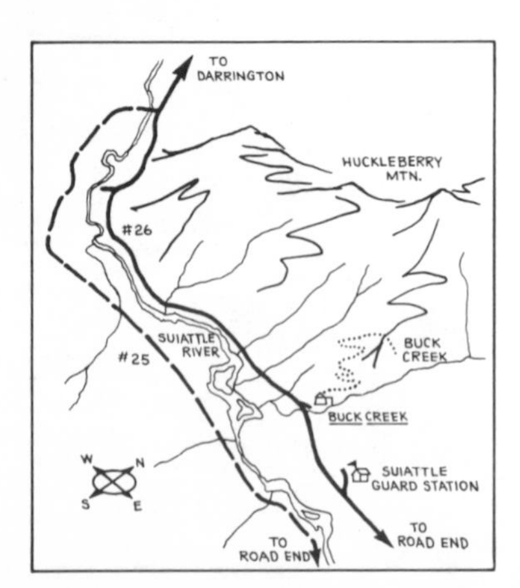

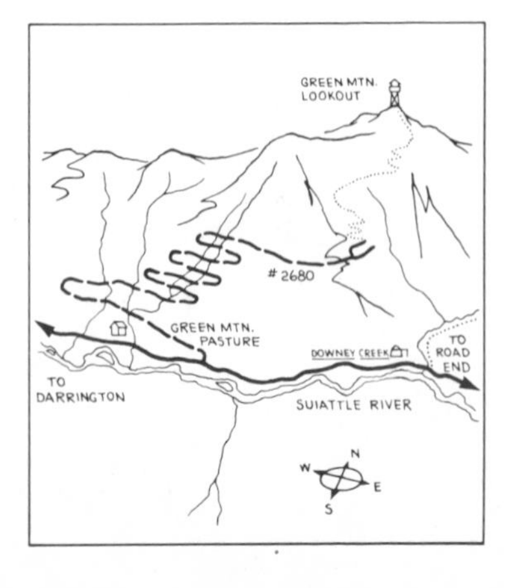

Suiattle River Valley from Green Mountain Road

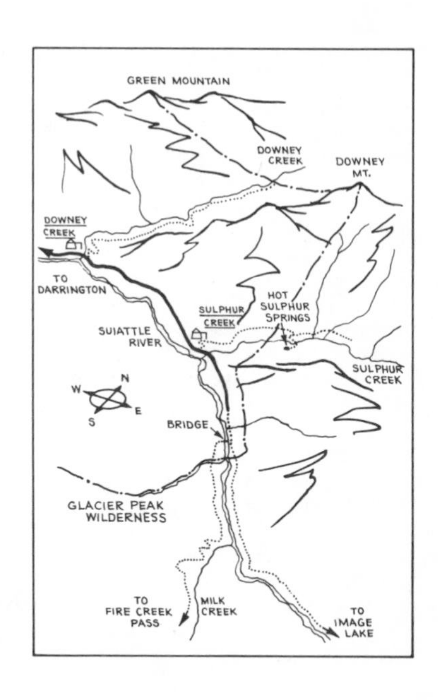

Nurse log on Buck Creek Trail

SUIATTLE RIVER TRAIL

Huge trees, ferns, and nurse logs along two fine forest trails at the end of the Suiattle River Road.

Find the trails out of the developed parking area at the end of the road. Follow an abandoned road to the junction of the Milk Creek and Suiattle River trails in about 1 mile.

The Milk Creek trail starts at a bridge over the Suiattle River and climbs almost immediately into rain-forestlike growth, gloriously rich with huge trees and understory greenery. A walk of a mile or so leads past tumbling creeks. Turn back when you feel like it.

The Suiattle River trail turns uphill slightly at the junction and plunges into stately forest. In about .5 mile watch for an unmarked trail back downhill toward the river. It ends at an old shelter and a number of sand bars in maybe .25 mile. (You can also reach the shelter from the Milk Creek trail bridge by following faint footpaths which pass a fern-covered rock wall of folded schists.)

But the shelter may be gone by the time you get there. It was included in the Glacier Peak Wilderness. However, as some in the Forest Service saw it, the shelter did not have the historic significance that would have qualified it for preservation in the wilderness. Indeed, some would argue that regulations forbid such structures. If it's still up when you visit, let rangers at Darrington know what you think about the situation. If it's gone, write about that too.

DOWNEY CREEK TRAIL

Another pleasant forest walk as far as you want to go.

Find trail on the north side of the road east of Downey Creek. Watch for sign. Trail climbs steeply at first then traverses above the river, returning to river level in about 3 miles.

N MOUNTAIN LOOP HIGHWAY

Less than a decade ago (in the mid-1970s), a Sunday drive around the Mountain Loop Highway was a prime tourist adventure featured almost yearly by newspapers and area outdoor magazines.

It took time. It took care. But it gave back a sense of adventure. A sense of accomplishment. And a sense—even from the road—that you were driving in a forest, amid mountains, and along a noisy river.

Drive the "improved" road today and wonder what was so exciting about it. Dull. With no personality at all. A highway for logging trucks. Nothing more.

MEADOW MOUNTAIN—CRYSTAL LAKE

One used to be able to walk to these places in far less than 2 miles. Beautiful meadows and pretty lake.

But in the 1970s the Forest Service poured nearly $300,000 of the public's money into improving the road so loggers could get their big trucks into a few clear-cuts. And then they closed the road. Loggers and trail bikers can drive it. Others can't.

In the past, you could reach Meadow Mountain by trail in 1.5 miles. Now you must walk 4.5 miles farther—on the road.

And it was the same with Crystal Lake. A 1-mile hike by trail is now a 3-mile walk, most of it by road.

The reason the Forest Service gives for closing the road without any prior public notice is to protect the lake and meadows from overuse—brought about by the agency's construction of the road.

To see where the bikers ride and the loggers drive and where you have to walk, drive east from the White Chuck Campground on Road No. 23 (along the White Chuck River) about 5 miles, turning north on Road No. 27 and then right onto Road No. 2710 to the infamous gate.

BEAVER LAKE TRAIL

A pleasant walk of about 2 miles leads through lush forest to ponds busy with beavers. Not that they'll be waiting for your visit. More than likely they'll have hurried home before you get there. But you can still see their handiwork (toothwork?) everywhere.

Find the trail at the end of a short spur road off the Mountain Loop Highway, toward the river, just south of the new concrete Sauk River bridge southeast of Darrington. Trail on the left, beyond a fallen log.

Path follows an old railroad bed through lots of thick green mossy and misty forest. Polliwog pools, occasional glimpse of surrounding peaks (Pugh, Sloan, and Forgotten),

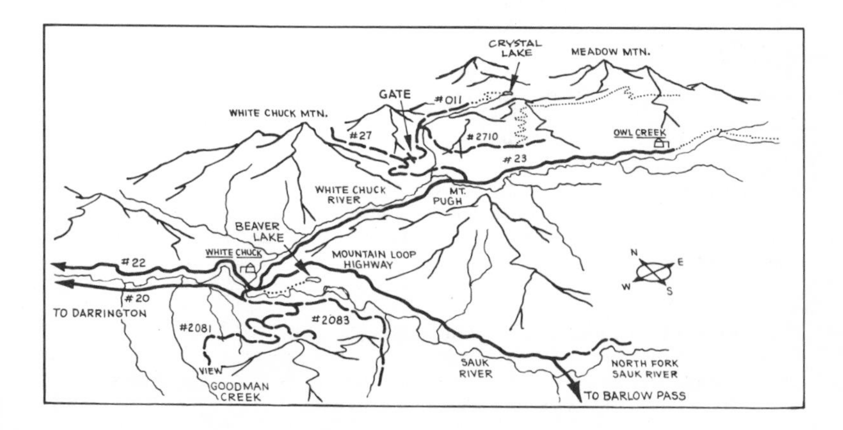

Meadow Mountain Road and Mount Pugh

lots of birds, salmonberries, and devils club. Puncheon bridges at the beaver ponds, along with old railway trestles. The best part of the trail ends at the river, but a spur to the left heads uphill back to the highway and a sign.

VISTA DRIVES

For view of **Glacier Peak,** not often seen from these low roads, turn off the loop highway at the new bridge (not-so-old-timers will remember a more interesting bridge) about 6 miles from the Clear Creek Campground on Road No. 23. Vistas at the end in 7 miles.

For high views over the Sauk Valley, along with Glacier, White Chuck, Pugh, and Bedal peaks, turn west at the bridge onto Road No. 2080 up Falls Creek, turning uphill onto No. 2081 in 2 miles. Take all turns to the right. Road ends along Goodman Creek.

CAMPGROUNDS

Owl Creek—4 sites. Primitive trailhead camp at the end of the White Chuck River Road No. 23.

White Chuck—10 units. Where the White Chuck River joins the Sauk. Tent and car-camper sites, 11 miles from Darrington. Pit toilets.

O SAUK RIVER

NORTH FORK FALLS

A roaring torrent less than .25 mile by trail from North Fork Road No. 49. Turn east off the Mountain Loop Highway about 18 miles south of Darrington or 7 miles north of Barlow Pass onto the North Fork Road. Drive about 1 mile. Watch for sign. The steep trail drops from a parking pull-off on the south side of the road. Can be slippery when wet.

RED MOUNTAIN VIEWPOINT

A 1-mile hike leads to a viewpoint, once the site of a lookout, with limited views of the North Fork Valley of the Sauk, including the snow-crested Bedal and Sloan peaks.

Take the Glacier Peak Wilderness trail out of Sloan Creek Campground, finding the Red Mountain trail to the left in about 100 yards, just beyond and behind a Forest Service display board.

Trail switchbacks steadily to the lookout site and then continues another few hundred yards to no better views. In Glacier Peak Wilderness.

MINERAL SPRINGS

Continue on the wilderness trail out of Sloan Creek Campground past the shelter to a salt-lick seep, a red-mud area to the left of the trail. Watch for path on left in about 100 yards. Take care here and you may see wildlife. Lots of tracks in the mud any time of year.

FOREST WALK

An easy forest walk past awe inspiring trees in a valley which is now, thankfully, part of the wilderness system.

Take the Glacier Peak Wilderness trail out of Sloan Creek Campground (see above), following it along the river as far as you want. Pleasant forest and huge trees for better than a mile. A magnificent place to forget the pettiness of the city.

HIGH VIEW DRIVE

Follow the North Fork Road No. 49 past the Sloan Creek Campground turnoff to clear-day views of the peaks around both Cadet and Sloan creeks. Take either fork at the "Y" about 2 miles beyond the campground. The road left up Sloan Creek leads to the highest views, looping back above Cadet Creek. See Sloan, Foggy, Monte Cristo, and Cadet peaks and a large glacier in Pride Basin. Good picnicking. Nice creeks. But watch for logging trucks.

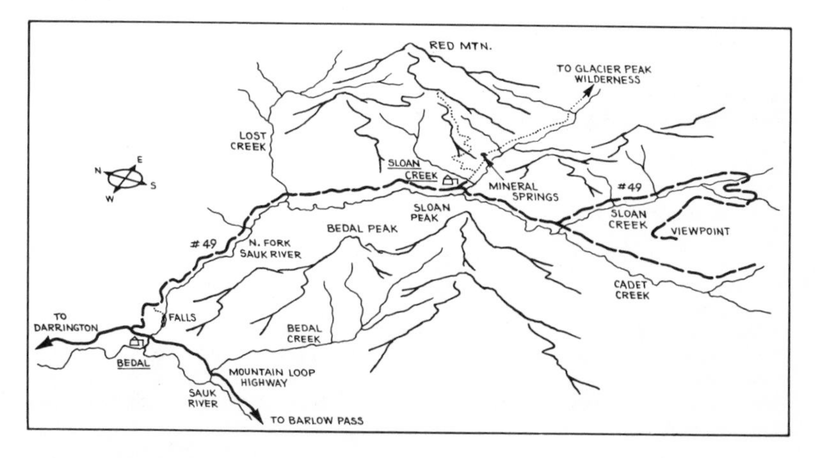

Buck Creek Campground

CAMPGROUNDS

Sloan Creek—8 walk-in units in a beautiful, stately old stand of Douglas fir and cedar. Trailhead camp to the Glacier Peak Wilderness, 6 miles from Mountain Loop Highway on Road No. 49. Watch for sign, campground on a short spur to the left (east). Pit toilets.

Bedal—19 units and a shelter. Very pleasant campground—one of the nicest on the Sauk. Some sites on the river. Others on open-timbered ledge overlooking the river, 18 miles from Darrington. Pit toilets. Piped water.

24 SOUTH FORK SAUK RIVER

GOAT LAKE

It's still 4.5 miles into scenic and popular Goat Lake, now in the Henry M. Jackson Wilderness. And it is still well worth the effort it takes to get there. But the hike is no longer as pleasant as it used to be.

A decade or two ago, you could drive to the end of a logging road and walk 1.5 miles to the lake. Then the Forest Service closed the road and routed hikers up a pleasant trail along Elliott Creek.

Now they've abandoned the trail because in the eyes of some it costs too much to maintain. And hikers must follow the gated "dual purpose" Road No. 4080—a trail for hikers and a road for loggers. (It was cleared out most recently for the ceremony dedicating the wilderness.) Now 3 miles by road and 1.5 miles by trail. Primarily a day-use area.

Old railroad trestle alongside the Beaver Lake Trail

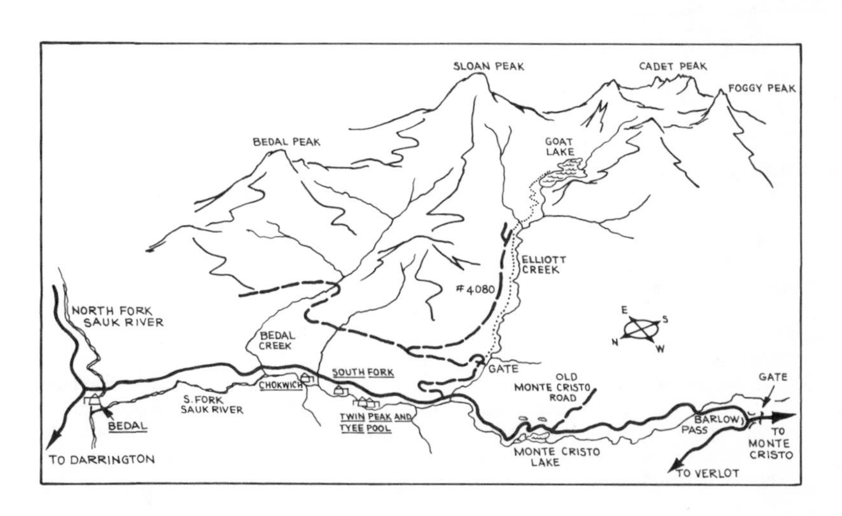

Monte Cristo Lake

MONTE CRISTO LAKE

No great spectacles here. No vast stretches of water. But the small ponds invite exploration by kayak and canoe. Not that you'll get lost. Impossible. But you won't be able to avoid the sense of secrecy the place presents.

Find the lakes (ponds?) about 2 miles north of Barlow Pass on the Mountain Loop Highway. One small pond on the right of the road. Others on the left. Water levels vary from year to year and from season to season.

CAMPGROUNDS

All of the campgrounds along this section of the Mountain Loop Highway have been abandoned. Signs are gone. In some cases, even the pit toilets have been eliminated. But most of the tables, road spurs, and camp spots remain. None are maintained. No funds, the Forest Service says. Note, however, how many of the logging roads have been improved.

P STILLAGUAMISH

The Stillaguamish River valley from Verlot to Barlow Pass and on to Darrington offers far more than scenery. History, fossil-bearing rock, mountain lakes, and high alpine trails—all in a single package.

An extremely popular place, crowded—and overcrowded—most summer weekends.

Drive east from Granite Falls on the Mountain Loop Highway. The Verlot Forest Information Station in 12.3 miles; Barlow Pass, 33 miles. Turn north at Barlow Pass and take the Mountain Loop Highway on to Darrington.

CAMPGROUNDS

Turlo—19 tent sites in a wooded area across from the Verlot Information Station. Some sites near the river. Others on a shaded loop. All well separated. A busy area. Vault toilets. Piped water. A fee camp.

Verlot—20 sites, 10 for tent campers only. The rest for tent or trailer use. Most heavily developed and popular campground in the valley. Full on weekends. But pleasantly private during the week. Restrooms. Piped water. Fee camp.

Hemple Creek—3 camping sites, 13 picnic-only sites. Fisherman trails and a pool to the east. Pit toilets. Piped water.

Gold Basin—67 sites, 20 for tent campers. The rest for tent or trailer use. Largest campground in the valley. Some sites near the river but most on pleasant wooded loops. Pit toilets. Piped water. Fee camp.

Red Bridge—10 sites on a forested bend in the river. Gets heavy trailer use, 8 miles from Verlot. Pit toilets.

River Bar—A gravel bar on the north side of the road across from the Red Bridge Campground, 6 sites for trailers. Pit toilets.

Boardman Creek—4 units. A group rental camp. On spur road just beyond Boardman Creek, 6 miles from Verlot.

Esswine—5 units. Group rental camp.

Note: There are a number of smaller primitive camps all along the river near almost every stream. Most are oriented to trailer-camper use. But a few provide tent camping opportunities. Pit toilets at some.

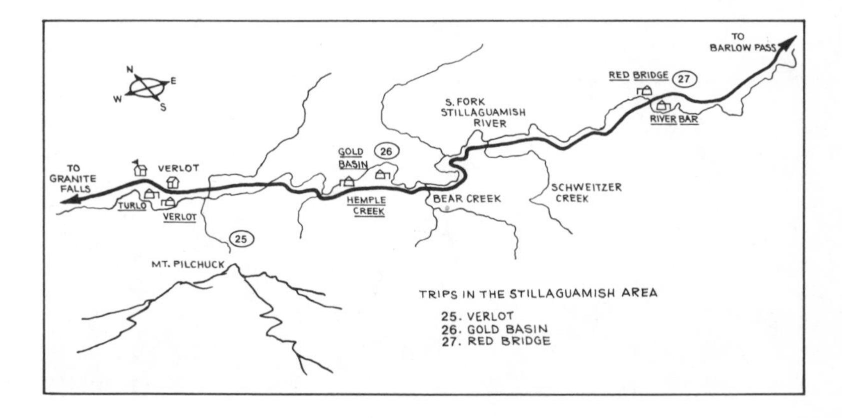

Maiden of the Woods

25 VERLOT

Turn south onto the Mount Pilchuck Road No. 42 just east of the bridge 1 mile east of the Verlot Information Station. Views along the way, with the best vista from the ski lodge area at the end of the road and from the top of the mountain itself.

PILCHUCK LOOKOUT

Vistas here of about everything from Puget Sound and the Olympics to the Cascade peaks.

A steep 2-mile trail leads from the road to the abandoned lookout. Find the trailhead uphill near the end of the road. The path at the start looks more like a cattle run than a trail; mud and roots several yards wide.

Snow often remains on the trail above timberline until midsummer or later. Stay on the trail coming down. Some shortcuts lead to cliffs.

HEATHER LAKE

A 2-mile hike to a cirque lake in subalpine forest and meadow.

Trail leaves the Pilchuck Road No. 42 at 1.5 miles from the valley turnoff, leading up an old logging road at first and into a logged-off area before entering lovely old forest in the valley of Heather Creek. Open meadows in the basin before reaching the lake, at 2,450 feet are filling up with little silver firs. No camping within 100 feet of the lake. Very fragile shore.

LAKE TWENTY-TWO

An extremely popular 2.4-mile trail through a grove of giant cedar and past a series of secluded waterfalls to a spectacular mountain lake (2,460) with an almost permanent snowfield at the end. In a Research Natural Area.

Find the trail from a parking area east of Verlot Information Station beyond Twenty-two Creek. Watch for sign. No camping and no fires either at the lake or on the trail.

A very popular walk. Hundreds of people every weekend. So don't expect much privacy. And treat the lakeside kindly.

MAIDEN OF THE WOODS

A .75-mile hike to a wooden lady clinging to the side of a cedar tree—despite fire and time—in the middle of the forest. Dudley Carter, a Seattle wood sculptor, carved the huge lady for a movie about wood carving.

Turn north on Road No. 4005 east of the Verlot store—watch for the trail sign in about 1.5 miles, just after the road turns sharply up a hill. A pleasant trail.

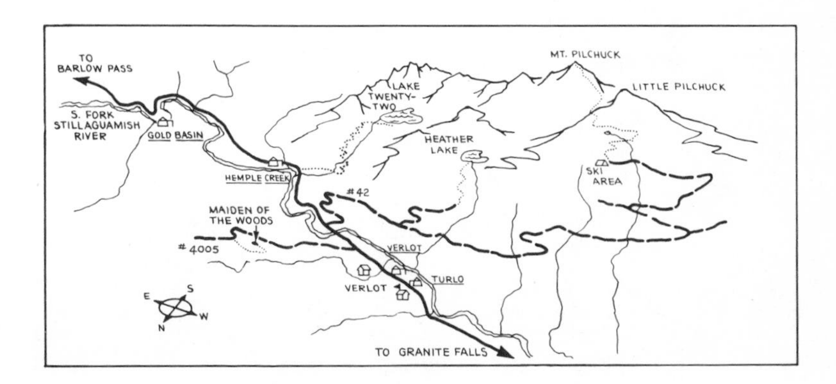

SADDLE LAKE

Struggle 2 miles to a subalpine lake that marks the entrance to an inspiring world of alpine meadows.

Turn north of the Mountain Loop Highway about 4 miles west of the Verlot Information Station (close to 7 miles east of Granite Falls) onto Road No. 41, following the road some 17 miles to Tupso Pass. Find the trail off a short spur to the right.

The trail enters the Boulder River Wilderness and promptly begins an unmaintained and heavily rooted and eroded struggle up a ridge (vistas now and then) to the lake, in what will seem much longer than 2 miles.

Admire the lake, with its marsh-loving flowers and scurrying salamanders, and then press on at least another mile (this path is not so rough) to a rolling subalpine meadow tucked with tarns. Find your own hummock of heather and give thanks to the hundreds who did political battle to preserve this corner of heaven.

For further thanks in an even bigger corner, hike another 1.5 miles to Goat Flats—a decorated altar of nature's splendor. And treat all these tarns and meadows with the respect due any place of worship.

26 GOLD BASIN

A single logging road with high views over the Stillaguamish River valley leads to a whole handful of pretty trails to mountain lakes.

Turn south on Road No. 4020, east of the Gold Basin Campground. At about 2.3 miles, turn west onto Road No. 4021 for trails to Bear and Pinnacle lakes and to Ashland and Twin Falls lakes. Keep straight ahead on Road No. 4020 for the trailhead to Boardman and Evan lakes.

EVAN AND BOARDMAN LAKES

An easy trail of about 1 mile leads first past Lake Evan and then climbs gradually through timber to Boardman. Trail gets sloppy when wet.

Lake Evan—A 12-acre lake at 2,981 feet only a few hundred yards from the road. Watch for trail sign on the left after the road makes a sharp switchback to the right about 2 miles from the junction. Shallow, weedy shoreline.

Boardman Lake—A pretty 50-acre lake at 3,370 feet, surrounded by big timber and rock bluffs. The trail reaches the lake near the inlet. Camping on a bench above the lake.

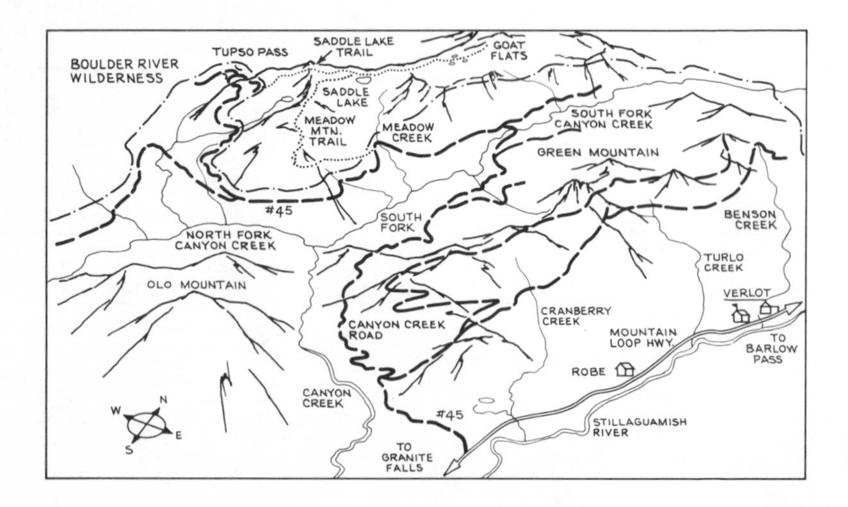

Boardman Lake

BEAR AND PINNACLE LAKES

A smooth, level trail—crested and finished with crushed rock—leads to Bear Lake in less than .5 mile. But it takes a low-gear, tedious, sometimes sloppy 2-mile effort to reach the alpine Pinnacle Lake.

Bear Lake—A path—it's much too posh to be called a trail—leads along the edge of a clear-cut—turn right at the junction to a timbered lake at 2,775 feet. Push a baby carriage down it if you like. An expansive but undeveloped area near the lake for picnicking. Heavily used. Fisherman's paths around most of the lake.

Pinnacle Lake—Turn left at the junction. Posh path for another .5 mile gives way to a sloppy forest trail. Occasional views down on Bear Lake and over the valley break up the tedium of the climb. Trail tops out across a series of marshy flower-huckleberry meadows to reach the lake at 3,820 feet surrounded by patches of timber, steep meadows, and scenic rock bluffs, 1.7 miles from road. Treat the meadows here with kindness so others also may enjoy.

ASHLAND AND TWIN FALLS LAKES

A world of small lakes and rich forest to explore off easy trails that extend 2 miles to the last of the Ashland lakes and another 1.5 miles to the seclusion of Twin Falls Lake.

These trails and lakes, mostly on state land, were developed by the state's Department of Natural Resources.

After turning up the Schweitzer Creek Road No. 4020 off the Mountain Loop Highway, beyond the Gold Basin Campground, turn right onto Road No. 4021, driving about 1.5 miles to a junction with Road No. 016. Turn uphill here and follow signs (generally bearing right) to the signed Bald Mountain trail parking area in less than a mile.

Walk up a steep road spur from the parking lot to a trail that crosses a grown-over area before entering old forest, reaching Beaver Plant Lake in less than a mile. A short spur path circles the pond.

Keep right for Ashland Lakes at a junction just beyond the pond. (Trail left goes out Bald Mountain Ridge.) Upper Ashland Lake, still within a mile, and Lower Ashland Lake in another .5 mile. Explore trails around both lakes before pressing on.

Follow the main trail beyond Lower Ashland over a ridge and then down around mossy rocks and cliffs to Twin Falls Lake. The main falls—the only one you can easily see—plunges off a 125-foot cliff into the lake. The other drops over another cliff at the lake outlet into the valley below. Approach the lip of the lower falls with extreme care.

Note: Most of the trails here consist of puncheon slabs and upended cedar rounds which can be slippery when wet.

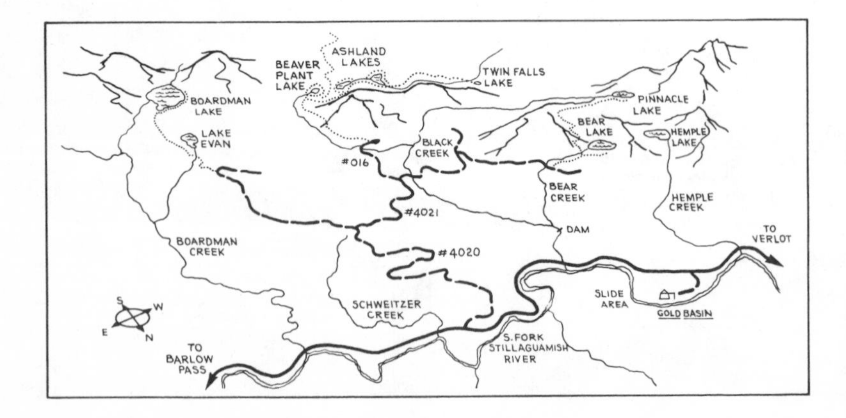

Skunk cabbage near Silverton

Devil's club

27 RED BRIDGE

BLACK CHIEF MINE

An old mine tunnel extends 125 feet into a mountain only a few yards off the highway. Mine entrance through the trees across from the Red Bridge Campground just east of the Red Bridge. In the northeast quadrant of the road junction. The mine was abandoned in 1926 after no ore had been found in an operation begun in the early 1900s. The shaft is not timbered.

MONTE CRISTO RAILROAD

Old pilings and occasional signs of an old roadbed cut are all that's left of the railroad that once ran as far as Monte Cristo.

Best signs of piling can be seen in the river at Boardman Creek and just off the highway through the trees to the south at the gravel section (washout) in the road west of Silverton.

Parts of the old roadbed are visible at Big Four, Barlow Pass, and along the road to Monte Cristo (now closed). The old tunnels have been plugged.

GOLD PANNING

No promises, now. But some campers have been seen panning for gold along the upper reaches of the river, particularly in the Gold Basin and Red Bridge Campground areas. Some of the smaller streams also attract an occasional prospector.

NATURE TRAIL

A short nature trail, signed as the Youth-on-Age Trail, east of the Red Bridge, leads through a rich forest with, as you'd expect, ample samples of this quiet and subdued moist-forest flower with its greenish brown-to-purple blossoms. Its name comes from the fact that it reproduces from buds (new) that grow from the base of the (old) leaf blade.

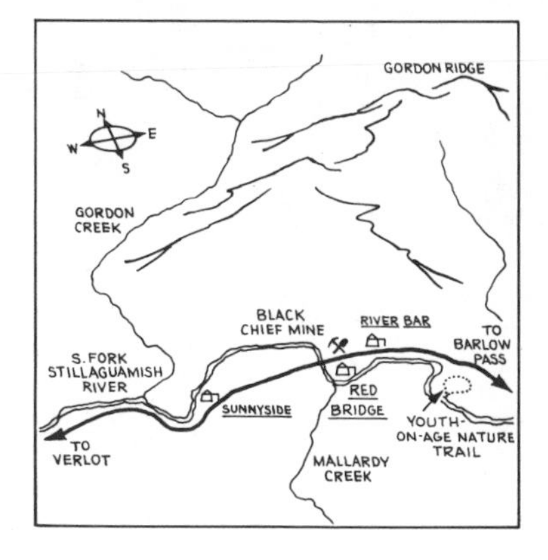

Cascade golden-mantled ground squirrel

Big Four Mountain and South Fork Stillaguamish River

Q SILVERTON

The town of Silverton—across the (private) log bridge 12 miles from Verlot—is now a summer-home area on private land, where public access is often denied.

But long ago the area was the center of mining activities. Many of the old mines lie abandoned along the south side of Silver Gulch: collapsed sheds, rusty machinery, old—now-dangerous—tunnels. No public roads or trails lead into the area.

BIG FOUR VIEW

If the road's open, drive. But if it's gated, walk the 2-plus miles to a full-sky view of Big Four Mountain and small secrets of the ancient past.

Turn north off the Mountain Loop Highway onto Deer Creek Road No. 4052 driving less than 1 mile to a junction with No. 4054 on the right. Drive if you can. Otherwise, park and walk.

Vistas as the road switchbacks uphill in about 1.5 miles. For secrets of the past, look for fragments of leaf-imprint rocks in the road-cut at the very end.

KELCEMA LAKE

A half-mile by easy trail that starts near the end of Road No. 4052. Watch for sign and parking area on the left. A mountain cirque lake on the north side of Bald Mountain in the Boulder Creek Wilderness.

Drive north on Deer Creek Road No. 4052, turning left at the junction within a mile. Trailhead in about another 3 miles.

A heavily used area. Don't camp near the lake. Best camping across the logjam at the outlet.

DEER CREEK PASS

A .5 mile walk leads into a tiny political battle ground with a view out at Three Fingers Mountain. At the end of Road No. 4052.

This single, short piece of trail between south-flowing Deer Creek and north-flowing Clear Creek was made part of the Boulder River Wilderness for one reason: to prevent the construction of a road where the trail is now.

So enjoy. Walk up to where you can see the mountain and then explore the ridges to the west (drop down to Kelcema Lake, if you like) for a fuller appreciation of what the wilderness is all about.

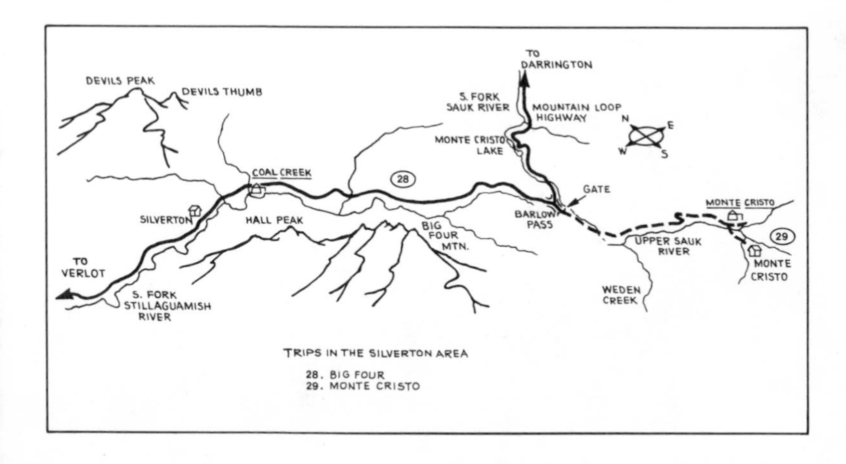

Ice Cave on Big Four Mountain

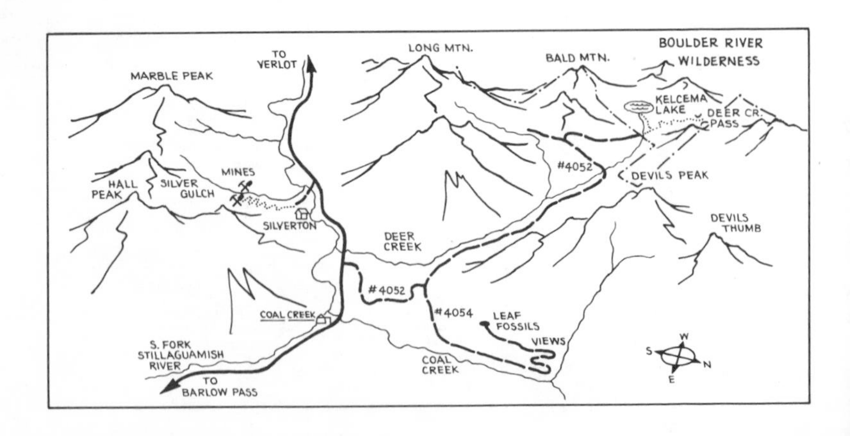

CAMPGROUNDS

Dick Sperry—4 units, 1 mile west of Silverton on the river side of the highway.
Marten Creek—5 units. A group rental camp, 1.5 miles west of Silverton.

Note: Group rental camps are closed to general public use. They must be rented by groups at the Verlot Information Center.

28 BIG FOUR

Site of an old resort in what was once advertised as the "Alps of America." Ruins of an old fireplace and concrete powerhouse are all that is left of the complex that almost filled the flat. Drive 15 miles east of Verlot. Watch for the Big Four sign.

ICE CAVES

Caves in snowfields at the base of Big Four Mountain about 1 mile by trail from a picnic area on the site of the old Big Four resort. Number and size of the caves vary from year to year.

The trail starts directly from the parking area at Big Four (find sign) and heads toward the Stillaguamish River over an old concrete sidewalk, part of the original resort complex. A new big bridge fords the river and the trail continues through pleasant forest to the base of the Big Four cliffs and the sun-sheltered snowfields.

One warning. The caves are not usually open until mid-July or later and can be hazardous, as can the snow above them. So explore with extreme care. Call Verlot Information Station to find out conditions in advance.

INDEPENDENCE AND COAL LAKES

Drive past one to hike to another. Both pretty mountain lakes. Turn north beyond Big Four on Road No. 4060. Big views of the valley and Big Four Mountain at a viewpoint, 2.2 miles. And look for leaf-imprint rocks in the road cut behind the formal vista display.

Coal Lake—About 50 yards off the road to the right. Watch for sign. An easy canoe or kayak carry. No powerboats here. A few camping spots on the south shore. A narrow snow-fed lake of 64 acres at 3,420 feet surrounded by steep timber and rock slopes.

Independence Lake—Worth every step of the .75-mile trail. Drive to the end of the road. Trail climbs through a clear-cut and then drops into timber down one of the branches of Coal Creek before climbing up sharply to the lake at 3,700 feet. Noisy little falls at the outlet.

Hike around the south side of the crystal blue lake to the open meadow at the inlet end. Camping off the meadows in the timber.

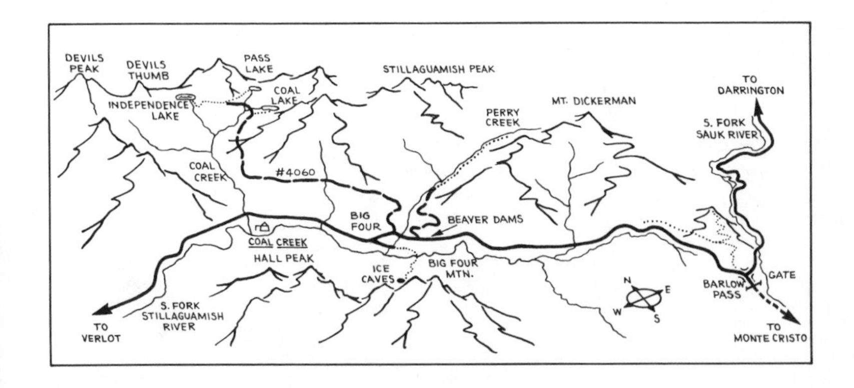

BARLOW LOOKOUT SITE

A 1-mile switchback trail to modest views of Big Four, Dickerman, and Sheep mountains, Monte Cristo Lakes, and the Stillaguamish Valley. Lots of mushrooms on lower levels in the fall.

Trail starts at Barlow Pass, skirting the south side of the ridge above the highway on the old government trail before turning up the mountain in a series of switchbacks through timber to the viewpoint.

The old government trail—which was the early route over Barlow Pass to Monte Cristo—continues downhill a total of 3 miles. In timber mostly.

CAMPGROUNDS

Perry Creek—8 units. East of Big Four, between Roads Nos. 4060 and 4063. No water.
Beaver Creek—4 units. Group rental camp.
Coal Creek Bar—10 units. Group rental camp. Spectacular views of Big Four Mountain.

Note: Group rental camps are now gated and closed to general public use. They must be rented in advance through the Verlot Information Center.

29 MONTE CRISTO

If the political game of logging interests you, here's a spot to place your bet.

Since 1983, the 4-mile mine-to-market road to Monte Cristo has been closed at Barlow Pass because, as Snohomish County officials were still saying in 1985, the county hasn't got the money to fix it. And the Forest Service says it can't fix it either because it would cost too much.

But there are still trees uncut on both sides of the road and as sure as lumber mills flourish, some logger is going to cut them. In fact, the Forest Service is already considering a road on the other side of the river to get the trees there.

So place your bets. Who's gonna pay? Who's gonna benefit? And who's gonna lose?

SAUK RIVER CROSSING

While the road is still gated at Barlow Pass, walk a mile to the ill-fated Sauk River crossing where the bridge washed out. Pleasant forest. Pleasant river. Pleasant crossing (on foot). And not many people either.

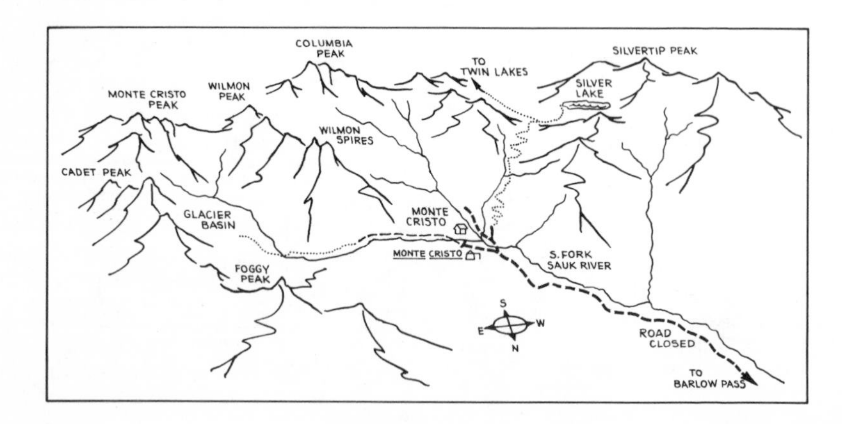

Beaver dam near Big Four Ice Caves

FROM MONTE CRISTO:

Note: closure of the Monte Cristo Road has added 4 miles each way to the following hikes.

Glacier Basin—It's a scramble to get there but the spectacle is hard to beat! Just over 2 miles.

Find the trail out of the Monte Cristo Forest Service Campground near the end of the road to Monte Cristo. To reach the campground follow an uphill spur to the left before the road crosses a bridge into the Monte Cristo complex.

The trail follows an old jeep road for about 1 mile and then scrambles sharply upward another mile along an old iron flume to a waterfall and then to a valley marred by mine operations. Continue to the spectacular alpine cirque at the end.

Don't camp on the meadows here. Find spots on the ridges, up in the rocks, or on Ray's Knoll. Heavy use is rapidly destroying the place.

Silver Lake—A steep and sloppy 2-mile trail climbs Poodle Dog Pass to a heather meadow and lake on the south side of the ridge above the resort. The trail starts at the end of a spur road uphill, to the right, just beyond the bridge into the Monte Cristo area. The path climbs sharply through open areas with views of the valley. Just beyond the pass a long, rough trail turns left to Twin Lakes. Trail to the right drops down to Silver Lake.

Skykomish River

R GOLDBAR TO STEVENS PASS

Spur roads off busy Stevens Pass Highway 2 lead to lakes, waterfalls, mine areas, high meadows, and quiet forest trails.

Drive east from Monroe through Sultan, Startup, Goldbar and on to Stevens Pass, exploring every side road along the way.

CAMPGROUNDS

Wallace Falls State Park—6 walk-in tent sites with tables and firepits. No camping facilities for trailers or camper trucks. In pleasant wooded area. Restrooms. Closed Mondays and Tuesdays in the winter.

Troublesome Creek—24 sites. Most of the sites along the North Fork of the Skykomish and Troublesome Creek. Sites both east and west of the bridge, in old-growth Douglas fir and hemlock. Half the sites can be reserved by groups, 10 miles northeast of Index. Pit toilets.

San Juan—8 campsites along the river in shaded hardwood area. A pleasant camp, 12 miles from Index. Pit toilets.

Beckler River Camp—24 developed sites in an open, gravel second-growth area. Some sites near the river, a few in the shade, 1 mile north of Skykomish. Pit toilets. Pump.

Money Creek—24 sites, some near the river, some on forest loops. Part of the camp in open timber. Some in undergrowth. A busy camp just off the highway, 4 miles west of Skykomish. Pit toilets.

Miller River—15 units in old-growth timber area. All on forested loops. Just over 3 miles south of Highway 2. Pit toilets. Group loops. Well.

Foss River—Primitive sites near the Foss River in a wooded area. Gets heavy hiker use. Near trailhead to Trout Lake. Pit toilets.

Tye Canyon—A pleasant but primitive camp off the Tye Canyon road about .5 mile east of the Martin Creek bridge. Places to camp in timber. One on the river. Generally full on weekends.

30 INDEX

Just because you aren't very far from civilization doesn't mean you can't find exciting places to explore just off the busy highway.

WALLACE FALLS

It wasn't too long ago that Wallace Falls was strictly something to be viewed from the highway. Today, however, you can stroll up and feel its spray after a modest hike down pleasant trails.

One of the most popular—and spectacular—waterfalls in the area.

Turn north off Highway 2 at the west end of Goldbar (watch for sign) and drive to Wallace Falls State Park. Trail to the falls is clearly marked off the parking area.

The path follows a powerline right-of-way to a viewpoint over the valley and then heads generally uphill through forest to the falls along two paths. The woody trail (to the right) reaches the falls in 2.25 miles. Upper trail in 3.25 miles. Both join about .25 mile from the falls.

Stop at the picnic shelter for one view or hike onward—and upward—to a middle viewpoint in .25 mile—and finally—at .5 mile—an explosive view of everything: down

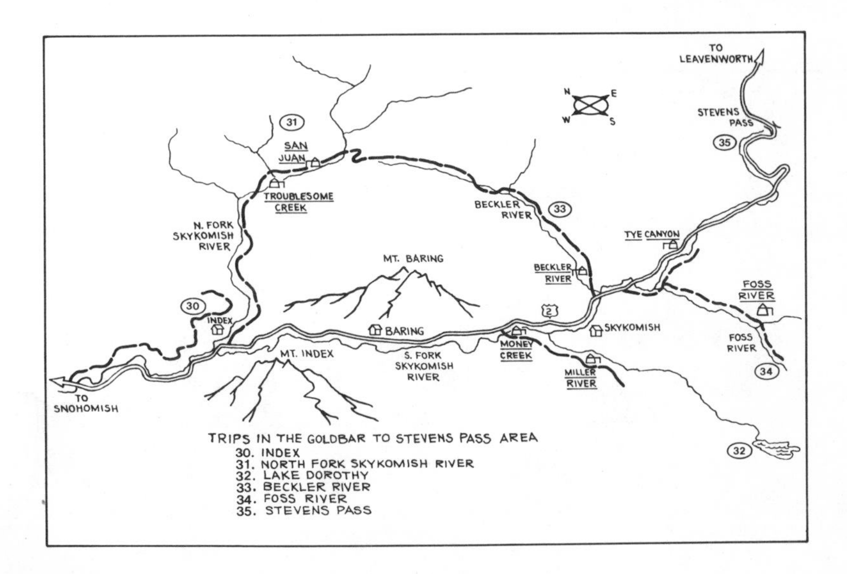

on the falls, across to the mountains on the other side of the valley, and out on the string of villages along the river.

MOUNTAIN VIEWS

Vistas opening with Mounts Index and Baring and ending with sweeping high views to the peaks in the Monte Cristo area.

Turn north off Highway 2 onto paved Rieter Road about 1.5 miles east of Goldbar. In less than 1 mile take rough, gravel Road No. 6010 straight ahead where the paved road turns sharply left.

Mount Index views over the Skykomish River valley in about 5 miles. Views of the North Fork Valley, Kyes and Columbia peaks of the Monte Cristo group, and Gunn and Baring between the forks of the Skykomish—in 10 miles.

HEYBROOK LOOKOUT

Hike a sharp 1 mile to one of the most popular vista points in the Cascade lowlands.

Find the trail here on the north side of the road about 2 miles east of Index, just beyond the Mount Baker–Snoqualmie National Forest sign. Limited parking. Watch for a wide place in the road. And use extreme care—particularly with children—near this busy highway. Most drivers here are rushing somewhere else and won't even see you until they've passed.

The trail parallels the highway for a short distance and then gets down to work, climbing some 900 feet to the Heybrook Lookout.

Climb the tower or just soak up the spectacle from the ground: Mount Index, Bridal Veil Falls, Index, and even the Olympics.

BARCLAY LAKE

Think ahead here to a pretty, forested lake tucked in the shadow of Baring Mountain, with lots of places to sit and dream.

Shun the clear-cuts at the start of the trail and wait for the peace of the forest as the trail climbs along Barclay Creek to the lake in a little more than a mile.

A rough way-trail climbs 1,400 feet in less than 2 miles from the far end of the lake up to Eagle Lake.

Turn north of Highway 2 about 6 miles from Index onto Baring Road No. 6024. Find the trail downhill to the left, before the road ends, in about 4.5 miles. Watch for signs.

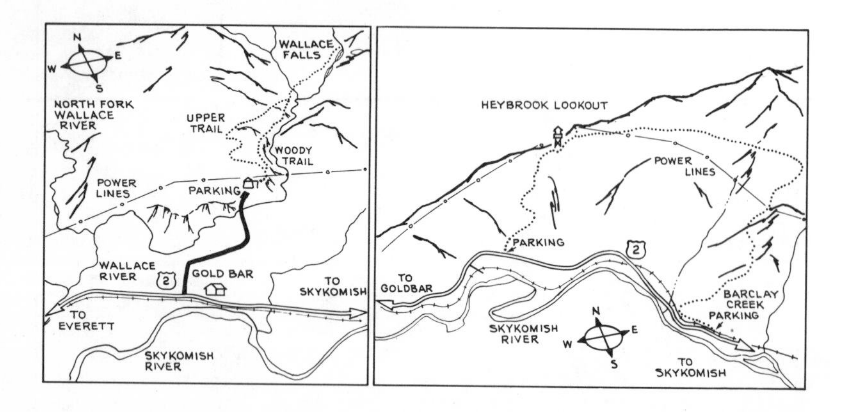

Mount Index from Heybrook Lookout

31 NORTH FORK SKYKOMISH RIVER

The first section—Index to Jack Pass—of a loop drive that starts from Highway 2 at Index, circles north, returning to the highway at Skykomish. Forty-five miles round trip. Index to Skykomish, 28.8 miles. Road paved almost 12 miles.

TROUBLESOME CREEK TRAIL

What was once an old miner's trail is now a busy—and pretty—interpretive trail along and around a tumbling creek.

Find the trail under the bridge out of the Troublesome Creek Campground on the west side of the creek. The path winds upstream past stately old-growth Douglas fir and along a tumble of cascades to a bridge. Cross the creek and return to the road on a trail that climbs through forest to still other views of the creek.

BEAR CREEK FALLS

A squat torrent that pours out of a rock gap into a beautiful pool. Less than .25 mile from the road.

Trail drops off the south side of the road about 1 mile east of Troublesome Creek bridge. Watch for a small turnoff where the trail drops through trees on a curve. No formal sign.

Trail leads to rock outcropping below the falls. Watch your footing when rocks are wet.

SAN JUAN FALLS

During the spring and fall, a pretty falls about .5 mile east of the San Juan Campground. A part-time stream tumbles off a high rock bluff on the south side of the road. A thin trickle in summer. Flows best during high-water seasons.

DEER FALLS

North Fork of the Skykomish River drops 70 feet over a slab cliff. Highest falls in the North Fork area and a good place to wonder about Forest Service recreation policy.

Take North Fork Road No. 63 east from Garland Springs (be sure to bear left at Jack Pass junction), driving 3.2 miles to Goblin Creek. About .2 mile beyond creek, turn right toward river down a logging road, bearing left at the bottom of the hill.

Find the trail off the road, as it starts paralleling the creek, by picking your way through logging debris toward the river. Walk downstream about .4 mile to the falls. You'll hear the roar.

Then note how this area was logged. The trail at one time wandered through stately

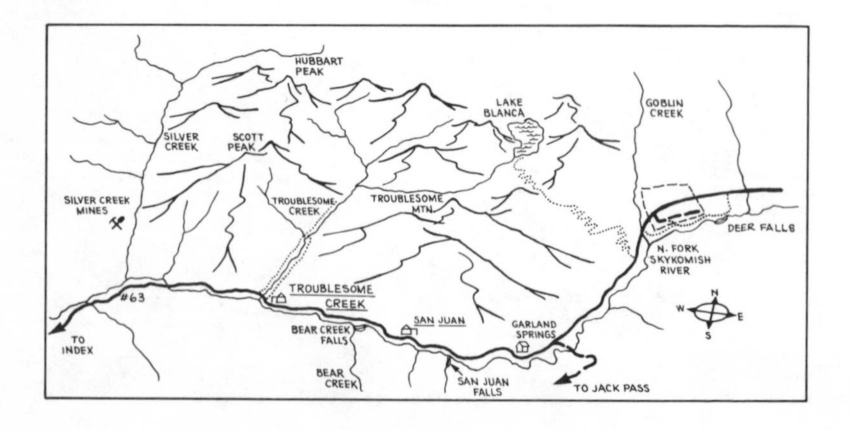

Lake Dorothy

forest to the falls. The walk itself was worthwhile! And then the Forest Service decided to make it "less hazardous" but still "undisturbed" by conducting what it euphemistically called a "sanitation-salvage" timber sale.

You judge. And then write the Mount Baker–Snoqualmie National Forest and let them know what you think about the matter.

32 LAKE DOROTHY

The biggest alpine lake and one of the most beautiful on the west side of the Cascade Crest, 1.5 miles through forest and past a junction of waterfalls from the end of the Miller River Road.

At 3,052 feet the lake, dotted with small rocky islands, stretches 2 miles down a long alpine-timbered valley. Trail touches the outlets (good views here) and then skirts the steep east side of the lake before turning westward, across the marshy south end of the lake, and climbing toward Bear, Deer, and Snoqualmie lakes (another 2 miles).

Take at least two snacks on this easy walk. Eat the first at the waterfall-filled stream junction at the footbridge about two-thirds of the way. Save the rest for the lake. Picnic spots at the outlet. Best camping farther down the trail near the lake.

Turn south off Highway 2 about 4 miles west of Skykomish—watch for Money Creek Campground signs. Turn south again in about 1 mile onto Miller River Road. Drive to the end, 9.3 miles from Highway 2. Lots of parking.

33 BECKLER RIVER

Eastern half of the loop drive into the mountains from Index to Skykomish. Jack Pass to Highway 2, 12.5 miles.

JACK PASS

Expansive views of the North Fork Valley and the Monte Cristo area peaks including Twin, Columbia, and Kyes.

Take Road No. 6570 west out of the Jack Pass complex, keeping right at the first fork. Viewpoint in less than 1 mile. Continuing views out over the valley and into the North Fork Skykomish River area on the road from Jack Pass to Garland Springs.

EVERGREEN MOUNTAIN

Hike only 1.5 miles to one of the most spectacular clear-day views in this section of the Cascades.

Trail takes off at the end of the road, switchbacks up a clear-cut and partially burned ridge, traverses an unburned area, and then bursts suddenly, in the last .5 mile, into open, flower-filled meadows.

Lookout tower (5,585) at the top, with 360-degree views of Glacier Peak, Mount Rainier, and the Monte Cristo peaks. But wander a way down the ridge on an abandoned trail for a lunch spot with your own private view. Bring your water.

Drive south from Jack Pass, taking the lower East Beckler Road No. 65. Evergreen Road No. 6554 turns east in about 1 mile, crossing Evergreen Creek before starting its climb, first to the south and then switching back to the north. Take the first spur to the right beyond the switchback to reach the trailhead and parking area. Big views, even from the road.

BECKLER PEAK

Drive to about 3,000 feet for views of most of the major peaks in the Stevens

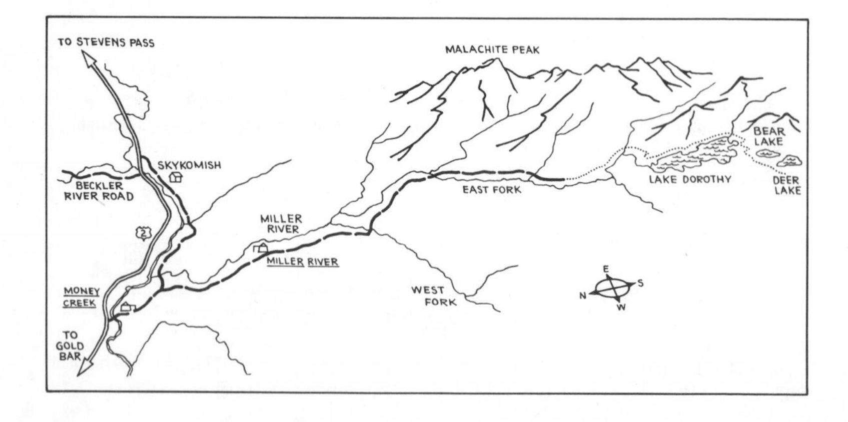

Foss River Valley from Beckler Peak Road

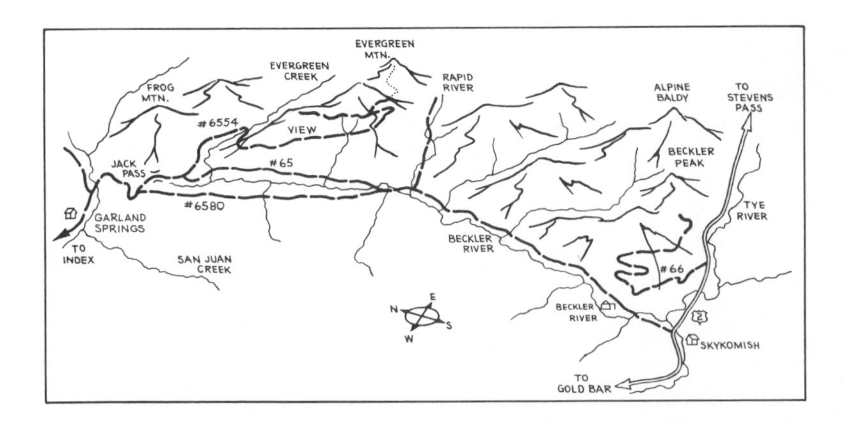

Tonga Ridge Trail

Pass–Skykomish area.

Turn north off Highway 2 onto the Beckler Peak Road No. 66, 2.5 miles east of the Beckler River road, 2 miles from the new Skykomish District Ranger Station.

Striking views of Mount Baring as the road climbs westward. The vista expands as the road switchbacks through clear-cuts to the east, with open views of the Tye River valley, the Hinman Glacier on Mount Hinman, Mount Daniels, Surprise, and other peaks of the Cascade Crest.

Watch for logging traffic.

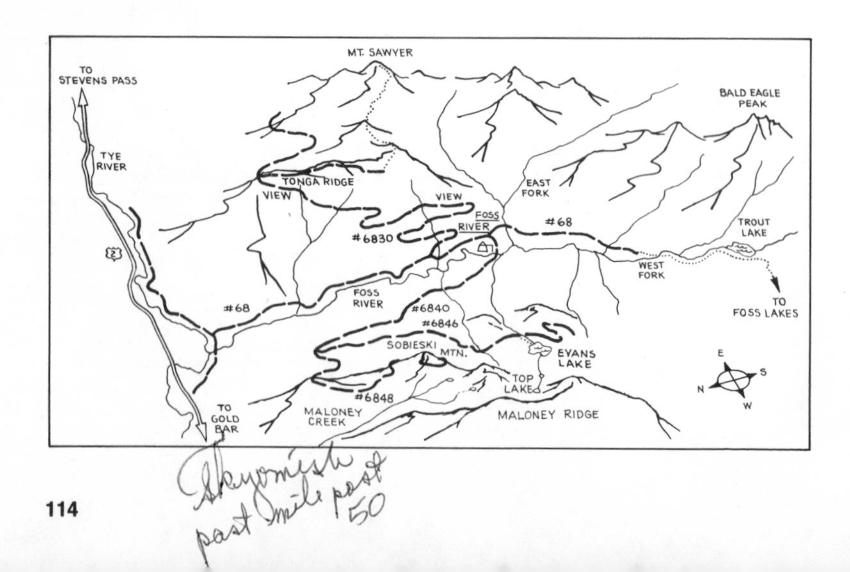

Skykomish past mile post 50

34 FOSS RIVER

TONGA RIDGE ROAD

A high mountain road offering continually changing vistas of the major peaks in the Stevens Pass area.

Turn south off Highway 2 on the first road east of the Skykomish District Ranger Station, about .5 mile. Keep right at Road No. 68, turning east onto Road No. 6830 at the Y, 3.2 miles.

At 6.9 miles from Highway 2, views of Hinman Glacier, Mount Daniel, the Necklace Valley area, and the West Fork of the Foss River. At 8.3 miles: Mount Index, Mount Baring, Eagle Rock, Glacier Peak, and Beckler River drainage. At 10.3 miles add Mount Fernow to all the rest. Road reaches 3,850 feet at highest point.

TONGA RIDGE TRAIL

In less than 1.5 miles, grass meadows at 4,000 feet along Tonga Ridge with views sweeping from Glacier Peak south through the glaciers on Mount Hinman.

Turn south off the Tonga Ridge Road No. 6830, about 6.8 miles from the Y (see above). Watch for signs.

Trail starts at end of the road and climbs quickly to the ridge. The main trail remains generally on the south side of the ridge, but spur paths lead north to vistas both ways. Lots of places to enjoy, enjoy, and enjoy. On the trail and off.

TROUT LAKE

A moderately steep trail to a small lake at 2,102 feet and past one of the biggest trees in Snoqualmie National Forest. 1.5 miles.

Trail leads through an old mine area past remnants of pipelines and mining equipment. Tunnel in brush and timber above the trail. Unmarked. The biggest tree—a 12-foot Douglas fir—marked next to the trail, about 1 mile.

Trail at end of Road No. 68.

SOBIESKI MOUNTAIN VIEWS

Drive to the end of a logging road atop Sobieski Mountain for grand views over the Skykomish Valley to Mount Baker and the snowy peaks of the Cascades around Stevens Pass.

Turn west on Road No. 68 at the Y, and west again in little more than 1 mile onto No. 6840, driving beyond the microwave towers in 9.6 miles onto Road No. 6848. Near the top, take the middle uphill spur road for the best vistas. About 12 miles from the highway.

EVANS LAKE

An easy .5-mile path leads to a small, pretty, wooded lake just inside the Alpine Lakes Wilderness boundary. Way-trails lead around the lake to picnic spots of your choice.

A good midweek walk. Busy on weekends.

From Road No. 6840 (see Sobieski Mountain) turn south on Road No. 6846, finding the trail on the right in 2-plus miles.

Unmarked and unclear fisherman way-trails lead up an inlet stream on the west side of the lake to Top Lake in less than 1 mile.

35 STEVENS PASS

DECEPTION FALLS

A roadside falls about 2 miles west of Scenic on Highway 2. Parking and restrooms on the north side of the busy highway. Falls on the south side.

Find a short nature trail to two more falls downstream from the parking lot. Noises of the highway disappear in a quiet stand of old-growth timber.

TYE CANYON ROAD

A pleasant respite from the rushing highway. A 3-mile winding drive through timber alongside the tumbling Tye River.

Turn north on Road No. 6700 just west of Scenic and the main highway bridge across the Tye. Road wends westward along the north side of the river, rejoining the highway just west of the Alpine Falls. The old Stevens Pass Highway.

HOPE LAKE

You don't have to walk far, but you do have to climb persistently to a pretty little mountain lake tucked into the very crest of the Cascades.

Drive east from Scenic a little more than 1 mile on Highway 2, turning right onto Road No. 6095 in the middle of a switchback-turn on the highway.

Follow traveled roads to the right.

The trail and trailhead here may change from year to year as the Forest Service continues to log in the area. (In 1985, the road was blocked at a creek at about 1 mile. The trail branched off the road to the left—on the other side of the creek—in another .25 mile.) Eventual plans call for a parking area and trailhead.

The path starts in forest (much of it was built and maintained by The Mountaineers Singles) and then settles down to a steady climb above Tunnel Creek, reaching the small lake and the Crest trail at 4,400 feet. A gain of about 1,400 feet.

But don't hurry away. If you've got time, walk north and south on the Crest trail, exploring the meadows and heathered tarns. And don't pass up the views. Finally, make a pledge to come back again.

RAILWAY RUINS

The west entrance of the abandoned Great Northern railroad tunnel, showshed, and townsite of Wellington just off the old Stevens Pass Highway.

Drive the old highway downhill from Stevens Pass. The road is blocked uphill from Scenic by a slide. Take the road off to the north, just west of the summit, and turn off to the right onto a gravel spur about halfway down, at the bottom of the switchbacks. Watch for what appears to be a gravel pit on the right.

Old tunnel entrance about 50 yards to the left off the spur road. Watch for it through the brush. If the tunnel is open, walk a short way into it for faint glimmers of light from the eastern entrance.

Old townsite of Wellington—renamed Tye by the railroad the day after 96 train passengers were killed in a nearby avalanche—lies between the tunnel entrance and snowshed, and to the north.

Hike down the old railroad through the snowsheds for further views of the valley. About 1.5 miles to Windy Point tunnel. Way is washed out in spots, rough, and brushy.

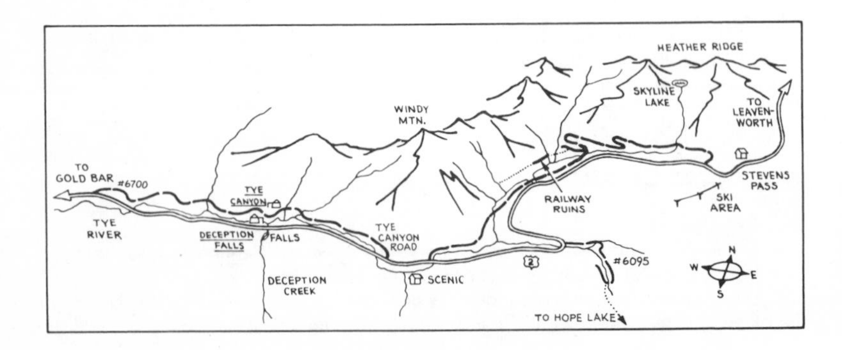

Deception Falls

Middle Fork Snoqualmie River Valley

S SNOQUALMIE PASS

Waterfalls, rock forms, nature trails, and high views—all practically at the edge of Seattle.

Drive east from Seattle on I-90 past North Bend, taking side roads up the Middle Fork of the Snoqualmie River, Taylor River, and Denny Creek. Snoqualmie Pass, 24 miles east of North Bend.

Campgrounds here are generally full throughout the summer. But there's always hiking room on trails and side roads.

CAMPGROUNDS

Tinkham—47 units in a new forested campground across the river from I-90. Turn south off I-90 at Exit No. 42 (Tinkham Road). Campground on the river side of the road in 2 miles. Water at pump.

Denny Creek—42 units on a series of loops, with 12 or so near the river, the rest in timber. A very busy, heavily used campground, particularly on weekends. Pit toilets.

Taylor River—Sites on a bar formed by the Middle Fork of the Snoqualmie River and Taylor River. A timbered area with undergrowth of vine maple and alder. Some sites near the rivers. Others back from the streams. All off several spurs near the entrance. Pit toilets.

Middle Fork—Primitive sites along the Middle Fork of the Snoqualmie River, beyond the Taylor River Campground. Camp spots start at the forest boundary and continue to the end of the road at Hardscrabble Creek. No facilities.

Commonwealth—12-unit primitive camp at Snoqualmie Pass. No water. Turn off I-90 at Exit No. 52 at Snoqualmie Pass, looping north beneath the freeway and then west, downhill, on the old Snoqualmie Highway (avoid freeway entrance). On the right.

36 MIDDLE FORK

Delicate stone forms near a campground and a trail that climbs to open views of mountains in the Alpine Lakes area—all off the road up the Middle Fork of the Snoqualmie River.

Drive east past North Bend on I-90, turning right at the Edgewick Interchange No. 34, looping north onto Road No. 56, driving to the Taylor River bridge in about 15 miles. Turn right on Road No. 5620 for the Taylor River Campground and Middle Fork trail. Turn left on No. 5630 to reach the end of the Taylor River road.

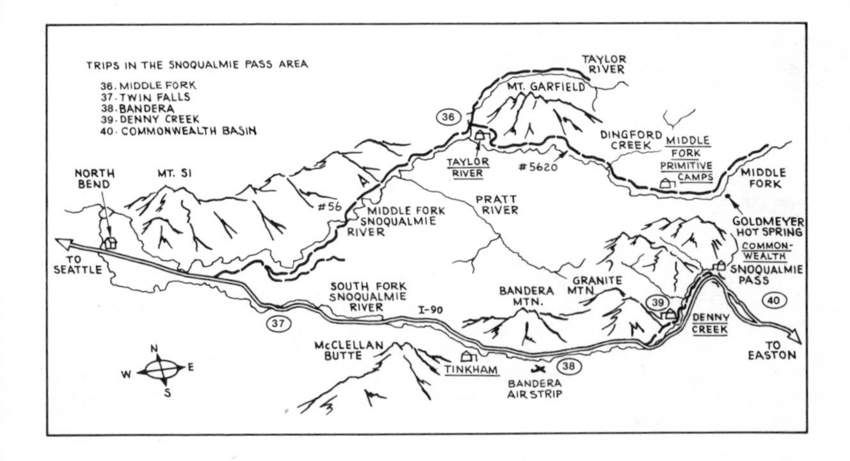

Middle Fork Snoqualmie River and Mount Garfield

TAYLOR RIVER ROAD

The Taylor River Road has been barricaded at Quartz Creek (1985), but the Forest Service has plans to open it (for logging, of course) about another 1.5 miles.

(The agency will spend public funds to build the road, but may close it to the public again after logging is completed. Wonder first if you think the road should be built, and then whether your money should be spent on a road to be used only for logging.)

Park at the end of the road and walk up the Taylor River past Marten Creek to Otter Falls—at least. If the road has been opened past Quartz Creek, walk about 1 mile to Marten Creek, and explore an old forest of cedars in a grove north of the road on the west side of the falls-filled creek.

(An undeveloped, steep fisherman's path scrambles about a mile sharply uphill to Marten Lake.)

Continue down the road to find Otter Falls in less than 1.5 miles. The falls—one of several along this stretch of road, plumes some 500 feet over tiered slabs into a blue pool called Lipsy Lake. Best early in the spring. Little more than a trickle later some years.

To reach the pool, find an unmarked path about 500 feet to the right of Otter Creek. About .25 mile.

Still more falls farther down the road, if you've got the time.

CLAYSTONE FORMS

Small, oddly rounded limestone forms found along the Taylor River. Some resemble animals, while others look more like first-grader experiments in clay. No two are alike.

Called concretions, the small forms were created through a lengthy process in which dissolved limestone was deposited around particles of rock or fossil in beds of blue clay laid down in lakes at the front of the ancient Puget Glacier.

Find the small forms in the sharp rocks along the Taylor River, starting about 100 yards north of the Taylor River Campground. Look closely for any small, round form. Some even look, at first, like sticks. Most are covered with a slick layer of brown silt. Once you've found one, however, the others come more easily. The supply is more plentiful the farther away you get from camp.

DUTCH MILLER GAP

Walk first through valley forests and then through more open places with views out at peaks in the Alpine Lakes Wilderness—2 miles, or as far and high as you want to go.

Find the trail at the end of Road No. 5620, about 12 miles from the Taylor River crossing. Parking area and trailhead at the end of the road.

The trail climbs higher and higher through forest, entering the Alpine Lakes Wilderness in about .5 mile. A camping spot near the river in another 1 mile. In about 4 miles the trail climbs to high valley filled with flowers and surrounded by peaks. Wander as far as you will.

MIDDLE FORK TRAIL

Find the upper end of this trail a little more than a mile from the end of the Middle Fork Road No. 5620. The trail crosses the river and then winds westward through forest for 3.8 miles to the junction with the Rock Creek–Snow Lake trail.

The downriver trail ends there, as of 1985, with no bridge back across the river. But the Forest Service has plans to extend it to a crossing at Dingford Creek, another 2.5 miles.

Until the trail is extended, wander down it as far as you want and turn back. Or wait until the new work is completed and arrange for a pleasant one-way trip.

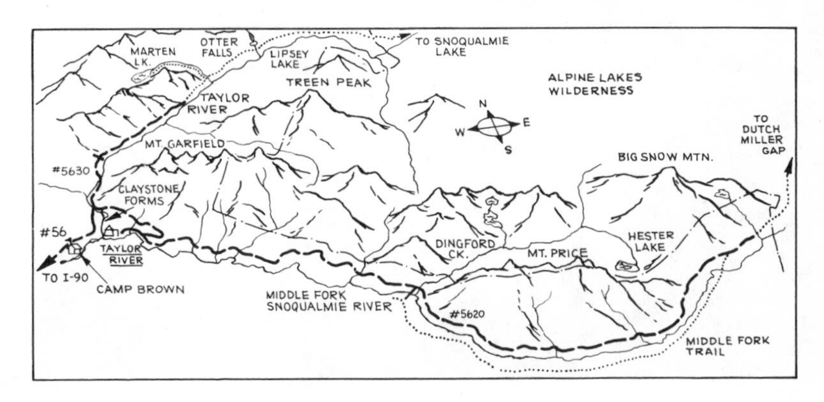

Lower Twin Falls

37 TWIN FALLS

Two spectacular waterfalls plunging full and free just off I-90 east of North Bend. But you can't see them anymore. In fact, you may never see them again in their natural state.

The falls, which have been listed in **Trips and Trails** for 20 years awaiting the development of a state park, are about to be converted into a private power generating site. A Snoqualmie Pass company appears to have obtained the private right to make a profit off the public park waterfall and land.

The Washington State Parks Commission—with little objection, little public notice, and even less public discussion—stood by for three years while the private firm obtained a license from the Federal Energy Regulating Commission to build a dam and power plant on the state park falls for the generation of electricity that's not needed in the Northwest but will bring in some $3 million a year to the developers.

Once the nature of the proposal was revealed, The Mountaineers and others tried to stop the project, or at least have public hearings on the proposal. But to no avail.

After the Federal Commission granted the license, the Parks Commission—again at a hearing called without any general public announcement—refused even to appeal the decision, deciding instead to resist any future attempts to build dams in state parks.

Basically, the Snoqualmie Pass firm, South Fork Resources, Inc., will operate the dam, powerhouse, weirs, flumes, powerlines, roads, and other "parklike" power plant facilities at the falls—on what was park land—and sell all of the energy it can generate at a guaranteed price to Puget Sound Power and Light for the next 35 years. Oddly, Puget Power was the company that sold the waterfalls land to the Parks Commission 35 years ago.

The Northwest Power Planning Council, which now-Senator Dan Evans once headed, determined earlier that there was no predictable need for the power from such a waterfall. The Federal Energy Commission, however, dismissed the Council's finding out of hand, deciding that the contract between South Fork and Puget Power was proof enough of need, even though there was no showing that the energy was or would be required by the firm to meet its needs in the state.

Although the Park Commission entered into an agreement with South Fork on the operation of the power facility, efforts (in late 1985) to save the falls continued. The developers then were still seeking permits from the county and state; and conservation groups, including The Mountaineers, were still trying to preserve the site. All lovers of waterfalls should join their efforts.

TALAPUS LAKE TRAIL

A 1.4-mile trail starts in brushy second growth—lots of berries in season—and then leads through a stand of marshy old growth to a lake with its own (sometimes) osprey.

Turn north off I-90 at Exit No. 45, following Road No. 9031 to the first road on the right, Talapus Road No. 9030. Trailhead at the end of the road. Views down on the valley from the parking area.

Trail starts on an old, overgrown logging road to the right of the trail sign. The trail near the lake was rebuilt recently. A heavily used area, not likely to afford any privacy on a weekend. 🚶

38 BANDERA

Short drives up logging roads on either side of I-90 west of Snoqualmie Pass lead to big views of the Snoqualmie River valley and its bordering mountain ridges.

HIGH ROAD VISTAS

For vistas out over the river valley, turn off the freeway at Exit No. 45 (see above), driving north and keeping left, as far as you can go. The road may be blocked at the final switchback.

If the road is blocked, park and hike out the old road as far as you want. Increasing vistas along the way. A 2-mile messy, unmaintained way trail leads sharply uphill beyond Mason Creek to Mason Lake. More of an effort than a pleasure.

HANSEN CREEK ROAD NO. 5510

Turn right (south) off I-90 at the Denny Creek Interchange. Drive back westerly on Road No. 55, taking the Hansen Creek Road to the left in about 2 miles. Follow the road, keeping left again at the Y, onto a spur with view of Bandera, Granite, and Snoqualmie Pass peaks. The road is gated at the top (Seattle watershed).

ASAHEL CURTIS NATURE TRAIL

Follow a pleasant .75-mile trail through an old-growth stand of Douglas fir, western red cedar, hemlock, and noble fir just off the freeway. Find the trail off the Forest Service parking area south of I-90 at the Denny Creek Interchange. Or take a path under the freeway from the picnic area north of I-90.

The grove of old-growth trees was named after Asahel Curtis, an early-day naturalist, photographer, and conservationist who played an active role in the preservation of such places.

39 DENNY CREEK

Seems incongruous to look for peace and quiet between two freeways. But that's what you'll find on this twisty, forested, but not-very-well-maintained old Denny Creek Road to Snoqualmie Pass.

Turn off I-90 about 17 miles from North Bend at the Denny Creek Interchange. Drive 2 miles to the Denny Creek Campground. Or to the end of the road at the pass. And take time to enjoy!

FRANKLIN FALLS

Hike here and measure for yourself the cost of progress. Compare the past beauty of this 70-foot plume of water, draped with late afternoon rainbows and rimmed by forests, with its setting today below a stilted freeway bridge.

An easy 1.5-mile walk from Denny Creek Campground. For an even easier stroll of half that distance, drive north from the campground on the Denny Creek Road and pick up the trail near the Forest Service Old Wagon Road display.

WAGON TRAIL

Long before automobiles wobbled over the rocks of Snoqualmie Pass, wagons made

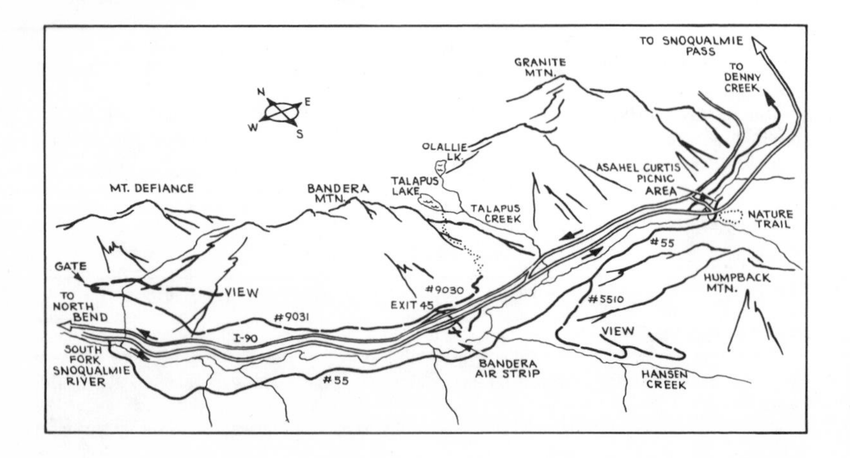

Bathing rocks on Denny Creek

the trip down roads that were even worse. One section of the original wagon road near the campground is being preserved in a project undertaken by Chief Seattle Boy Scout Council.

First section of the road starts directly opposite the turnoff onto the road across the bridge above the campground. Look for the wagon wheel display on the east side of the road. The trail is cleared to Franklin Falls.

BATHING ROCKS

A pleasant walk on a sunny summer day to basking places on water-washed rock slabs in Denny Creek. The creek fans out over smooth rock chutes to provide places in which even small children can play.

Hike less than 1.5 miles to the second crossing of Denny Creek on the Denny Creek trail to Melakwa Lake. After a rest, walk another .5 mile for a view of Keekwulee Falls.

Find the trail out of the campground or from a hiker's parking lot north of the campground. To reach the parking lot, drive north from the campground on Road No. 58, turning left and crossing a bridge. Trail is signed.

(The trail here goes beneath the freeway, which is built on stilts in European fashion, doing little damage to the mountain. The roadway is 150 feet above your path. Chances are you may not even hear it.)

LODGE LAKE

The noise of the big trucks on I-90 yields to silence on the timbered shores of Lodge Lake less than .5 mile—as the decibels travel—from the highway.

Take the Pacific Crest trail—it's signed—out of east end of the Snoqualmie Pass ski area. The trail starts in timber, crosses a section of ski slope, and then passes Beaver Lake before entering timber again and climbing to Lodge Lake and beyond. About 2.5 miles.

The Mountaineers built its first lodge (hence the name) at the lake in 1914. It burned in the late 1930s. Skiing and climbing in the vicinity got their start as a result of the lodge activity.

40 COMMONWEALTH BASIN

A 2-mile walk leads into a peaceful forest with glimpses of mountaintops through the trees. Add another mile and gain clearer views from the trail to Red Mountain Pass.

From Seattle, turn off I-90 at Snoqualmie Pass (Exit No. 52), turning left beneath the freeway and then right to a parking area for the Pacific Crest trail.

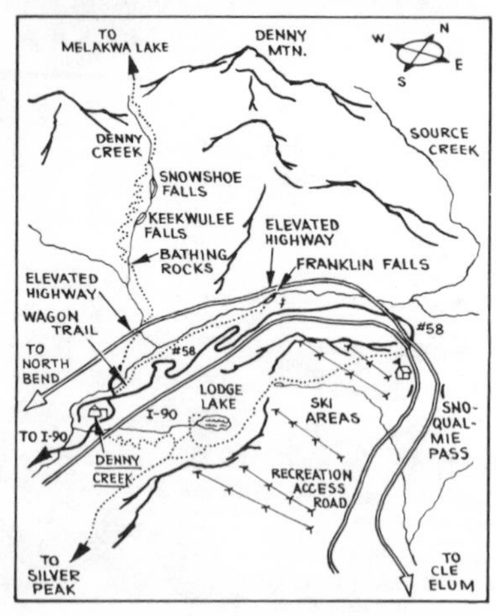

Lodge Lake and Denny Mountain

Follow the Crest trail north through forest, then bear straight ahead as the Crest trail turns uphill in something more than 2 miles. The path now drops through a rich forest past camp spots and along soggy creeks before climbing sharply up an open slope toward its end on Red Mountain, in 5 miles.

Don't feel you were robbed when you look up in the basin or on the side of Red Mountain and see hikers way above you on the Crest trail. They had to walk about 4 miles from the junction with your trail to get there. And besides, you'll have more privacy than they have.

SNOW LAKE

A longer walk here than most others in this book. But it's so popular—12,000 people a year—that it cannot be ignored, even by the novice. Four miles one way, so allow a full day.

And treat the slopes here kindly!

Find the trail off a parking lot at the end of the ski area road about 2 miles from the freeway (see above).

Red Mountain from Commonwealth Basin

The trail climbs gradually through forest and across open slopes above Source Creek, making its way to a point above little Source Lake before switchbacking through alpine slopes to a saddle in about 3.5 miles. Stop here if you like, certainly to rest. The trail drops to the lake in another .5 mile.

A busy place on weekends. But picnic spots abound. Don't leave any trash—even though lots of others have.

HYAK FOREST ROAD

For view up Gold Creek to Rampart and Chikamin ridges, take the rough forest road that climbs through the Pacific West ski area.

Best views from the top of the ridge, but the road continues another 2.5 miles along the powerline.

Find the road near the ski area parking lot.

KENDALL PEAK WALK

Roads, even old ones, generally aren't for walking. But a walk of 2 miles or less up an unused road just **east** of the summit leads to big views of the pass and the mountains around it.

Drive eastward down the pass to the Hyak Interchange, Exit No. 54, turning north under the freeway and then straight ahead up Road No. 2235 to a gate in little more than a mile.

Walk uphill to vistas of your choice. A trail leads up Coal Creek to Kendall Peak Lakes.

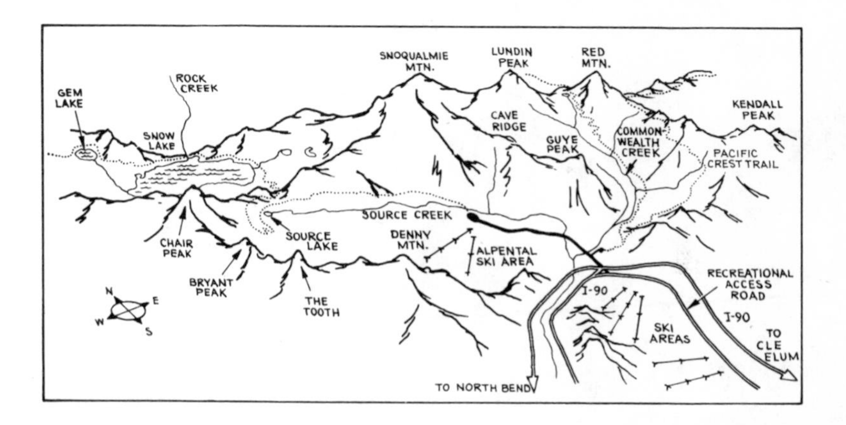

View from Lookout Mountain near Twisp

T THE EAST SLOPE

Sunshine and sagebrush, certainly. But much, much more: high mountains, crisp ridges, waterfalls, rushing rivers, quiet valleys, and breathtaking vistas. With all of them to be found on the eastern slope of the Cascade range from just south of Ellensburg to the Canadian border.

Snoqualmie Pass, Stevens Pass, and the North Cascades Highway lead to the edges of this expansive countryside.

From Snoqualmie Pass, main highways lead into the high country of Cle Elum River, the Taneum and the Teanaway. From Stevens Pass, other roads lead to the enormous Wenatchee recreation area, the Icicle, the Swauk, and north to Entiat, Chelan, and the even higher roads of Harts Pass and the Pasayten.

As always, roads are only the beginning. The best, certainly, is reserved for the hiker willing to wander any of the hundreds of trails that leave campgrounds, road ends, and waysides for lookouts, lakes, waterfalls—the natural lot.

The outdoor season on this side of the Cascades is a little longer than on the west side of the range. Spring comes sooner; fall, a little later. Summers, though, are hotter and winters, colder, with both varying year to year, as you would expect.

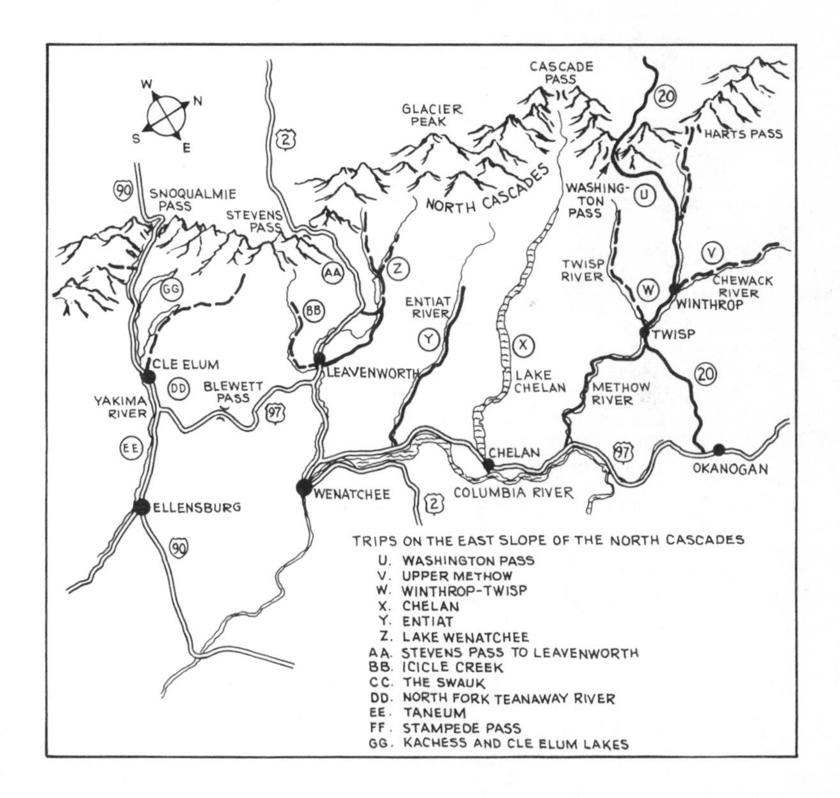

U WASHINGTON PASS

The quiet wildness of this once remote area has most certainly been disturbed by the new North Cascades Highway. But remnants of the area's original beauty can still be found if you're willing to park your car and walk.

Drive 36.8 miles east up the North Cascades Highway from Newhalem or 35.9 miles west from Winthrop, through what admittedly has to be the most magnificent "highway" scenery in the state, to the highlight of the trip—Washington Pass.

A formal overlook north of the highway will give you a hint of what's to be seen here. But for greater vistas in more private settings, plan to walk—not hike—over any of the several gradual trails to nearby mountain lakes.

In 1985, the Forest Service said it had banned camping at all of the lakes and many of the high places near Washington Pass. But agency maps don't show that prohibition, and very few of the trails to the lakes or high places are signed to indicate it. And there is no indication that the agency enforces its bans.

Obviously agency regulations should be made known to the public and then applied equally to all. So if you see parties camping in these places, scream—not at the campers, but at the Forest Service for adopting rules and then taking no steps to either announce or enforce them.

And by all means, urge the restrictions. None of these areas can withstand the stress of uncontrolled heavy use.

RAINY LAKE

A paved, easy trail, primarily for the handicapped. You can watch waterfalls plunge off Lyall glacier on Frisco Mountain into the clear blue lake.

Find the trail at Rainy Pass—about 5 miles west from the Washington Pass complex. The very gradual path leads through pleasant forest to the small cirque lake at 4,790 feet.

Less than 1 mile. The shortest walk to a lake in the area. And thus, the busiest.

LAKE ANN

Hike 2 miles to a pretty alpine lake in a snow-fringed, scenic cirque. Hike another 1.5 miles and reach Maple Pass, with views of Glacier Peak country to the south and the Pacific crests to the north.

Find the trail on the east side of the picnic grounds at Rainy Pass. It climbs through timber to a spur trail (left) to the lake. Occasional vistas en route down on meadows and up at nearby peaks.

Continue up the trail to sweeping views down on Lake Ann before reaching, first,

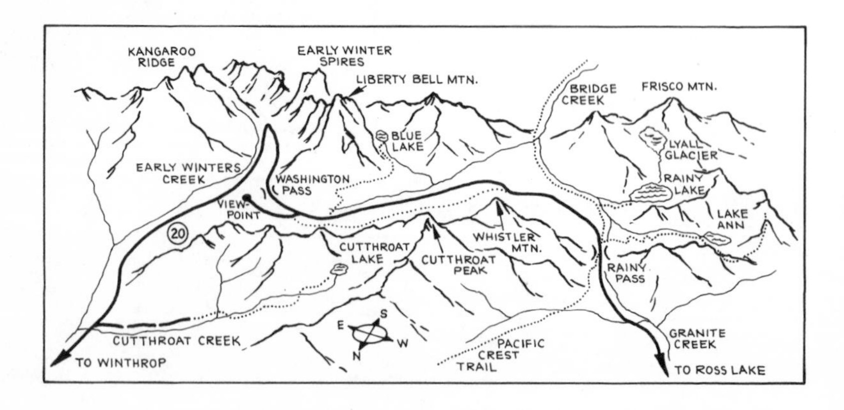

Liberty Bell (Mountain) from Washington Pass

Heather Pass—a heather-covered place to rest and wander—and then on to Maple Pass, with more heather, marmots, and the most spectacular vistas. One of the grandest of places.

BLUE LAKE

Look up at the cliffs of Liberty Bell and the Early Winters Spires and out at Cutthroat Peak from the shores of a rock-rimmed mountain lake.

Find the trail on the east side of the trail sign on the south side of the highway, just west of the Washington Pass overlook area. It does **not** start from the small parking area.

The path switchbacks 2 miles through forest and occasional subalpine meadows to the outlet of the lake, with its tumbled log shelter and rock outcrop ideal for picnicking, resting, and looking. Take a sandwich and a bag of your most private thoughts.

41 EARLY WINTERS CREEK

Don't misunderstand. Washington Pass is a great place to stop on any trip from Seattle. But the Pass isn't the end. The road **east** of the pass, down Early Winters Creek to Mazama, offers its share of trail adventures too.

CUTTHROAT LAKE

The signs say 2 miles, but it seems little over a mile to this lake surrounded on three sides by snow-patched peaks.

Turn uphill off the North Cascades Highway onto the Cutthroat Lake Road less than 5 miles east of Washington Pass. Trail leads from a picnic area at the end of the 1-mile spur road.

Views from the trail about halfway to the lake. Either stay on the main path or take tourist trails to the left (before you cross a wooden bridge) to reach the shore, picnic spots, and all sorts of views.

WASHINGTON MEADOWS

The beauty of soaring Liberty Bell and Cutthroat peaks almost—but not quite—drowns out the highway noise once you've hiked away from the road on this trail through Washington Meadows.

Walk into the meadow down any of a number of unmarked paths north of the highway or out of the picnic area. The old trail makes its way leisurely along the north side of the meadows in a general westward direction, reaching the highway in about 4 miles at Bridge Creek, west of the pass.

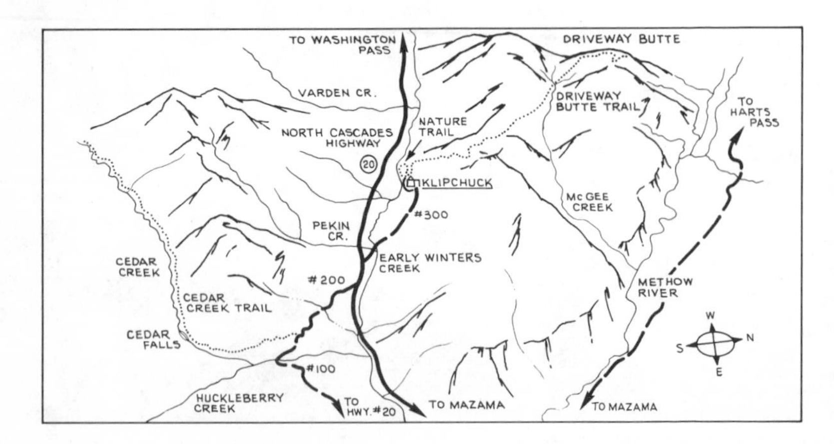

Blue Lake and Cutthroat Peak

Follow established trails whenever you can. The meadows can't stand much human abuse.

Vistas here are bigger than any you'll find either from the road or the formal overlook. Snowy peaks on every horizon. And fields of flowers in season, too.

DRIVEWAY BUTTE TRAIL

It's 7 miles over Delancy Ridge to the Methow River trail. But spend an evening wandering less than 1 mile out of Klipchuck Campground to views toward Silver Star Mountain.

Take the Driveway Butte trail out of the campground through an old logging site and up switchbacks to whatever vista pleases you. Before you go—or as you return—explore the short Creek Side Loop nature trail through a stand of old red cedar along Early Winters Creek. A cooling respite after a hot day.

CEDAR FALLS

Walk an easy 2 miles to a wild waterfall on Cedar Creek.

To find the trail, turn right off the North Cascades Highway about .3 mile east of the

Fawn only a few days old

road to Klipchuck Campground. Follow Road No. 200 another long .5 mile to a gravel pit on the right. Park there.

The trail climbs gradually well above Cedar Creek to an overlook and picnic point above the falls on the left. You'll hear it before you see it. A classic for any falls collector. Beware of slippery rocks.

CAMPGROUNDS

Early Winters—12 formal sites in a heavily used trailer-camper area off the North Cascades Highway near the Early Winters Information Station and Visitor Center, 16 miles from Winthrop. Pit toilets. Well water.

Lone Fir—20 units in wooded area, 5 miles east of Washington Pass at 3,600 feet. Views of nearby peaks. Pit toilets. Water system.

Klipchuck—46 units in pleasant, open pine forest. Nature trail, 3 miles west of the Early Winters Information Station. Flush toilets. Water system.

Slate Peak Road

V UPPER METHOW

This back country of the Okanogan National Forest offers surprises on almost every trail and road through forests north of this turbulent river.

From Washington Pass, cross north across the river at Mazama, turning in either—and any—direction for your particular recreation specialty.

42 HARTS PASS

A winding and switchbacking forest road climbs 13 miles from Mazama to high views of the North Cascades.

Turn north off the North Cascades Highway a long 1 mile southeast of the Early Winters Forest Service Visitor Information Station to Mazama, and then left in Mazama onto the Harts Pass Road. **No trailers** beyond Ballard Campground, 7 miles from Mazama.

PACIFIC CREST TRAIL

Hike out the Pacific Crest trail either north or south of the pass for spacious views of valleys, flower meadows, and peaks.

For views out over Ninety-Nine Basin and Trout Creek Canyon, walk the Crest trail to the south from the end of Road No. 500 beyond the Meadows Campground. The trail climbs to a sharp ridge over the basin to the north and the canyon to the south. Less than 2 miles. But give yourself time enough to explore farther if you want.

For vistas off the trail to the north, turn right at the pass, finding the trailhead on the ridge where the road switchbacks on its way to the lookout. The path here winds north, over open meadows with wide vistas, toward Windy and Buffalo passes and—eventually—Canada. Snow often blocks the road here through July 4.

Or, for yet another walk, follow a spur trail west and then south around the west side of the ridge. Views over Ninety-Nine Basin before the trail drops down to the road end south of Meadows Campground.

(All those buildings you see there are on mining claims, even though the claims haven't been worked for years. Maybe decades.)

SLATE PEAK

The lookout tower here may be burned, but the vistas will remain.

Take the road north at the top of Harts Pass, following it uphill past the Pacific Crest trailhead to a gate just below the tower. Park and walk the rest of the way, giving yourself enough time to enjoy the 360-degree views from 7,440 feet. It's the highest point in the state to be reached by road. The top of the mountain was flattened by the Army for a radar station.

Displays identify surrounding ridges and peaks.

SLATE MEADOW

For one of the best walks in the pass vicinity, drive up the Slate Peak road toward the lookout about .25 mile, then wander out into Slate Meadow, a broad green meadow bench.

Hike a mile or so or saunter up to the ridgetop. There are some secret crystal "mines" and fossil beds in the vicinity of the ridge. Rockhounds won't tell where they are. But they're there. That's all they'll say.

CHANCELLOR-BARRON

Tumbling shacks and occasional signs of old machinery in an area which saw heavy

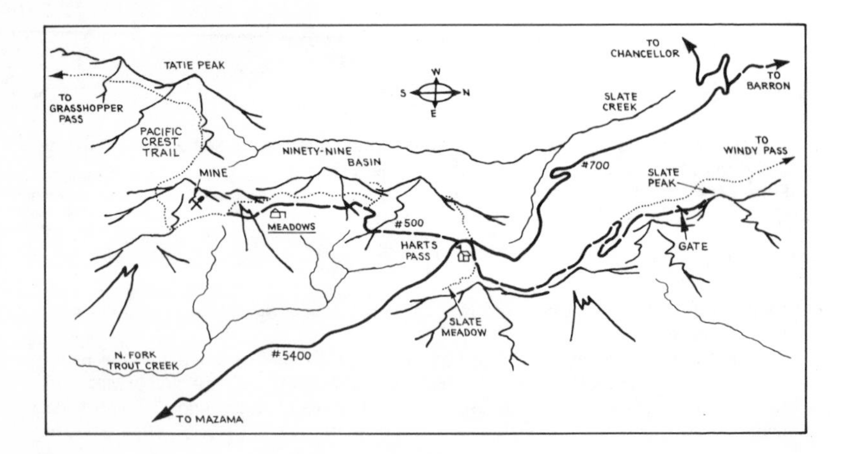

mining activity in the 1880s and 90s.

Drive west from Harts Pass down a narrow road, No. 700, often rough and sometimes not well maintained, turning north on rougher spur to Barron below Windy Pass. (Road is sometimes gated, barring access to patented mining claims.) Rockhounds look for crystals and ore.

Or continue down the road to Chancellor—12 miles from the pass—for summer homes, more ruins, and a pleasant trail along Canyon Creek.

Cross the bridge at the end of the road, following the trail downstream as it goes along the creek toward Ross Lake. The dying house in the first mile once served as a stage stop and post office on a road that then ended at Barron, before the Harts Pass road was built.

CAMPGROUNDS

Gate Creek—4 sites near juncture of Gate Creek and the Methow River, 18 miles from Winthrop.

River Bend—5 sites. Turn east on Road No. 060 about 7 miles from Mazama. Campground in 1 mile. Pit toilets. Well water.

Ballard—7 sites near the Methow River, 7 miles from Mazama. Pit toilets. Well water.

Meadows—Pleasant camp at 6,300 feet on Spur Road No. 500, south from pass, 14 sites. In flat alpine timber area. Pit toilets. Carry water.

Chancellor—6 sites in shaded timber along Canyon Creek, 30 miles from Mazama. Pit toilets.

Harts Pass—5 sites. The original camp. Pit toilets. No water.

Camping at Harts Pass

43 MAZAMA

Leave the heavily traveled North Cascades Highway for high and still higher views, waterfalls, and flower meadows off logging roads north and west of Mazama and Winthrop.

GOAT WALL

An easy drive to spectacular views up the North Cascades Highway, down on the Methow Valley, and out toward Silver Star Mountain (8,901), with its glacier patches, and Gardner Mountain (8,974) to the left of it.

Turn north off the North Cascades Highway to Mazama, less than 2 miles east of the Early Winters Information Station. Turn right (east) at Mazama to Forest Road No. 52 and then sharply uphill to the left in about 2.5 miles. In another 2.8 miles turn left again onto Road No. 5225.

Best views in about 4.5 miles from the start of Road No. 5225. A great place to stop for lunch and to gawk at all the mountains.

GOAT PEAK

Walk to absolutely the best views in this entire area from a lookout atop Goat Peak. You can see the tower from almost any corner of the Methow Valley around Mazama. And conversely, you can see all of the valley plus peaks in every direction from the lookout at 7,000 feet. Manned some seasons.

From the valley, as above, drive up Road No. 52 and then west and uphill on Road No. 5225 to a signed Spur No. 200 (total of less than 9 miles from the county road). Find the trail uphill (keeping right) at the end of the road in about 3 miles.

The trail starts out up a ridge climbing alternately through meadows and forest. At about 1 mile it settles down to the serious work of getting uphill, topping out on the ridge and then wandering up and down to the lookout perched on the valley rim.

Wildflowers, naturally, in their proper season.

SWEETGRASS BUTTE

Lots of blue sky and mountains in a 360-degree view from a meadow-topped mountain at 6,100 feet. Camping spots off the road. But no water.

From Mazama, drive toward Winthrop, turning north on Road No. 52 (see Goat Wall), continuing up Goat Creek to Banker Pass and then, in another 2 miles, turning north on Road No. 5220. At Cub Pass, turn left (north) on Spur No. 100 to the top of the butte.

Leave time for wandering and admiring all the Pasayten peaks, and in spring, the flowers.

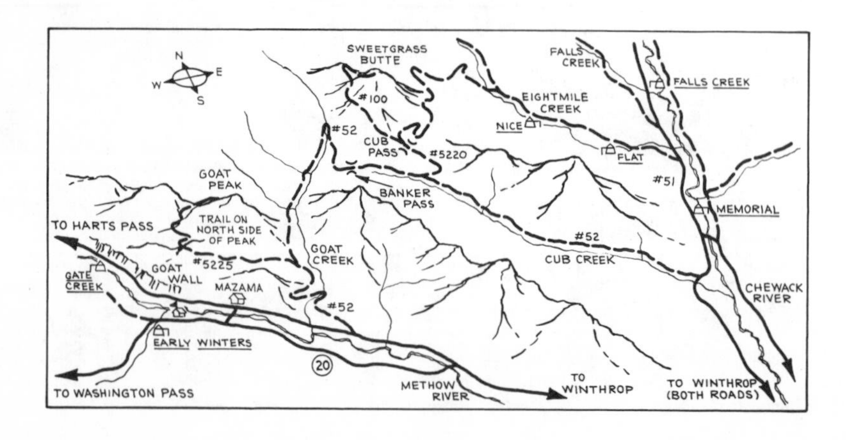

Isabella Ridge from Sweetgrass Butte Road

FALLS CREEK FALLS

A short walk leads to a frothy, talkative, pretty 50-foot waterfall, with lots of rock ledges for viewing.

Drive north of Winthrop on the county road along the **east** side of the Chewack River (follow Pearrygin Lake signs out of town). In nearly 6 miles, turn left to paved Road No. 51. Falls Creek and Falls Creek Campground in about 5.5 miles more.

Find the first falls off a path that starts across the road from the campground, north of the creek. The path continues uphill, to the right, beyond the first torrent to the second falls and then uphill again to a viewpoint over the valley from a rock ledge. Cross a bridge when you return to walk a path on the south side of the creek.

Pretty, even in the fall. Violent in spring.

CAMPGROUNDS

Memorial—2 sites near the Chewack River, 7 miles north of Winthrop. Pit toilets. Well water.

Falls Creek—7 sites in open timber near the river, 2 sites east of the road near waterfall trail, 13 miles from Winthrop. Pit toilets. Well water.

Chewack—6 sites near the river, 15 miles from Winthrop. Pit toilets.

Camp 4—4 sites in open timber on the river, 18 miles from Winthrop. Pit toilets.
Flat—9 sites in timber on Eightmile Creek, 12 miles from Winthrop on Road No. 5130. Fenced. Pit toilets. Well water.
Nice—3 sites that are just that off Eightmile Creek, 14 miles from Winthrop on Road No. 5130. Pit toilets. Well water.

44 TIFFANY MOUNTAIN

Backcountry roads—some paved, some not, and a few even closed until late in the spring—between Winthrop and Conconully lead to lookouts, beaver-dam lakes, and trails up ridges to still more lakes.

From Winthrop, drive 7 miles north on the paved county road **east** of the Chewack River (on the road to Pearrygin Lake State Park), turning east on Forest Road No. 37 and then north at Roger Lake on No. 39. (Road may be gated in the spring and early summer.) Follow No. 39 north around Tiffany Mountain, turning toward Conconully on Road No. 3820 and then No. 38.

FIRST BUTTE LOOKOUT

Not as exciting, perhaps, as some of the lookouts in the state that you have to hike and climb to. But still worth the drive to views not to be seen any other way.

From Road No. 37 off the county road north out of Winthrop (see above), turn north on the First Butte Lookout Road No. 800, jogging sharply left onto No. 825 in about 2.5 miles. Lookout at the end in another 2 miles.

View into North Cascades and out at the Tiffany peaks to the northeast.

ROGER LAKE

If you have always thought of beavers as creatures that dam small streams, stop here and enlarge your vision.

Follow the county road north from Winthrop (see above), turning east onto Road No. 37 and then, in about 18-19 miles from Winthrop, north on Road No. 39, finding the lake in little more than 1 mile. On the right. Very primitive camp spots near the lake. Road No. 39, labeled too steep for trailers, may be closed some years until late in the summer.

Can't guarantee you'll find a grand display of beaver construction every year. Sometimes people do the beavers in and sometimes the beavers change their own plans.

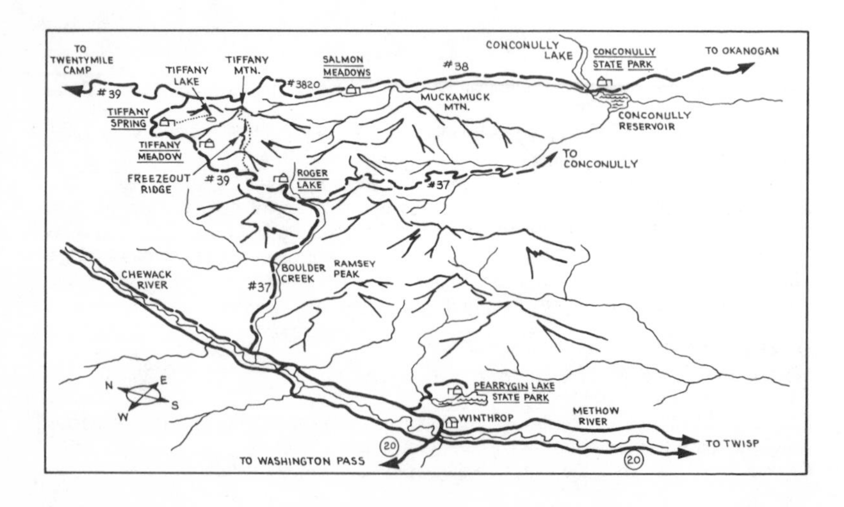

Freezeout Ridge from Tiffany Mountain

But in good years, beavers here build dams that extend for hundreds of yards around the lake shore, making a cattail pond into much larger cattail lake. Wonder how many beavers it took to build this elaborate network of dams, and further, how they ever agreed on what they would do. No low spots. No high spots. Everything perfect—in proper beaver style. Wonder if engineers without tools and gauging devices could do so well.

TIFFANY MOUNTAIN AND FREEZEOUT RIDGE

Farmhouses of the Okanogan Valley, Glacier, and Baker from Tiffany (8,242) or more modest views of the Boulder Creek drainage and the Cascades from Freezeout Ridge.

Hike 1.5 miles through pine forests to reach alpine meadows on the south side of Freezeout Ridge, and first views. At 2.7 miles, Whistler Pass. A .5-mile side trip leads to the top of Tiffany for a 360-degree vista sweeping from the Cascades to the hot plateaus of the Columbia Basin and eastward into the Okanogan Highlands.

Watch for trail sign at Freezeout Pass, about 4 miles north of Roger Lake. Leave the trail after a .25-mile hike in the meadows to start climb across easy grass slopes to Tiffany's top.

TIFFANY LAKE

An easy mile walk to the open shores of a pretty mountain lake. Lots of places to camp and usually no other campers.

Find trail at Tiffany Spring Campground. Trail drops down from the road. Trail ends on the ridgetop, but go as far as you want. Soggy marshes at the start, with vistas later.

CAMPGROUNDS

Note: The sites here are the formal campgrounds listed by the Forest Service. Campers, however, will find hundreds of primitive spots used in the fall by hunters.

Roger Lake—Primitive site. A poor campground near a marshy lake, 22 miles from Winthrop. Pit toilet.

Tiffany Meadow—Primitive site. A high camp at 6,800 feet, 23 miles from Winthrop. Pit toilets.

Tiffany Spring—3 formal sites at the trailhead to Tiffany Lake, 25 miles from Winthrop, 22 miles from Conconully. Pit toilets. Spring water.

Salmon Meadows—14 sites, 8 miles from Conconully. Pit toilets. Piped water.

Conconully State Park—81 sites on Conconully Reservoir. Restrooms. Piped water. Showers. Boat launching. Swimming. State fee.

Main street of Winthrop

W WINTHROP—TWISP

More here—at the east end of the North Cascades Highway—than the fake fronts of the redone western town of Winthrop. Take forest roads and trails nearby to lakes, lookouts, and lovely views.

NORTH CASCADES SMOKE JUMPER BASE

Watch smoke jumpers fold their chutes and inspect their equipment at the Forest Service Smoke Jumping base at the Intercity Airport.

Cross the Methow River at Twisp, driving north on the county road toward Winthrop. Watch for signs indicating the airport and school in about 5 miles. Or drive south on the north side of the river from Winthrop toward Twisp.

Stop at the Visitor Information Service for an explanation of the aerial activities at the base.

SHAFER MUSEUM

Pioneer furniture, tools, ancient bicycles, mining relics, sleighs, carriages, a bathtub, and even a Model T Ford.

Turn north off Highway 20, crossing the bridge into Winthrop, turning right again down the main street of the town. Watch for signs. The museum, in several old cabins, overlooks the town, the Methow River, and the mountains.

Always open on weekends and most weekdays. Hours vary, however. No admission. But donations help.

SULLIVAN'S POND

A small, but busy (bird-filled) marsh just off a high-view road.

From Pearrygin Lake State Park, turn east at the junction with the Winthrop Road, then north in less than .25 mile onto Forest Spur No. 100.

Sweeping views down on the lake and valley between the junction and the pond. At the pond, be patient. The small swamp is a world by itself. Yellow-headed blackbirds some years. And other marsh creatures, too.

Road crosses part of the Winthrop Game Refuge. In fall or early spring watch for herds of deer migrating from one part of the range to the other.

LOOKOUT MOUNTAIN

A lookout, naturally, on a mountain of the same name. With sweeping vistas over Twisp, the Methow Valley, the Columbia Basin, and all the surrounding mountains.

Drive west out of Twisp on the Black Pine–Twisp River Road, turning uphill to the left onto paved Road No. 200, signed "Lookout Mountain trail" in about a .25 mile. Limited views of the valley on the way up. End of the road in about 6 miles.

The trail makes its way uphill for about a mile, ultimately topping out on a ridge reaching the lookout after a short spurt upward in another .25 mile. The lookout is signed at 5,692 feet. A forest map sets the elevation at 5,522 and contour maps say it's at 5,515. Lots of wildflowers. Mariposa lilies in the spring.

BUTTERMILK BUTTE

Panoramic views of the Methow Valley, Twisp River, and Sawtooth Ridge from the end of a road.

Drive out the Twisp River Highway from downtown Twisp, turning left on Road No. 43 for 7 miles and then right for another 5 miles on a primitive but passable Road No. 400 to a formal overlook of the area.

CAMPGROUNDS

Pearrygin Lake State Park—88 sites, most along the open shores of the lake, 5 miles from Winthrop. Restrooms. Piped water. Showers. Swimming. Popular trailer-camper area. State fee.

Blackpine Lake—21 sites on a pretty forested mountain lake with views of Hoodoo Peak. Take the river highway from Twisp, turning left on Road No. 43. In about 7 miles, turn left to the campground. Pit toilets. Piped water.

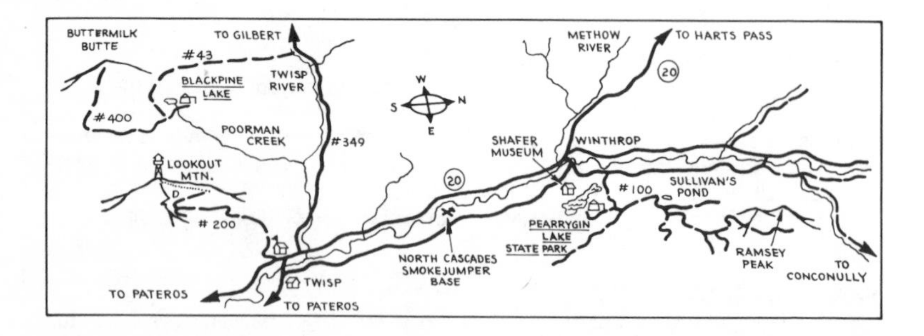

Lake Chelan from Grade Creek Road

X CHELAN

An 86-mile loop drive to spectacular high-ridge views of both the Chelan and Methow valleys, the Columbia River, the glacier trench of Lake Chelan, and the Cascade Crest.

But—and it's a very big **BUT**—the higher parts of the road may be too rough to travel. Some years those stretches are not maintained at all. You may have to stop every inch or two and pick boulders—not stones—off the road. And one more **but:** the road here at 6,500 feet, and higher, has got views that won't quit.

Turn north off Highway 150, 2 miles east of Manson, turning left in .25 mile, and right beyond Roses Lake onto the Upper Joe Creek road. Continue past Antilon Lake on

Road No. 8200. (Smoothest road to the top of the ridge is from the Methow Valley on Gold Creek Road No. 4330/600, off the highway between Methow and Carlton.)

Best views of the Lake Chelan Valley from No. 8200 between the lake and the junction with No. 8200.

Lake, orchard, and mountain views from South Navarre Campground, midway point on the loop.

Passing the campground, the road skirts burned-over Coyote Ridge for 10 miles, reaching views into the Methow at Saint Luise Pass–Gold Creek junction with Road No. 4330/600 to the Methow. A rare mixture here of desert and alpine plants.

In late July the roadside is blue with lupine between the junction and Cooper Mountain, 12.2 miles on Road No. 8020. From Cooper Mountain to Chelan, 19 miles.

COOPER MOUNTAIN VIEWPOINT

See Rainier, Stuart, the Cascades, the high peaks of the Chelan Range, the Big Bend, and the Columbia, Methow, and Lake Chelan valleys. By road from 5,800 feet.

Either take the Grade Creek Loop Road (see above) or drive 19 miles directly from Chelan.

Take Highway 150 west from Chelan, turning north in about 2 miles onto a paved road uphill. In another 2.5 miles turn north again near an abandoned schoolhouse, turning right in another mile. Follow signs up Cooper Gulch and past Echo Valley ski area.

At the forest boundary sign, just north of Echo Valley, turn left on Road No. 8020. From here it's 8.1 miles to the viewpoint, mostly through heavily burned forest. A grim scene, but one worth noting, nonetheless.

Viewpoint area, unburned, is a former lookout site. Camp here for supreme sunsets, night-light and dawn views.

CAMPGROUNDS

Antilon Lake—4 developed units and many undeveloped camps in a wooded area at the head of the reservoir lake located along the lake and a stream. Pit toilets. Boating, but no motors allowed. Swimming. Lake likely to be low at the peak of the irrigation season. Occasional rattlers.

South Navarre—4 units. A cool site with no mosquitoes in open pine grass and timber. Midway point on loop road. Trailhead for Chelan Summit trail. Pit toilets.

Roadside camps—On the ridgecrest section of the road overlooking Lake Chelan. Carry water. Pick the view of your choice. But remember an ax, shovel, and bucket. Fires may be banned outside formal camps in dry periods.

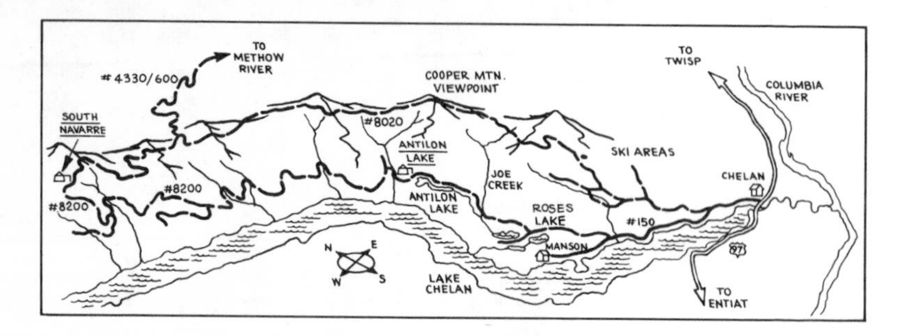

45 CHELAN SUMMIT

CHELAN SUMMIT TRAIL

A high trail leads across pine grass meadows painted with lupine and Indian paintbrush. Views to the south and the west. No views of Lake Chelan.

Find the trail sign out of South Navarre Campground. A spring in .5 mile. Pass up the ones you hear gurgling in the grass below the trail for the ones that flow across the path a little farther on. Follow the trail along the mountain slope until it drops into timber in about 1 mile. Views cease here. Trail continues on to Stehekin in 36 miles. A cool respite at the end of a hot day.

Chelan Summit from side of South Navarre Peak

SUMMER BLOSSOM TRAIL

Just as the name implies: flowers here range from lilies to lupines and from marsh marigolds to heather, depending on the whims of the slopes and the season.

Drive 2.5 miles north of South Navarre Campground. Park in an improved spot on the right and find the trail uphill to the left. Road toward Saint Luise Pass beyond this point turns bad and gets worse.

The trail climbs first to a rocky basin—some camps here—in less than a mile and then switchbacks its way up the side of a bluff to high meadows in something under 2 miles, with views out over Lake Chelan, the Columbia Basin, and nearby ridges.

The tread tends to become a little vague as the path climbs to the meadows—watch for cairns—before dropping down (well beyond 2 miles) and then climbing to a ridge. Summit trail in 7.5 miles.

46 LAKE CHELAN

See the entire length of the 55-mile lake in one day from Chelan to Stehekin aboard the **Lady of the Lake** from Chelan. Or stretch the trip over several days by camping along the way at any of the remote campgrounds on the lake.

A spectacular winter trip, too. Goat and deer near the shore and snow on all the hills. Gateway also to Holden and the Stehekin River valley.

CHELAN BUTTE

Sweeping views of Chelan, the green, regimented orchard country around it, the lake, the high, dry plateaus of the Columbia Basin, and the broad curves of the Columbia River from an overlook point just outside the city.

Turn south (away from the lake) about 1.75 miles west of the bridge in Chelan. Watch for Chelan Butte sign. Top of the butte by gravel road in 3 miles, 3,892 feet.

BEAR MOUNTAIN VIEWS

Look down on Lake Chelan and across onto the community of Manson from a high road above Lake Chelan State Park.

Turn away from the lake up the Navarre Coulee Road across from the State Park entrance. Turn left (east) about .5 mile beyond the switchback on the road up, following the logging road, uphill at all junctions, for the highest views. Thirteen miles.

CAMPGROUNDS

Chelan City Park—160 sites, most with hookups, in grassy open area on Lake Chelan in Chelan. Restrooms. Water. **No tents.** Reservations recommended. Fee.

Lake Chelan State Park—201 sites. An extremely popular campground. Restrooms. Piped water. Swimming. Boat launching. Lots of trailers. Showers. State fee.

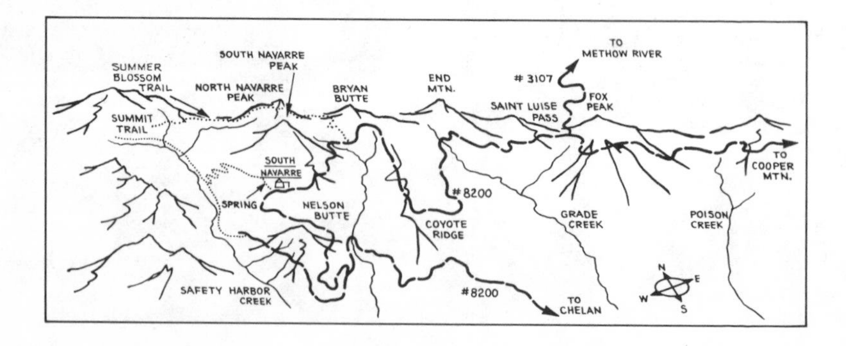

(Note: All the following campgrounds can be reached by water only, either by **Lady of the Lake** or private boat.)

Mitchell Creek—5 units, 15 miles from Chelan. Pit toilets. Lake water. Sheltered dock. Watch for snakes.

Deer Point—4 sites on a small harbor well-protected from down-lake winds, 22 miles from Chelan. Popular with small-boat owners. Pit toilets. Lake water. Watch for snakes.

Safety Harbor—Undeveloped sites in an open area near the lake, 25 miles. Pit toilets. Lake water.

Big Creek—4 units and a shelter. Shaded camp on southwest side of the lake. Small falls 300 feet by trail from campground, 27 miles. Pit toilets. Lake water.

Corral Creek—2 units, 28 miles. Pit toilet. Lake water.

Graham Harbor—10 units and shelter, 31 miles. Pit toilets. Lake or creek water.

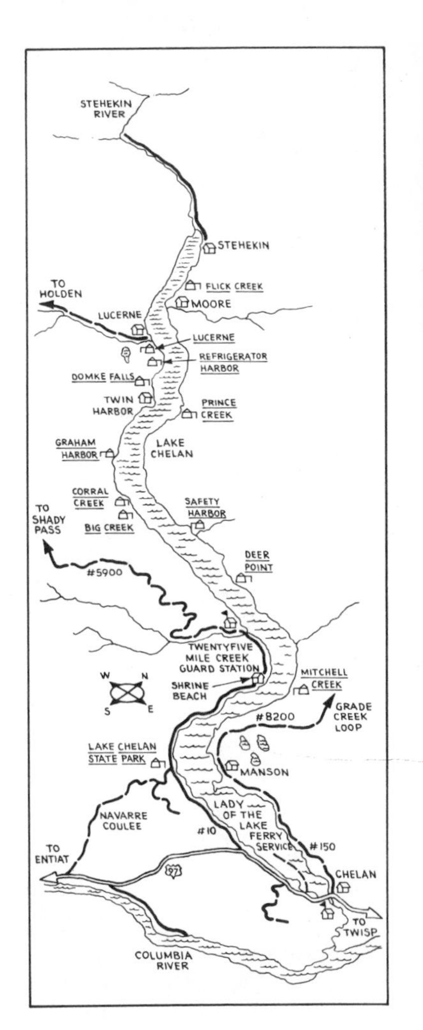

Lupine

Lake Chelan and Castle Rock from Stehekin

Prince Creek—5 units, 35 miles. On shaded bench above heavy outwash area. A newer camp. Trailhead for Lakeshore and Prince Creek trails. Pit toilet. Lake or creek water.

Domke Falls—3 units but room for other campers if the sites are taken, 37 miles. About 100 yards by trail from a spectacular falls that plunges into a pool just off the lake. Pit toilets. Lake water.

Refrigerator Harbor—4 units in a protected cove. Connected by a .25-mile road to Lucerne, 41 miles. Pit toilets. Lake water.

Lucerne—2 units, near guard station on a little manmade cove. 41 miles. Attractive camp. Good base for trips to Domke Lake and Holden. Pit toilets. Piped water.

Flick Creek—1 unit and shelter off lakeshore trail, 5 miles. Pit toilets. Lake water.

Moore Point—Undeveloped sites. Pit toilets.

47 STORMY MOUNTAIN

Drive a logging road through panoramas of Lake Chelan or the Entiat Valley and then hike to a circle of spectacle from the site of an abandoned lookout.

From Twenty-five Mile Creek on Lake Chelan, turn uphill on Road No. 5900 and then left on the Slide Ridge Road No. 8410 in about 2.5 miles.

In about .25 mile, the Slide Ridge Road passes through a pleasant corner of river greenery (Ramona Park) and then starts twisting uphill. Views out over Lake Chelan, Chelan, Manson, and the Columbia Basin begin about 10.5 miles from Twenty-five Mile. A great place to gain a sense of how this part of the country was put together.

From Ardenvoir in the Entiat Valley, drive upriver about a mile, turning right onto Road No. 287 and 5300, turning left onto the Slide Ridge Road No. 8410.

Find the trail at the top of the ridge, about 20 miles from Lake Chelan and 21 miles from Ardenvoir. The path climbs from the west side of the road along a fireline to the old trail and then to a saddle with vistas north over Lake Chelan and as far south as Mount Adams. A long mile.

Hike on another .25 to .5 mile, watching for the hint of an old path uphill before the trail you're on starts down slightly.

The uphill spur—if you miss it, just scramble to the ridgetop—leads to the crest of Stormy Mountain. Everything from the gaping maw of Mount St. Helens, the orchards of the Wenatchee Valley, glistening sheds in the Columbia Basin (again), Glacier Peak, and the North Cascades

CAMPGROUNDS

Grouse Mountain—3 sites in open timber. Isolated. Pleasant. Water from spring .5 mile down the road. Primarily a fall hunter's camp. Pit toilet.

Ramona Park—Undeveloped area. A cool camp in ponderosa pine and Douglas fir. On a spur road. Pit toilet.

48 LUCERNE

HOLDEN

Popular entrance point to the Glacier Peak Wilderness, 12 miles by taxi from the small resort town of Lucerne on Lake Chelan. Make reservations in advance with Lucerne Resort.

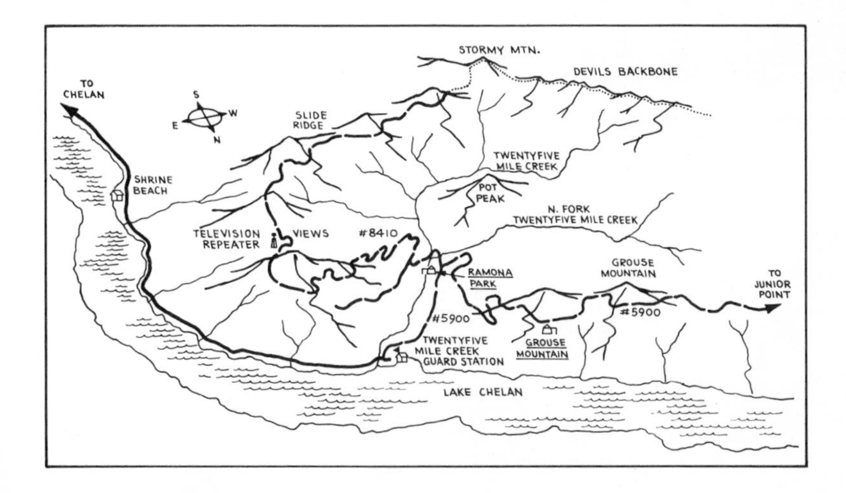

A church now operates Holden Village as a church camp under a special permit from the Forest Service. A snackbar and general store offer limited hiking supplies and equipment, but no hiking food. Housing is limited to those registered in the camp programs. Emergency communication and medical facilities available.

The mining property is closed to the public. Some old mines and buildings on the south side of Railroad Creek are on private property. A visitor can, however, get a good idea of what tailing piles would look like near Image Lake if mining should ever be permitted in the wilderness.

DOMKE LAKE

A 2.5-mile trail to a remote but extremely popular lake.

A good-grade trail leaves Lucerne at the boat dock—watch for signs—climbing gradually through timber to 2-site Domke Lake Camp. Resort nearby. Rent a boat and row across the lake to another small campground, Hatchery Camp, even more remote.

A Chelan air charter firm also flies campers to the lake.

LAKESHORE TRAIL

From Prince Creek Campground to Stehekin, 17.5 miles, up rock gullies, beneath steep cliffs, and along the dry, steep slopes above Lake Chelan.

The **Lady of the Lake** will drop you off at any of the way-points along the trail and pick you up at another. Make arrangements for dates and signals with the boat captain.

CAMPGROUND

Holden Campground—3 sites and other undeveloped areas along Railroad Creek just beyond the village. Views of Buckskin, Copper, Bonanza, and North Star peaks. Pit toilets.

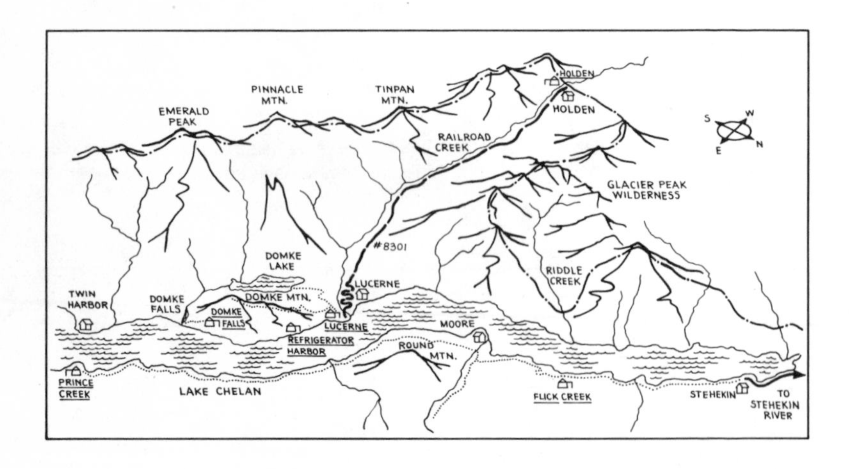

Domke Falls and Lake Chelan

Stehekin River Road

49 STEHEKIN RIVER

Hike or take a bus to a series of remote campsites in a beautiful valley along the park road that ends at 23 miles in the midst of North Cascades National Park.

Take the boat from Chelan to Stehekin and then catch a park bus to any of several campgrounds along a 23-mile back-country road.

The Park operates the bus several times daily from mid-June to Labor Day—road conditions and budgets permitting—as far as Cottonwood Camp, with stops—wherever you want them—along the way. Fees and schedules vary from year to year.

Go up the road one day, camp, and return several days later. Or make a series of stops. Anything you wish.

Permits are required for camping or if you plan a back-country trip. Camping is restricted to designated areas unless you camp at least a mile from any trail.

CAMPGROUNDS

Purple Point—4 sites on a pleasant, wooded slope. Road between the river and the campground. About .25 mile from the Stehekin boat landing. Pit toilets.

Harlequin—7 units in a timbered area along the river, 5 miles from Stehekin. Popular camp with Boy Scout groups. Pit toilets.

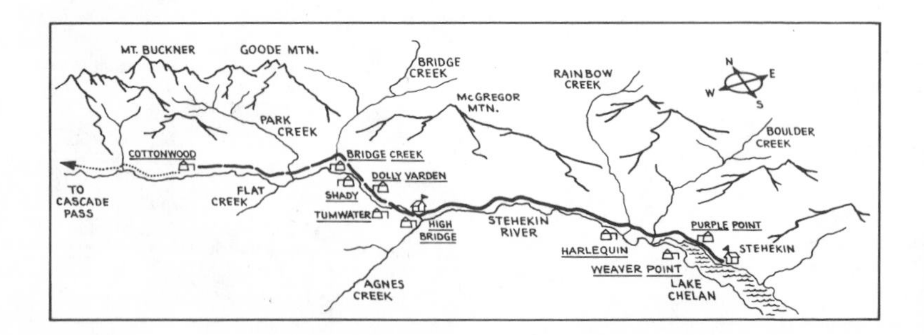

Stehekin landing and McGregor Mountain

High Bridge—3 units and a shelter on a bench about 100 feet above the river, 11 miles from Stehekin. Pit toilets. Climb down to the river for water.
Tumwater—2 units on a ledge above the river, 13 miles from dock. Pit toilets.
Dolly Varden—1 site near the river, 14 miles. Pit toilet across the road.
Shady—1 site near the river, 15 miles. As the name implies, a shady spot. Pit toilets.
Bridge Creek—7 units and a shelter on Clear Creek, 16 miles. Beginning of Pacific Crest trail to the north. Walk up the road to Bridge Creek for views of a falls. Private land nearby. Pit toilets.
Cottonwood—5 units at the end of the road, 23 miles. Trail starts here to the east side of Cascade Pass. Limited views from campground, but scenery all the way on the trail. Pit toilets.
Weaver Point—22 sites on Lake Chelan across the lake from the Stehekin boat dock near the mouth of the Stehekin River. Primarily a boat camp. But it can be reached by a 2-mile trail from the Harlequin Campground. Pit toilets.

PURPLE CREEK TRAIL

Look down on Stehekin and out over Lake Chelan and the mountains at the head of the lake.

A steep trail starts a series of switchbacks toward War Creek Pass, 8 miles, near the Stehekin post office. High views of the lake in 1 mile through an opening in the forest.

Better views in 2 miles when trail reaches a small meadow where one can look back at Stehekin and out at the up-valley mountains.

Rainbow Falls

Stehekin schoolhouse

RAINBOW FALLS

A 312-foot plume of white water plunging from a sheer cliff.

Beautiful in the summer. But in winter, a spectacle of ice-draped boulders hung with glistening icicles.

Hike up the road 4 miles from the Stehekin dock or take a park bus from the resort. A tour bus also makes the trip to the falls and back during the stopover of the boat from Chelan.

SCHOOLHOUSE

The only one-teacher log school still operating in the state. The building was constructed in 1921 of trees harvested from nearby forest land by local people who contributed their time to build the school. A half-mile downriver from the falls alongside the main road.

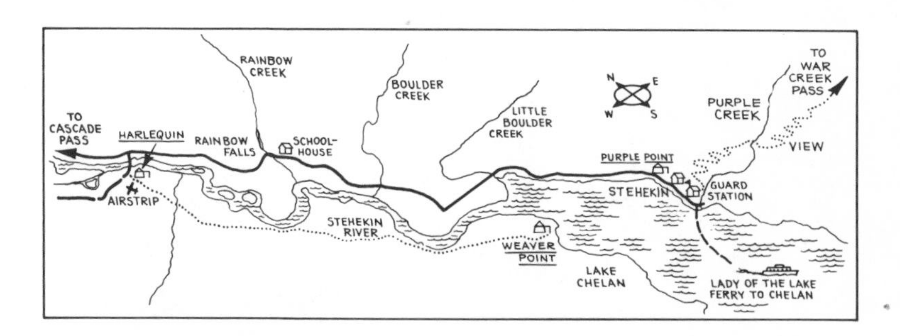

50 AGNES GORGE

A walk through high and dry forest leads to up-valley views of peaks in the Glacier Peak Wilderness.

Find the trail uphill beyond High Bridge and beyond the Pacific Crest trail about .25 mile, to the left. The path starts out in forest with no views anywhere until it reaches the wilderness boundary in about 1 mile.

From then on the trail winds above the Agnes Creek gorge with almost constant views ahead until it ends in pleasant forest at small waterfalls. Come back the same way.

COON LAKE

A 1-mile hike with occasional down-valley views to a boggy lake.

Take the McGregor Mountain trail near the High Bridge Guard Station. On the north side of the road. Trail climbs through timber to a rocky point near the lake for views down the Stehekin River valley.

A polliwog lake, high in spring, low in summer.

BASIN CREEK

An easy 2-mile walk leads to higher and higher vistas of ridges, peaks, and waterfalls on the east side of scenic Cascade Pass.

Take the trail out of Cottonwood Camp at the end of the road from Stehekin. Views increase as the trail steadily makes its way up the valley toward the pass, in 8 miles.

A spectacular short walk. Waterfalls at Basin Creek.

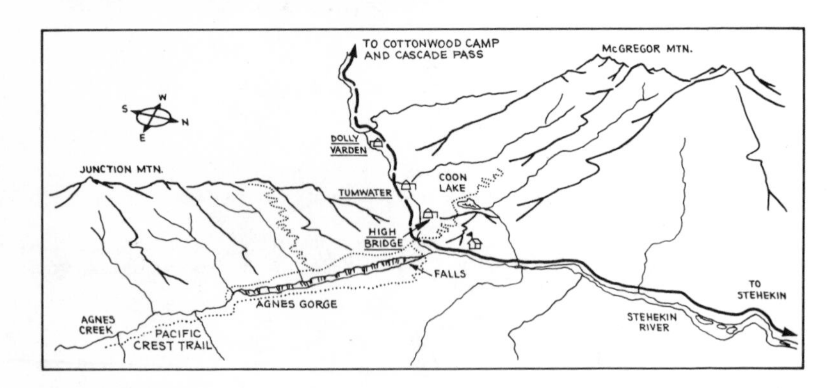

High Bridge on Stehekin River

Y ENTIAT

From hot, dry valleys to cool alpine meadows with waterfalls, river trails, and viewpoints in between.

From Road No. 19 and 51 up the Entiat River from Entiat explore high places on the Chelan Mountains to the north and the Entiat Mountains to the south. For Columbia River features, drive south on Highway 97.

Mountain roads here generally open in late June. But always check in advance.

Note: Over 65,000 acres of forest were swept by fire in this area during 1970. For overall views of the destruction—and how nature has repaired the damage—visit Sugarloaf Lookout, Tyee Mountain Lookout, Big Hill, and Junior Point.

ROCKY REACH DAM

Fish-viewing rooms, motion pictures, murals, Indian history, and industrial exhibits.

Drive north 7 miles from Wenatchee on Highway 97. Watch for signs to parking area on the right.

Lincoln Rock above the Swakane Canyon Road

Windows in the side of the fish ladder that climbs from the river to the top of the dam permit underwater views of migrating salmon, steelhead, and trout in a viewing gallery in the Visitor Center.

An Indian exhibit on early history of the Columbia Basin, an industrial display prepared by commercial power purchasers, and a topographic map of the state are features of a powerhouse display. Films on construction of the dam and about the Chelan-Wenatchee area are shown almost continuously in the Visitor Center Auditorium.

Self-guided tours include views of the dam, generators, murals, and occasional summertime art shows.

LINCOLN ROCK

Lincoln's profile in the side of a mountain overlooking the Columbia River behind Rocky Reach Dam.

Drive north of the dam on Highway 97 a little more than 1 mile, turning uphill at the Swakane Canyon Road. Stop and look up at the cliffs.

CAMPGROUNDS

Entiat—121 sites in a city park on the Columbia River. Separate area for tents. Restrooms. Water. Fee.

Pine Flat—9 units, designed for tents and small trailers in open ponderosa pine forest near the Mad River, 4 units near the river, the rest away, 11 miles from Entiat. An ideal spring and late-fall camp. Hot in summer. Pit toilets.

Fox Creek—8 units on a tree-shaded flat next to the Entiat River, 27 miles from Entiat. All units, however, are back from the river. The first campground to fill up on weekends. Pit toilets.

Lake Creek—12 units located on a bench above the river, 28 miles from Entiat. One unit on Lake Creek. Pit toilets.

Silver Falls—44 units in two campground areas on either side of Silver Creek. First—downriver—site in large, shady timber with about half the sites near the river. Upriver campground on one timbered loop with sites well separated. Pit toilets. Wells.

North Fork—8 units about 25 yards off the highway, 33 miles from Entiat. Tends to be dusty in summer. Pit toilets. Near river.

Spruce Grove—2 units next to the river in well-worn, heavily used area under big timber, 35 miles from Entiat. Often crowded on weekends. Pit toilets.

Three Creek—3 units about 50 yards from the river in lodgepole pine. On spur road off main Entiat Valley Road, 36 miles from Entiat. Pit toilets.

Cottonwood—26 units, most oriented to the river, 38 miles from Entiat. A few off the main road, tending to be dusty. Most across the bridge on a loop downriver. Pit toilets. Wells.

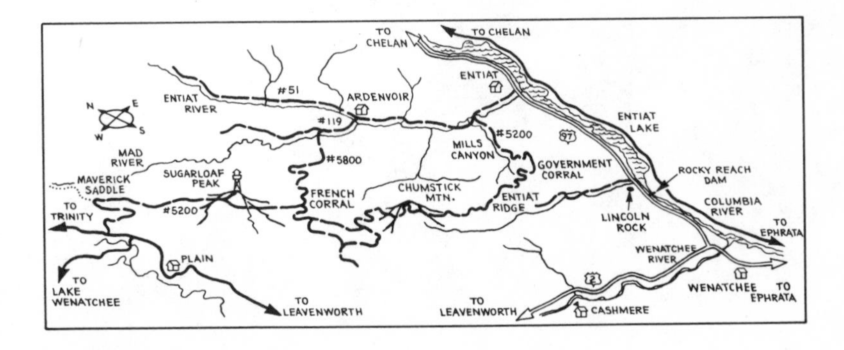

Shady Pass Road

51 ENTIAT MOUNTAINS

Superb vistas from the high points south of the Entiat River plus interesting features along the Columbia.

For the high places, drive west out of Entiat to Ardenvoir, crossing the river there to Road No. 119.

ENTIAT RIDGE

Airplane views of the Columbia, Lake Wenatchee, Glacier, Stuart, and the Cascades.

A high, sometimes steep and skittish road along the top of Entiat Ridge from Chumstick past Sugarloaf to Maverick Saddle. The airborne, squeamish sections are very real but short, thankfully, and safe. Road generally open late in June when country is at its best.

To start with high views of the Columbia, turn south off the Entiat River Road up the Entiat Summit Road No. 5200 at Mills Canyon, about 3.25 miles west of Entiat. First high views in about 10 miles. Chumstick—an abandoned lookout—in 17 miles. French Corral, at junction with No. 5800 from Ardenvoir, at 27 miles.

To start with views of Lake Wenatchee and mountains to the west, turn south off the Entiat River Road at Ardenvoir onto Road No. 119, and in a little more than 2 miles onto No. 5800. French Corral junction in 13 miles. Best views on Road No. 5200 **north** of French Corral.

To drop down into the Lake Wenatchee area, take Road No. 6101 west out of Maverick Saddle, dropping 6 miles to the Chiwawa River Road.

SUGARLOAF LOOKOUT

Expansive views of the Stuart Range, Stuart, Glacier, Snowgrass, Rainier's tip, Cashmere, the brown plains of the Columbia Basin, and the stark ridges of the Chelan–Okanogan mountains.

Five miles from French Corral. Watch for sign. A quarter-mile spur road leads past primitive camping area to lookout building perched atop an irregular group of basalt columns. Several other shafts of basalt stand alone on the slopes of the mountain.

MAD RIVER TRAIL

Walk 1.5 miles down to the Mad River, cross a bridge, and then settle down to an easy stroll along a pleasant river. Go as far as the spirit moves you.

Start your trip on the .25-mile primitive road that drops downhill at the end of Road No. 6101 at Maverick Saddle, turning left at the bottom onto the river trail. Hike midweek if you can. Motor bikes and horses take it over on weekends.

The path climbs through nice forest, dropping to the river's edge just enough to keep you intrigued, until it reaches the bridge. From then on, it's a magic mix of river, trail, and forests.

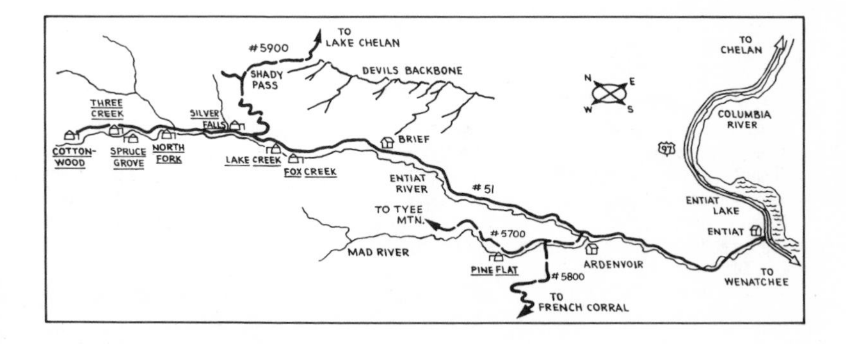

Lower Mad River Trail

52 TYEE RIDGE

TYEE MOUNTAIN LOOKOUT

Less than a decade ago this lookout was best known for its view of the damage wrought by fires which swept all across these ridges.

Today, it looks out on greenery again. Most of the burned snags have fallen, but the mountainsides and panoramas are worthy of your time. Lookout is manned some years.

From Ardenvoir, follow Road No. 5700, to an uphill spur (No. 5713) right at about 15 miles, reaching the end of the road in another 4.2 miles. (Avoid all downhill spurs after about 14 miles.)

A circle of mountains here: Stuart, Rainier, Adams, Glacier Peak, and all the Cascades.

And don't stop your vista-gawking at the tower. Hike out the Tyee Ridge trail (park at the switchback just below the tower) through a ghost forest created by fire as it struggles now to recover.

First, stand in awe of the furnace of flame that consumed this ridge. Then note that not every tree was destroyed in the holocaust. The few that survive live now to reseed the slope. Note, too, the birds that have returned. And the flowers. The tracks of deer and the scat of smaller animals.

LOWER MAD RIVER TRAIL

An easy and pleasant hike through a shady river canyon from the Pine Flat Campground off Road No. 5700.

Find trail off the turnaround in the campground. Trail follows the river to Hornet Creek and beyond. Touched only slightly by fire. Most pleasant in the first mile. And watch for a small grove of trees that a beaver once envisioned using for his dam. The beaver's efforts still show and the trees still live.

Note also how some of the older Douglas fir and cedar trees survived the blistering groundfires that crossed the trail in places.

YOUNG CREEK SHELTER

A 2-mile hike along the Mad River to a shelter in a small open meadow.

Turn south (left) off the road to Tyee Lookout Road No. 5700 onto Road No. 5703 and Spur 300. Drive to Camp 9—a primitive hunter's camp—at the end of the road.

Spur trail leads westerly from camp down to the Mad River trail, following the river upstream to the shelter near Young Creek.

53 SILVER FALLS

A lace-like veil of water hanging from a 50-foot cliff.

By nature trail from the Silver Falls Campground, .25 mile. Find sign on uphill side of the road across from the upper campground entrance.

Trail climbs a series of switchbacks with stone steps in steepest pitches and occasional places to rest. Views of the falls from the upper end of the trail. Or hike to the top and cool off behind the curtain of water.

BOX CANYON OVERLOOK

A 75-foot-deep narrow gorge gouged through solid rock, roaring its loudest in the spring.

Watch for sign about 2 miles downriver from the Silver Falls Campground. Follow a short spur road toward the river to a parking area, walking directly toward the river to a formal overlook area.

Fence protects a path over rock slabs for views into the canyon.

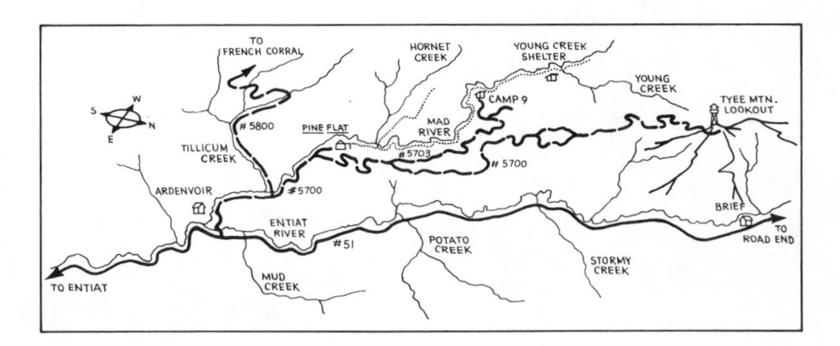

Silver Falls

Silver Falls Trail

ENTIAT FALLS

A stubby torrent plunges through a rock cleft. A cool place to rest.

Watch for sign about 3 miles upriver from the Silver Falls Campground. Find the waterfall just past the parking area.

Water ouzels (dippers) some years nest in corners of rock overhangs below the falls. Look for yellow mouths gaping from small nest-holes in moss.

VALLEY VIEW

One of the very few views up the forested Entiat Valley from the valley floor.

Watch for marked vista point on the south side of the road at the Shady Pass Road junction, 1 mile downriver from Silver Falls Campground.

Profile sign identifies Maude, Gopher, Saska, and Duncan Hill.

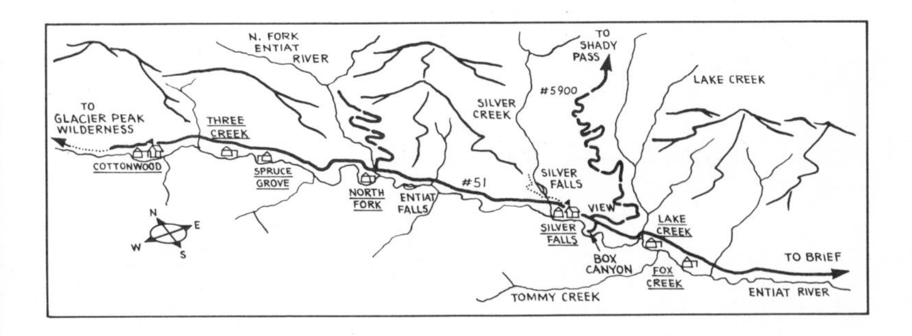

54 ENTIAT VALLEY TO LAKE CHELAN

High views off a narrow, sometimes steep, and often dusty forest road. Much of this area was burned over in the forest fires of 1970.

From the Entiat River north of the Lake Creek Forest Camp drive Road No. 5900 to Shady Pass and then on to Lake Chelan near the Twentyfive Mile Creek Guard Station. About 24 miles.

BIG HILL VIEW

Drive 2 miles northwest of Shady Pass along narrow Road No. 112 through timber to long views of Lake Chelan, Glacier, and Rainier and closer looks at the devastating effects of a wild forest fire.

A cool 6,800 feet on a hot summer day.

Walk past the cabin shelter at the end of the road to the one-time site of a lookout tower. But for bigger views, prowl along the ridge on open meadows.

JUNIOR POINT

Glacier, the top of Rainier, the Navarre peaks, and the scorched mountains of the Okanogans from a viewpoint (6,676) atop an alpine knoll.

Watch for Junior Point signs about 12 miles from Lake Chelan. Spur No. 115. Viewpoint about 100 yards beyond the Junior Point Campground.

CAMPGROUNDS

Halfway Spring—5 units. A pleasant camp at mid-elevation in open timber. All sites except one back away from the road. Pit toilets.

Shady Pass—1 unit at the junction of the Big Hill Road at the top of the pass. A pleasant, shaded, semialpine site. Pit toilet. Water from a spring downhill to the west of the camp.

Big Hill—A garage converted into a shelter with expansive views. Condition of the shelter is as good as the last visitor left it. Pit toilet. Haul water from Shady Pass.

Handy Spring—1 unit at the end of a short spur road. A primitive, unkempt site in a sometimes muddy area. Pit toilet. Piped spring water.

Junior Point—5 sites in a cool alpine (6,600) setting near viewpoint. Off the main road. Surrounded by lupine slopes and subalpine timber. Water in camp from cistern in summer. Pit toilets.

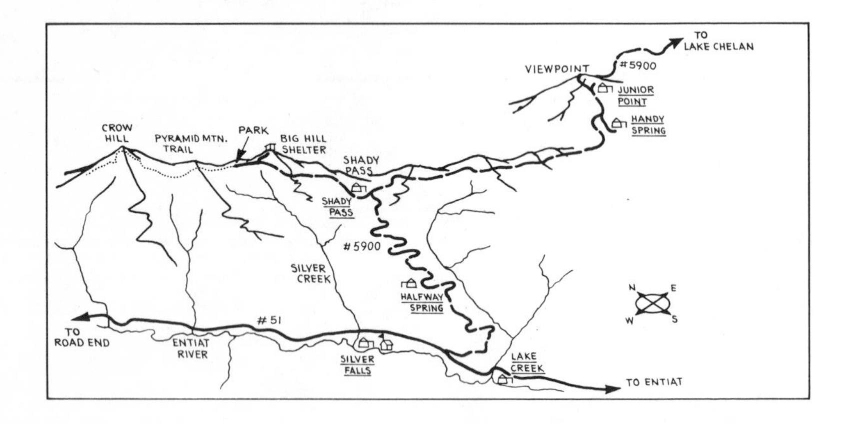

Entiat Burn of 1970 from the Shady Pass Road

Twin Lakes

Z LAKE WENATCHEE

Three valley recreation areas linked to the hub of a big lake.

Roads up the Little Wenatchee, White, and Chiwawa River valleys lead away from the heavy camping pressures on the lake to trails, falls, old mining towns, and high views.

Unpaved river roads are likely to be dusty or muddy, depending on the weather. But the river campgrounds, in many instances, offer some of the better camping opportunities in the area.

Note: Only campgrounds of more than 2 sites are listed here. Smaller camps can be found along valley roads, particularly up the Chiwawa River.

LAKE WENATCHEE CAMPGROUNDS

Lake Wenatchee State Park—197 sites on both sides of the Wenatchee River outlet. Mostly away from the lake. An extremely heavily used area. Swimming. Boating. Saturday evening movies. Restrooms. Piped water. Showers. State fee.

Nason Creek—75 sites on both sides of the road to the State Park. Often mistaken for the State Park. Popular trailer area. Group trailer loop. Pit toilets. Piped water.

Glacier View—23 sites. An extremely pleasant tent-only campground at the far end of the South Shore–Lake Wenatchee Road. Walk-in sites from parking spurs on campground loop. Some sites on lake. No trailers. Pit toilets. Federal fee.

LITTLE WENATCHEE RIVER CAMPGROUNDS

Riverside—6 units near Little Wenatchee River on spur off Rainy Creek Road, 8 miles from Lake Wenatchee. All sites near the river in timber. Pit toilets.

Soda Springs—5 sites near a soda spring, 8 miles west of Lake Wenatchee. Units on both sides of campground spur road. Mosquitoes, usually. Hot and dusty in late summer. Pit toilets. No trailers.

Lake Creek—8 sites in open timber area away from the road, 13 miles from Lake Wenatchee. A pleasant campground even though sites are not well defined. Pit toilets.

Little Wenatchee Ford—3 sites in open area at the end of the road, 18 miles from Lake Wenatchee. Modest views. Busy despite lack of development. Pit toilets. No trailers.

WHITE RIVER CAMPGROUNDS

Napeequa—5 sites near Napeequa River bridge. Pit toilets.

Grasshopper Meadows—5 sites on the west side of the road in wooded area, 8 miles from Lake Wenatchee. Meadow across the road. Short hike to the river. Pit toilets.

White River Falls—5 units along the White River, 9 miles from Lake Wenatchee. Waterfall attracts heavy vehicle traffic through camp. Pit toilets. No trailers.

55 LAKE WENATCHEE AREA

HIDDEN LAKE

A steep .5-mile walk leads to a pretty boulder-bound mountain lake about 500 feet above Lake Wenatchee.

Find trail off lakeshore at upper (west) end of Glacier View Campground. In parking area. Watch for sign. Trail crosses bridge then wends through timber to popular lake.

Paths around the boulder-strewn shore. Lots of places to picnic, contemplate, or just plain snooze.

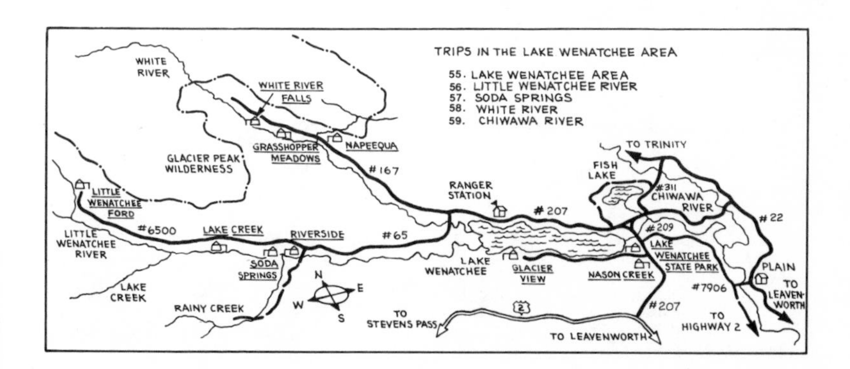

Porcupine

SOUTH SHORE LAKE TRAIL

An easy, level trail leads out of Glacier View Campground about 1.5 miles to a Campfire Girls camp to the east.

Pick up trail in the campground between tent sites and the lake, following it eastward past summer homes to the formal camp. Trail follows lakeshore all the way.

GLACIER PEAK VIEWS

Glacier Peak (10,568) framed up the White River valley between David (7,431) and the White Mountains.

Drive west past the Lake Wenatchee Ranger Station about 2 miles, turning south on the Little Wenatchee River Road No. 65. Viewpoint, marked with signs, at the bridge over the White River.

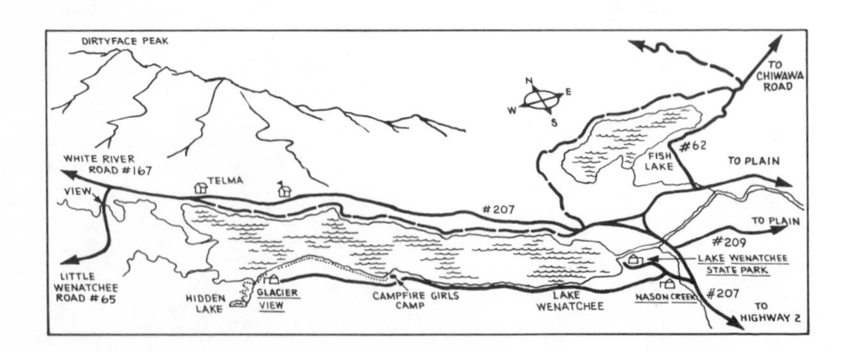

Hidden Lake

56 LITTLE WENATCHEE RIVER

BLACKBERRIES AND VIEWS

Blackberry thickets in clear-cuts, with high views of Lake Wenatchee, Nason Ridge, and the Little Wenatchee River valley.

Turn north on Line Creek Road No. 6502—the first road west of Lake Wenatchee off the Little Wenatchee River Road—keeping right at the first turn. Formal viewpoint in 3 miles. Best blackberries in logged-over areas on the way.

For views and berries along Soda Springs Road No. 6503, turn north from the Little Wenatchee Road just beyond the buildings of the sometime limestone quarry. Keep left at the first junction. Add Labyrinth (6,360) to the view.

LITTLE WENATCHEE TRAIL

A 1.5-mile trail along a pretty canyon on the sparkling Little Wenatchee River. Rocks, bluffs, tumbling rapids, and deep pools.

Trail leaves the back—southwest—corner of the Lake Creek Campground. Find sign. The trail climbs a ridge above the river before dropping down to pass a series of riffles and rapids, climbing again along the rim of the canyon near the end of the trail. Whenever the trail leaves the river, watch for spur paths leading to loops along the gorge. An extremely pleasant walk.

POE MOUNTAIN RIDGE

From a high logging road, climb to a ridge and then hike through better and better vistas either to Poe Mountain in 2.5 miles or to the most open part of the ridge in maybe 2 miles.

Turn north off the Little Wenatchee River Road No. 6500 onto the first road uphill to the right beyond the turnoff to Soda Springs Campground. The road, No. 6504, makes a long, gradual traverse to the west before switching up the mountain to the trailhead in about 6 miles—.5 mile from the end of the road.

Find the trail up through a clear-cut off a blocked logging spur about 30 yards from the road. At a junction in a forested saddle at the end of a long .5 mile, take the trail up the ridge to the left.

The path varies from good to so-so as it wends its way up and down along the ridge, offering most vistas through trees. But in less than 2 miles, the path climbs out onto a ridgetop meadow with views here up at Poe Mountain and north into the Glacier Peak Wilderness and south over the Little Wenatchee Valley. Stop here and soak up the scene or scramble on to the former lookout site on the mountain in .5 mile or more. Your choice.

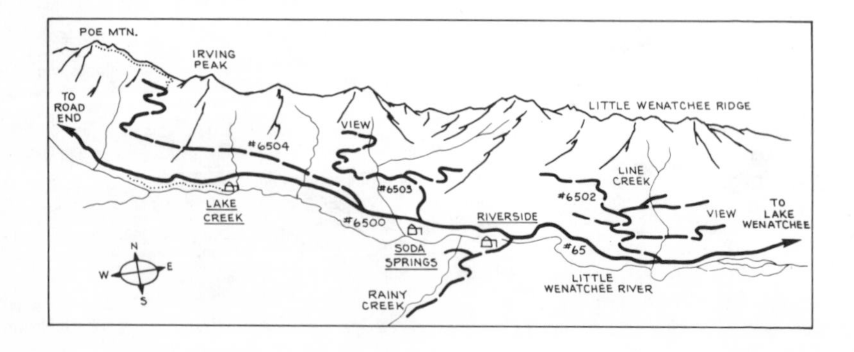

Lake Wenatchee from Line Creek Road No. 6502

57 SODA SPRINGS

Soda-pop spring, a rock to carve on, and trails through forests and to viewpoints.

Find the soda spring and the soft soapstone boulder to the left of the entrance road into Soda Springs Campground.

Dip soda water—bring your own flavoring, nature supplies the fizzin'—from a boxed spring about 20 feet from a parking area.

Find the initial rock up a short trail beyond the spring, turning right at the first fork.

And it's perfectly all right to carve here. In fact, the Forest Service encourages it—hoping to save a few tables and signs in the process.

BLUFF VIEW TRAIL

A modest view of an old limestone quarry and the Little Wenatchee River valley.

Turn left at the junction to Initial Rock, following tourist trails and old switchbacks constantly uphill to a former lookout site. A quarter-mile. Trail downhill is just as confusing. Note turning points on the way up.

Some years, if the quarry appears to be in operation, paths may be blocked with "private property keep out" signs. It is private land.

BIG TREE LOOP

A pleasant .5-mile loop trail through a creek-bottom stand of cedar. The "big" trees aren't the big trees of the Puget Sound region, but, rather, excellent examples of bigger timber found on the dry side of the Cascades.

Find trail at the far end of the Soda Springs Campground, bearing to the right. Watch for signs. Trail drops across a small creek to the Little Wenatchee River.

MINE VIEW TRAIL

A short trail to a bluff overlooking the Little Wenatchee River and glimpses through the trees of the limestone quarry to the east.

Find trail at the end of the campground road into Soda Springs Campground. From the river overlook point, follow trail to the left for view of quarry. Trail eventually drops down to rich cedar forest area along the river. To viewpoints, less than .25 mile.

Here, again, you may run into private property signs when the quarry is being operated.

LITTLE WENATCHEE FALLS

A pretty series of stubby torrents through huge boulders with crystal pools. At the lower end, massive snarls of logs.

Find unmarked way-trail off the paved Little Wenatchee River Road about 50 yards east of the junction with Rainy Creek Road No. 6700. The narrow trail, beyond rocks piled off the road, drops steeply but quickly to a faded Wenatchee Falls sign.

Rock slabs above the noisy river afford ideal lunch spots. Note bowls being eroded into the tops of some slabs. Small pebbles and stones, often still inside the dishes, grind the bowls larger in the swirling action of high water.

For a bigger spectacle, visit the falls in the spring.

58 WHITE RIVER

Viewpoints, history sites, waterfalls, and forest trails along a formal tour route. Watch for signs. Along Road No. 6400.

WHITE RIVER VIEWS

The "Poet Peaks" of Little Wenatchee Ridge—from the left, Irving, Poe, Longfellow, Whittier, and Bryant—and including Lake Wenatchee, Nason Ridge, and on the way down, Glacier.

Turn east off the White River Road about 2.5 miles from the intersection with the Little Wenatchee River Road. Watch for Dirty Face Logging Road sign. Drive 2.3 miles to a marked viewpoint.

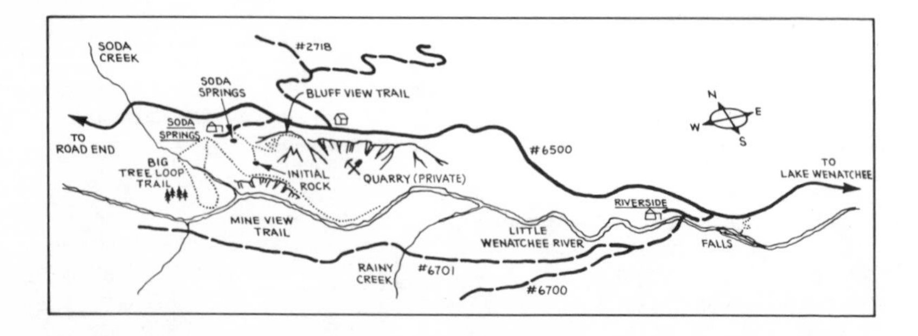

Little Wenatchee River Falls

Lake Wenatchee from Dirtyface Viewpoint

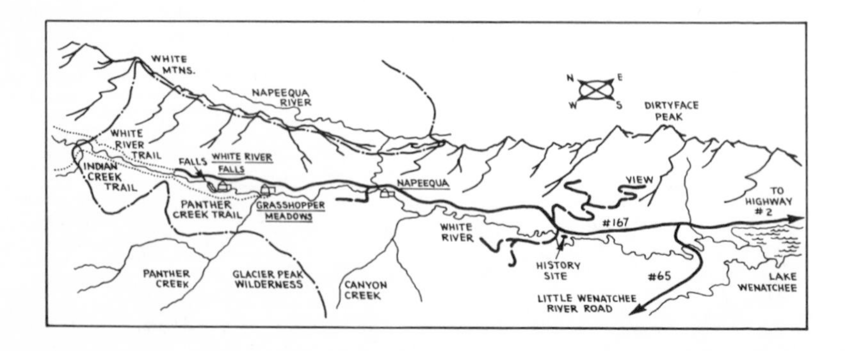

WHITE RIVER FALLS

The White River plunges over rock slabs into a narrow canyon.

Walk out over rock outcrops from the White River Falls Campground to views down over the water chute. No fence protects the area, and rocks can be extremely slippery when wet.

A way-trail leads around to the left through boulders to the bottom of the canyon and limited views of the falls. Best views across the river. See Panther Creek trail.

PANTHER CREEK TRAIL

A pleasant 1-mile walk back along the west side of the White River leads to full-face views of White River Falls.

Drive to the end of the White River Road, taking trail to the left across the footbridge. A spur trail forks left to the falls in a little less than 1 mile.

A narrow way-trail leads uphill from the first falls viewpoint to a second overlook with a fuller view.

GLACIER PEAK WILDERNESS TRAILS

Two trails on either side of the White River lead to the boundary of the Glacier Peak Wilderness in about 2 miles.

Both lead through pleasant timber, sometimes near the river, sometimes not. The two trails—the White River on the east bank and the Indian Creek on the west—are not connected at the wilderness boundary.

HISTORICAL SITE

A concrete cross on the west side of the White River Road No. 167/6400, 2 miles from the Little Wenatchee Road junction, marks the grave of Eunice Henry, a homesteader who died here in 1913. Remnants of her cabin and overgrown sections of the old wagon road to the east of the road on a short loop trail. See sign.

59 CHIWAWA RIVER

TRINITY

Buildings and old mill of the defunct Royal Development Mine at the end of the Chiwawa River Road No. 6200.

Trail to the Glacier Peak Wilderness leads across bridge, gated to vehicle traffic, through the center of the private town. All the buildings are posted and probably dangerous. Don't explore off the trail without permission of the caretaker.

PHELPS CREEK ROAD

High views of the icefields on Buck Mountain, Chiwawa Ridge, and the Chiwawa River valley.

Turn east on the first road (No. 6211) south of the Phelps Creek Campground. Best views in about 2.5 miles at about 3,000 feet.

Road is rough but passable to passenger cars.

HALFWAY HOUSE

An abandoned two-story log cabin on open meadows of an old homestead tract which once served as a halfway resting point for travelers bound for Trinity.

Watch for the cabin on the far side of meadows to the east of the road just north of Chikamin Creek, less than 1.25 miles north of Grouse Creek Campground.

Cabin and the meadows are privately owned.

CAMPGROUNDS

Goose Creek—4 units in wooded area next to Goose Creek. On Road No. 6100. Pit toilet.

Deep Creek—3 units at junction of Deep Creek and Lower Chiwawa roads. Pit toilet.

Grouse Creek—4 units in wooded area near Grouse Creek, 26 miles from Leavenworth. Pit toilets.

Rock Creek—4 units near road, 29 miles from Leavenworth. Likely to be very dusty. Pit toilets. Piped water.

Rock Creek Crossing—4 units in sparsely wooded area near Rock Creek, 31 miles from Leavenworth. Pit toilets.

Schaefer Creek—3 sites on Chiwawa River in timber, 33 miles from Leavenworth. Pit toilets.

Atkinson Flat—4 formal sites near the Chiwawa River in a huge meadow. Pit toilets.

19 mile—3 units above the river on a steep bank in a wooded area. Pit toilets.

Maple Creek—7 sites across the Chiwawa River on a spur road, 37 miles from Leavenworth. Watch for sign. Sites away from the river in shady timber. Pit toilets.

Alpine Meadow—4 units in pleasant open meadow near river, 38 miles from Leavenworth. Pickup and tent campers only. Pit toilets.

Phelps Creek—7 units on a very pleasant, shady spur along the Chiwawa River just below the end of the road at Trinity, 39 miles from Leavenworth. Pit toilets.

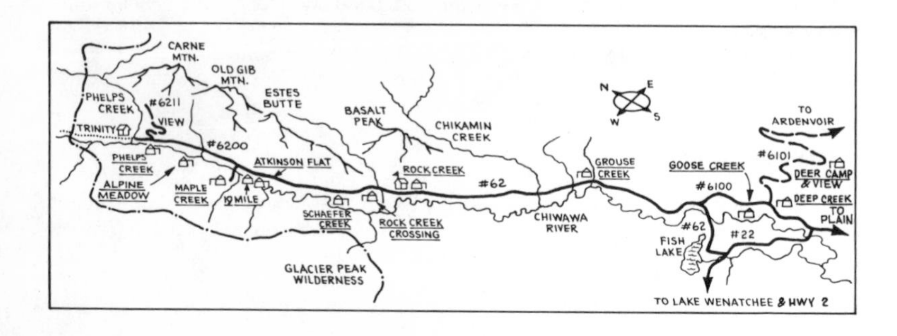

Trinity Mine buildings below Buck Mountain

Morning mist near Leavenworth

AA STEVENS PASS TO LEAVENWORTH

From the alpine slopes of Stevens Pass to the remodeled Bavarian-style town of Leavenworth.

A spectacular drive for color-seekers in the fall, with spur roads and trails leading to higher views, lakes, and quiet river drives.

SUSAN JANE AND JOSEPHINE LAKES

Sneak up on two alpine gems by taking a rough logging road to within a little more than 2 miles of both.

Turn south off Highway 2 about 6 miles east of Stevens Pass onto Mill Creek Road No. 6960. The road is sometimes gated in about 2 miles. But most summers it's open as far as you can carefully avoid the deepest ruts. A small patch of woods along the road beyond a sharp switchback at about 1.7 miles from the gate is a good place to stop. The road gets really rough after that.

Park and walk up the road—maybe a mile—to the Pacific Crest trail. Once you've turned left on the trail, no more ugly powerlines. Instant peace in the Alpine Lakes Wilderness.

Susan Jane in a pleasant mile is truly the diamond of this walk. Lots of private places to enjoy the beauty of the lake and ridges around it. Under no conditions should you hurry on.

The trail beyond Susan Jane climbs in .5 mile to a ridge between the two lakes. Explore its small meadows and tarns and search out the views down on Josephine. Trails branch at the ridge, left for the lake and straight ahead for the Pacific Crest trail.

As you return, watch for an unsigned, unmaintained, but obviously well-used way-trail that drops downhill east of Susan Jane. It ends up on the road at the big switchback you can see from the trail. About 1.6 miles from the gate. May save time. And avoid the ugliness of the powerline.

LANHAM LAKE

An easy 1.8-mile walk just off the Stevens Pass Highway to a pleasant mountain lake at 3,900 feet.

Find the trail to the east of Road No. 6960 just beyond Lanham Creek. Park in a clear area on the right. Trail starts in timber then breaks out into an ugly powerline right-of-way. Make your way generally uphill by walking first to the right and then left on roads, watching for an old logging track or blazes on trees.

Trail follows an old logging spur before entering timber again, ending at a very pleasant picnic or camp spot on the lake.

Turn south off Highway 2 about 6 miles from Stevens Pass (see Lake Susan Jane), finding trailhead in less than .25 mile.

LAKE JANUS

Walk uphill and down a little more than 2.5 miles to reach a glorious mountain lake surrounded by green cotton-grass meadows on the Pacific Crest trail.

Turn north off Highway 2, 4.5 miles east of Stevens Pass on the Smith Brook Road No. 6700, finding the trail uphill to the left just beyond the first big switchback, about 3 miles. Signed as the Smith Brook trail.

The trail starts with a long traverse to the ridge in the first .5 mile (turn right at the top onto the Pacific Crest trail) and then drops down about 600 feet in the next 1 mile before making its way upward again past a pretty waterfall and through meadows to the lake.

A tottering shelter and camp spots. And lots of places to lunch and enjoy and wonder why you didn't come to this place before.

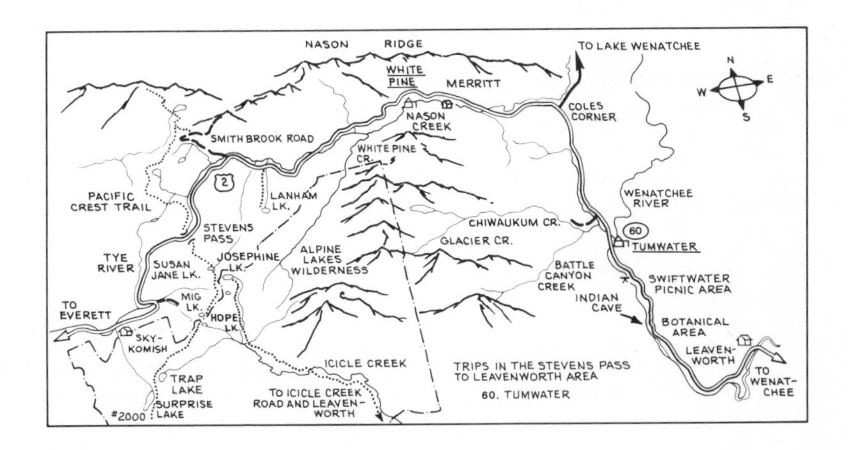

Tweedy's Lewisia (Lewisia tweedyi)

CAMPGROUNDS

White Pine—6 sites just off Highway 2 on White Pine Creek Road No. 6950. Turn south off Highway 2 about 1 mile west of Merritt. Pit toilets.

Tumwater—56 camping and 27 picnic units in a wooded area between Chiwaukum Creek and the Wenatchee River. A popular, heavily used campground, 9 miles northwest of Leavenworth on Highway 2. Toilets. Piped water. Federal fee.

60 TUMWATER

WENATCHEE RIVER ROAD

A quiet, beautiful section of the Wenatchee River away from the hubbub of highways. Riffles and rapids under bald cliffs between the community of Plain and Tumwater Canyon. But... **but... BUT...**

Turn right (east) onto the first Forest Road No. 7906, just north of the Tumwater Campground and the Chiwaukum Creek bridge. Sign says road not maintained by county—or by anybody else for that matter.

The road wanders 3.75 miles along the river before climbing along a clifflike ridge to a paved road leading to Plain, 9.3 miles.

The lower road is likely to be dusty in summer, muddy in spring, and full of holes all year. The narrow ridge-road section above the river—1.25 miles—can be even more hazardous after a rain. Dust turns to slime. So start out carefully with the understanding it may be wise to turn back. **Not** for low-slung passenger cars or squeamish drivers—in anything.

From Plain return either via Lake Wenatchee or through Chumstick to Leavenworth. Follow signs.

DRURY FALLS

Spring torrents pour off the cliffs of Icicle Ridge into the Wenatchee River Canyon.

One mile downriver from the Swiftwater Picnic Area. Watch for falls on cliffs across the river.

Indian cave in Tumwater Canyon

CASTLE ROCK

A favorite practice area for rock climbers, with airy views from the top of the Tumwater Canyon.

Drive 3 miles west of Leavenworth on Highway 2. Parking area at the base.

An unmarked scramble-route up grass and scree slopes leads to similar views without the necessity of rock climbing.

INDIAN CAVE

Nature trail from the Swiftwater Picnic Area leads to an Indian "cave" under the crest of a huge boulder on the Wenatchee River.

Drive 8 miles north of Leavenworth. Short trail upriver from the upper picnic area leads to the cave. Signs of smoke on the ceiling of the rock shelter establish setting for Indian fishermen waiting out a storm.

LEWISIA TWEEDYI

The rarest of three species of Lewisia.

Preserved in a two-square-mile botanical preserve about 5 miles north of Leavenworth but sometimes seen along the highway near the Swiftwater picnic area. Look for yellow or salmon colored blooms in May and June. But don't pick. They are extremely rare. Take a picture, leaving the blossom for others to enjoy too.

BB ICICLE CREEK

Clear, deep pools and chattering rapids on a creek as crisply beautiful as its name.

Turn south off Highway 2 at sign just west of Leavenworth. Road remains near the creek most of the way up the valley.

Catch glimpses of Stuart up the Eightmile Creek valley at the top of the hill just beyond the Eightmile Campground.

Coolest camping at Johnny Creek and above. Some rattlesnakes below Johnny Creek.

BOUNDARY BUTTE VIEWPOINT

From 3,168 feet, look down on the orchards of Leavenworth and Cashmere, out into the Enchantment Lake peaks and the Icicle Creek drainage and up to Glacier Peak. With wildflowers in the spring.

Cross the bridge over the Wenatchee River just east of the Leavenworth Ranger Station in Leavenworth, taking the first road right off the highway. In 100 yards turn left on

Cashmere Peak from Johnny Creek Road

the Mountain Home Road No. 7300. Follow signs. Road views down on Leavenworth in the first mile.

In 6 miles turn east onto the lookout spur road No. 570. Old lookout site in 2 more miles. (You may need to walk the last .25 mile.) Road No. 7300 continues southeast to the Blewett Pass Highway.

LEAVENWORTH NATIONAL FISH HATCHERY

Largest federal fish hatchery in the United States.

Built in 1939 after Grand Coulee Dam blocked upstream migration of salmon. Over 8 million coho and chinook salmon are hatched here each year.

Turn south onto the Icicle Creek road at the west end of Leavenworth. About 1.5 miles south of the Wenatchee River bridge. Watch for signs.

JOHNNY CREEK ROAD

Views of Cashmere Peak (8,520), the Icicle Valley, 6,600 Ridge, and Bootjack (6,700).

Turn north off the Icicle Creek Road, about 400 feet southeast of the Johnny Creek Campground. Views from Road No.7603 in less than 2 miles.

EIGHTMILE LAKE

Hike past a small lake to a much larger one tucked in timber below towering rock walls.

Turn south off the Icicle River Road at Bridge Creek Campground onto Road No. 7601. Trail is well signed about 3 miles up the road. Valley views en route.

The trail climbs sharply at the start, straight up a ridge to the end—you'll never believe it!—of a logging road. The steep part of the trail was logged in 1972, supposedly to protect recreation values. (Ask yourself if they succeeded.) The logging road, on private land, is closed to the public by a gate at the bottom.

But all is not lost. Once the trail enters the Alpine Lakes Wilderness, your day is saved. Little Eightmile Lake (4,400) in 2.5 miles and then, after a quick climb through a rock slide, Eightmile Lake itself with its spectacle, spectacle, spectacle in another .5 mile.

Treat the lakeshore kindly. It's suffered enough already.

CAMPGROUNDS

Eightmile—22 sites on loop near creek, 8 miles from Leavenworth. Group reservation area. Vault toilets. Water.

Bridge Creek—8 units, 9 miles from Leavenworth. Sites oriented to creek. Pit toilets.

Johnny Creek—16 units, 12 miles from Leavenworth. First of the cooler campgrounds. Sites off two spurs. Some away from the creek but most near it. Pit toilets. Piped water.

Black Pine Horse Camp—9 units at the end of the road on the south side of the creek. A trailhead camp for horse groups. Unloading ramps.

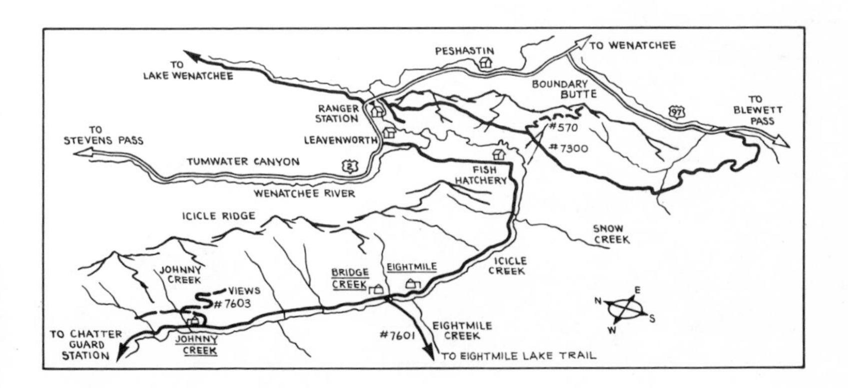

Icicle Creek at Chatter Creek Guard Station

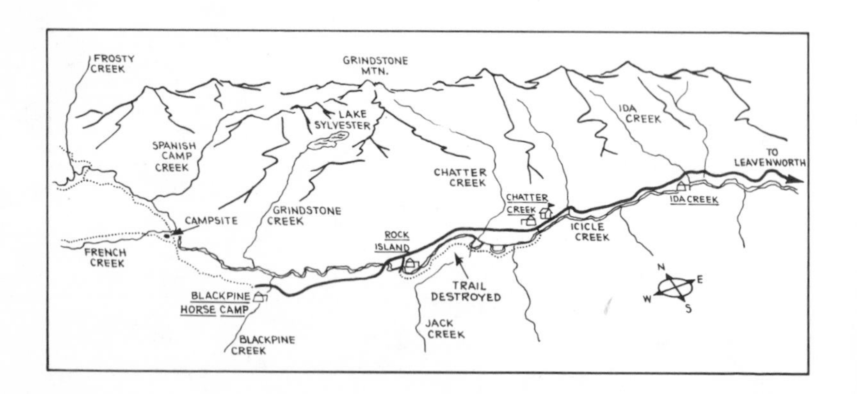

61 UPPER ICICLE CREEK

ICICLE CREEK BRIDLE TRAIL

Is it really true? If the Forest Service spots a tree big enough to cut, will it abandon a trail to chop it? The agency says not. But take a look at what happened here.

There used to be a pretty streamside trail past pools, big rocks, and more pools between the Chatter Creek Guard Station and Rock Island Campground. An easy 2 miles.

But not anymore. High water and floods used to block the trail early some springs. But now loggers have closed most of it entirely—clearcutting, you know. You can walk maybe .5 mile downriver along the south side of the creek from the Rock Island Campground and bridge. But that's about it.

The Forest Service may restore the trail in "five or six years." But don't hold your breath. Past history offers very little hope.

FRENCH CREEK CAMP

An easy 1.5-mile walk through timber down the Icicle Creek trail to a noisy rapids and a pleasant camping spot. A good place for a test-run backpacking trip.

Drive across Icicle Creek at Rock Island Campground, following the Blackpine Road to the end. Trail, at the end of the road, winds up the valley but away from the river until it reaches the camp.

Find the rapids—you'll hear them hustling—off to the right of the trail before it crosses the bridge.

CAMPGROUNDS

Ida Creek—7 units in timbered area near creek which has slowed down here to riffles over gravel, 15 miles from Leavenworth. Sites between road and creek. Pit toilets. Water.

Chatter Creek—13 units away from the Icicle on two small forks of Chatter Creek, 17 miles from Leavenworth. Three walk-in sites reached by log bridge in the middle of the campground. Pleasant shaded area. Pit toilets. Water planned.

Rock Island—19 units in four camping areas, 19 miles from Leavenworth. Three groups of sites off spurs above and below the bridge. One small camping area across the bridge. All are signed. Pit toilets. Water planned.

Mount Rainier from Tronsen Ridge

CC THE SWAUK

Highway 97 from Cle Elum to Wenatchee races up this valley but viewfinders and campers get off the main highway and into the surrounding hills. Mines once were the biggest attraction in the valley. Some prospectors still try for fortunes. Campers, however, will look for agates, views, and fossils.

Drive east from Seattle on I-90, turning off at Wenatchee Interchange No. 85, east of Cle Elum. Continue east on Highway 97. Liberty Guard Station 13 miles from the junction. Swauk Pass in another 11 miles.

CAMPGROUNDS

Mineral Springs—11 sites at the junction of Medicine and Swauk Creeks. A wooded area just off the highway, 3 miles north of Liberty Guard Station. Some sites oriented to the creek. Pit toilets. Spring water.

Swauk—22 sites in wooded loops below the highway on Swauk Creek. Some sites near the stream, others in shady timbers, 3,000 feet elevation. Restrooms and pit toilets. Piped water. Seven miles from guard station. Charge.
Tronsen—20 sites in heavy timber, 1 mile north of Swauk Pass. Most sites on Tronsen Creek. Some near a meadow at the upper end of the campground. Pit toilets.
Bonanza—5 sites in a small camp squeezed in open timber between the highway and Tronsen Creek. Pit toilets. Well.
Park—3 sites in wooded area along old Blewett Pass Highway, less than 1 mile north of Highway 97. Pit toilets.
Lion Rock—3 sites in a patch of timber near a fenced spring below Lion Rock, 8 miles from Swauk Pass. Horse corral. Pit toilets. Spring.

Undeveloped camp spots are to be found in most of the high areas on both sides of the highway. Pick your own but carry ax, bucket, shovel, and water.

62 BLEWETT PASS

Leaf fossils and history along an abandoned section of state highway that became so much a part of the state's transportation history that the new pass (the Swauk) still is called by the old name.

From Seattle, turn off I-90 at the Wenatchee Interchange east of Cle Elum, continuing north on Highway 97 to Swauk Pass (still called Blewett Pass on some highway reports) in 24 miles.

The old highway often is not free of snow until mid-June.

OLD BLEWETT PASS HIGHWAY

For an interesting respite from the usual freeway straightaway rush, drive a mountain highway built as highways used to be, full of curves, twists, and hairpin turns. One-way traffic in some places.

Realize that most of today's short-term and part-time back-country logging roads are wider than this main "highway" which once carried all of the state's truck, bus, and car traffic between Seattle, Wenatchee, the Columbia Basin, and Spokane.

Turn left (north) off Highway 97 about 16.5 miles from the Wenatchee Interchange. The old highway—now Forest Road No. 7320/9415—twists to the old pass at 4,064 feet and then snakes its way down to the new highway about 2 miles south of the old Blewett townsite. An 11-mile trip.

Occasional views and signs of old mining operations mark the trip. Heaviest mining near the summit.

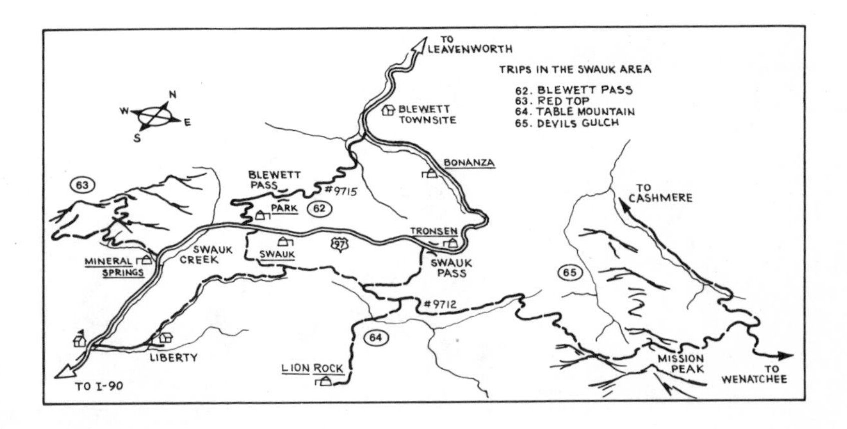

Arrastra, an ore grindstone, at Blewett townsite

LEAF FOSSILS

Find fossils and leaf imprints of plants that grew when the climate here was almost tropical.

Watch for dark bands in road-cut rock .5 mile west of Swauk Pass on Highway 97. Dark bands contain coallike fossils. Imprints are found in sandstone bordering the bands.

BLEWETT TOWNSITE

A tumbledown mining mill and an ore-grinding stone (arrastra) carved in solid rock are all that remain today of a mining town that boomed in the late 1800s.

Drive 10.5 miles north of Swauk Pass on Highway 97.

Look on the west side of the road for the collapsing mill where gold was once

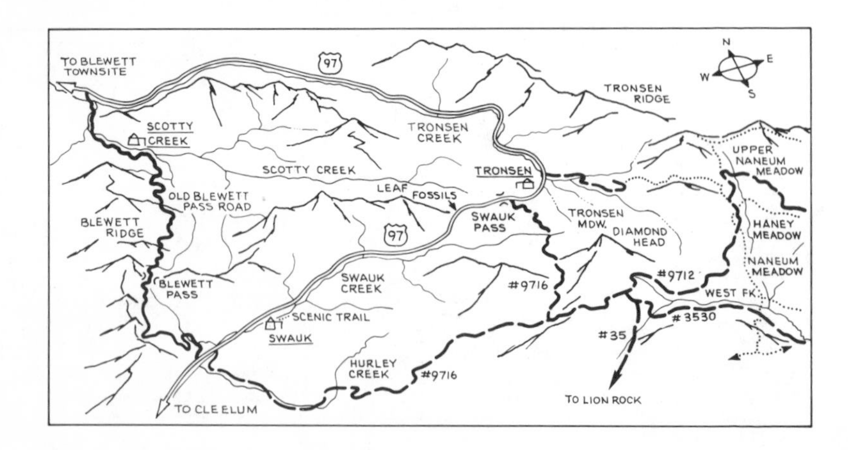

Searching for agates at the "battlefield" on Red Top Mountain

processed. Gold was taken from mines in Culver Gulch behind the mill.

The arrastra—base of a water-powered ore-grinding machine—is located to to the east of the highway over a bank several hundred yards south of the building.

SCULPTURE ROCK TRAIL

Geology of the Swauk area unfolds on an easy .75-mile nature trail out of the Swauk Campground.

Trail starts at the picnic shelter, crosses Swauk Creek, and then turns east, winding back to the far end of the campground.

The pathway loops around sandstone and basalt outcrops, past viewpoints and through timber typical of the entire area.

63 LIBERTY AND RED TOP

A cross-section view here of man's relationship to mineral.

Leave I-90 at the Wenatchee Interchange east of Cle Elum, driving north toward Wenatchee on Highway 97. Liberty Guard Station in 13 miles.

LIBERTY

If you've ever wondered what a mining dredge can do to a pretty creek take a long look at the private gold-dredging operation on Williams Creek in the old mining town of Liberty.

Turn east of Highway 97 at the Liberty Guard Station. Watch for sign. Liberty townsite in 2 miles. A national historic site.

Quaint houses on the north side of the single Liberty street belie the destruction of terrain on the south. Heaps of tailings often hide machinery that make them. Mining operation is all on private land and posted, so get your glimpses and do your cursing from the public street.

PROSPECTOR DRIVES

For glimpses of how mining used to be, explore the mining roads east, north, and south of Liberty. Old cabins still dot hillsides. Grown-over heaps of dirt attest to failures and probably a few modest successes. Some claims are still active.

RED TOP MOUNTAIN

A prime agate-hunting area but a fine view spot too.

From Highway 97, turn west up Road No. 9702 beyond the Mineral Springs Resort and just across the Blue Creek bridge. Follow signs. Park up a spur marked "Agate Bed Parking."

To reach the lookout—with views of Rainier, Stuart, the tip of Adams, other peaks in the Cascades, and Ellensburg and Cle Elum valleys—take trail from the parking area. Trail climbs the west side of the mountain across steep meadows.

Return on a trail that heads north from the lookout and then creeps around a steep bluff to the meadow trail system.

To reach the open agate meadows, which look like they had just undergone a shattering artillery barrage, follow signs beyond the parking area, hiking as far as you like. Spurs lead to Blue Creek Spring and other digging areas.

GOLD PANNING

As always, no promises. But gold is still being mined and panned in this area. Favorite creeks include Medicine Creek above the Mineral Springs Campground, Baker Creek above the Baker Campground, and all creeks in the Liberty area.

One warning. Some of the creeks may cross private land. Some may be part of patented mining claims. If posted, don't trespass.

64 TABLE MOUNTAIN

Leave the valley to enjoy the brisk silence of alpine meadows and ridgetops—all bursting with views.

Drive north on Highway 97 from the Wenatchee Interchange, near Cle Elum, to Swauk Pass, 24 miles, turning right (south) on Forest Road No. 9716 just below the

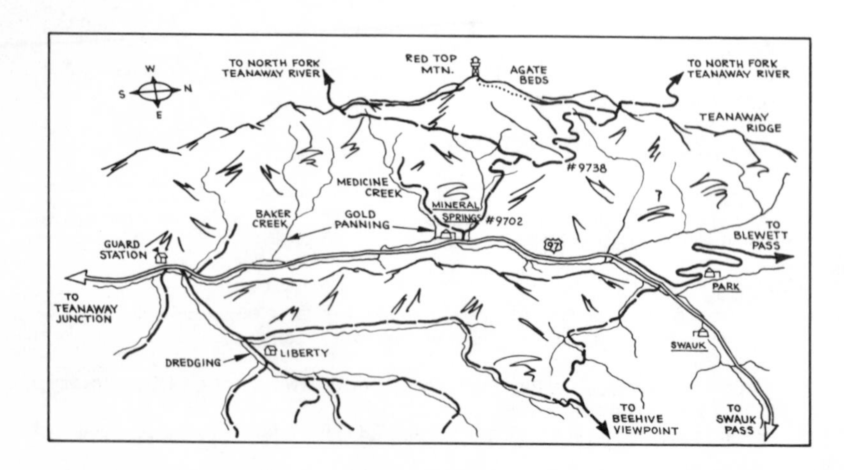

summit. Roads in this area are narrow with few turnouts and tend to get slippery and greasy after rains. But views from all of them are spectacular.

Or from Ellensburg, drive north on the Green Canyon Road off Highway 97, less than 2 miles west of Ellensburg toward Virden. Follow road to the Reece Canyon Road continuing uphill to the top of the Table Mountain plateau and Forest Road No. 35. Watch for campground signs. A smoother route. Paved almost to Lion Rock, in fact. About 23 miles. A spectacular drive through pretty meadows and grand vistas.

Roads on this plateau often range from rough to roughest, tending to get dangerously slippery and greasy after rains. But the panoramas from all of them are spectacular. Elk too if you watch carefully.

Snow may block some roads until July.

LION ROCK VIEW

A lonesome view out over the Swauk valley to the Enchantment Peaks, Stuart, and Mount Rainier. At night listen for coyotes in the valley.

From Swauk Pass follow Road No. 9716 and then No. 9712 along Swauk Ridge to a junction with Road No. 35 to the south. Turnoff to the viewpoint in 4 miles.

Devils Gulch

This road (35) can be rough beyond belief all the way, or just part of the way, depending on logging activity. If loggers want the road improved, it's done. If you'd like it improved, guess again.

For a smoother road drive north from Ellensburg to the plateau on Road No. 35 (see above). About 23 miles.

Camp either at the fenced campground (the fence keeps the cows out) away from the edge of Table Mountain or at any of many undeveloped open areas on the mountain's rim. (Carry water.) You may find a cow bawling at your tent door in the morning. Grazing is permitted. Agates and Indian artifacts are sometimes found in this area.

For a walk-in view, hike north .25 mile from the junction of Lion Rock Lookout Road.

NANEUM MEADOW

You can glimpse this meadow from the road, but to really enjoy its wet beauty in an otherwise dry landscape walk less than 1 mile.

From Swauk Pass drive south (it will seem like east) on Road No. 9716, turning left onto No. 9712 in about 5 miles and then right in about 1 mile onto No. 3530.

Watch for the trail downhill, in about 1.5 miles. The path drops in a few hundred yards to a soggy meadow surrounded by ridges of basalt with a creek down the middle. Elk if you're lucky. Tracks if you're not. Flowers in any case. In every direction. Or just sit and enjoy.

HANEY MEADOW

You can wander here if you like. Or you can drive, park, and wait. Elk, with luck.

Road No. 9712 circles the north side of this big meadow, about 10 miles from Swauk Pass Highway, 5 miles from the junction of the road to Naneum Meadows and Lion Rock.

Trails lead south around and across the meadows to Naneum Meadow (above), or along Howard Creek, or north to Upper Naneum Meadow. Or just wander the trails as you wish. Elk graze here, except after the first shots of hunting season. Stupid they're not.

65 DEVILS GULCH

Drive through high meadows on an atrocious road to look down on the stark, eroded-sandstone slab sides of Devils Gulch. And out toward Lake Wenatchee and Glacier Peak (providing you stop first).

Continue on Road No. 9712 from Swauk Pass, past the Lion Rock junction, driving

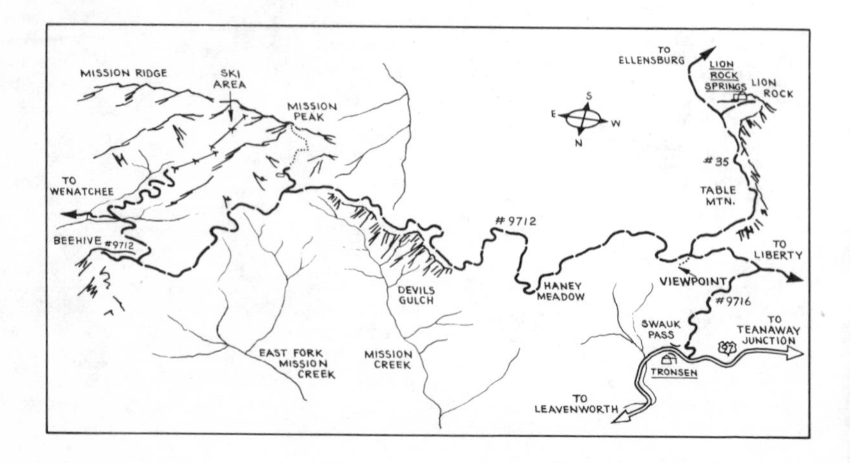

Sunflowers on Tronsen Ridge

first through Haney Meadow (watch for cabins and a fenced area) and then to the rim of the gulch at between 5,800 and 6,000 feet.

Views over the gulch to the north from occasional turnouts or stop almost anywhere along the high road and walk to the sharp canyon lip for a new view. Glimpses of Stuart over lupines on some turns.

(This road gets rougher and rougher every year. The Forest Service does practically nothing either to maintain it or control wet-weather spring and fall use—by hunters mostly—which causes the deep ruts. In the Forest Service view, the road "serves no purpose," which means it's not needed for logging. If you think the agency might preserve these roads just a little by closing them during the wet seasons, write to the agency **and** your congressman!)

MISSION PEAK

Hike up an abandoned road to one of the highest and best views in this area. See not only Rainier and Stuart but Glacier, Baker, Wenatchee, and Rocky Reach Dam on the Columbia River.

Watch for a road spur on the south side of Road No. 9712 east of Devils Gulch shortly after the road turns northerly. At one time you could drive to a small lake at 6,100 feet. But now walk up Road No. 330 to the lake and then another .75 mile to a long-abandoned lookout site at 6,878 feet.

BEEHIVE

Look down on Wenatchee, up the Columbia Gorge toward Chelan, south to the Mission Ridge ski area, and out at Stuart and the Cascades.

From Swauk Pass, drive about 22.5 miles past Devils Gulch (see above) on Road No. 9712 to a junction with Road No. 7100 to Cashmere. Take the first spur road turnoff on the right beyond the junction. Walk .25 mile to the former lookout site at 4,576 feet. Watch for sign.

From Wenatchee, drive southwest toward the Mission Ridge ski area, turning right onto Road No. 9712 about a mile beyond Squillchuck State Park. Turn right again beyond Beehive Reservoir, finding the spur trail to the right uphill in a .25 mile.

Esmeralda Peaks and North Fork Teanaway River Road

DD NORTH FORK TEANAWAY RIVER

A river that barely trickles across farmland in Swauk Prairie roars like a mountain stream should nearer its source. Irrigators drain most of the river at lower levels but have no effect on the river higher up.

From Seattle, drive east over Snoqualmie Pass, turning off I-90 at the Wenatchee Interchange, No. 85 east of Cle Elum, driving north on Highway 97. To reach the Teanaway River turn left (north) off 97 in about 6 miles on County Road No. 970. Follow North Fork signs.

CAMPGROUNDS

Beverly—13 sites in pleasant, open wooded area along the river, 17 miles from Highway 97. Most sites oriented to the river. Pit toilets.

DeRoux—2 sites near the river, 20 miles from Highway 97. An undeveloped camp in open timber. Pit toilets.

Undeveloped sites are to be found all along the river and off logging spurs. Find your own. Some are very nice.

66 TEANAWAY

From the Wenatchee junction east of Cle Elum, drive 6 miles north on Highway 97, turning left onto the Teanaway River Road, bearing north in about 7 miles onto the North Fork Road to Forest Road No. 9737.

RED TOP LOOP

Drive up one road and back another for views from the lookout and meadows on Red Top Mountain. (See the Swauk, above.)

Turn east off the river road just beyond the timber company campground at Dickey Creek. Watch for lookout turnout to the north at the top of the ridge.

To return with continuing vistas most of the way, follow Road No. 9702 downhill and eastward to its junction with No. 9738. Turn left, back toward the Teanaway, picking up a pleasant paved road with lots of downhill views at the top of the pass. The road wends its way along Jack Creek before reaching the Teanaway Road.

67 DE ROUX

Spring waits here until mid-July some years. Roads often plugged with snow until then.

From Seattle, drive east over Snoqualmie Pass, turning off I-90 at the Wenatchee Interchange east of Cle Elum. Continue east on Highway 97, turning left (north) in about 6 miles onto the Teanaway River Road. DeRoux Campground in about 20 miles.

ESMERALDA BASIN

Start with a rock-shredded waterfall and then hike onto flower meadows that offer fresh bouquets for each new week of summer. And one weekly display—truly—is no better than the other.

Don't forget your flower book—or camera. And look up at the ridges occasionally for

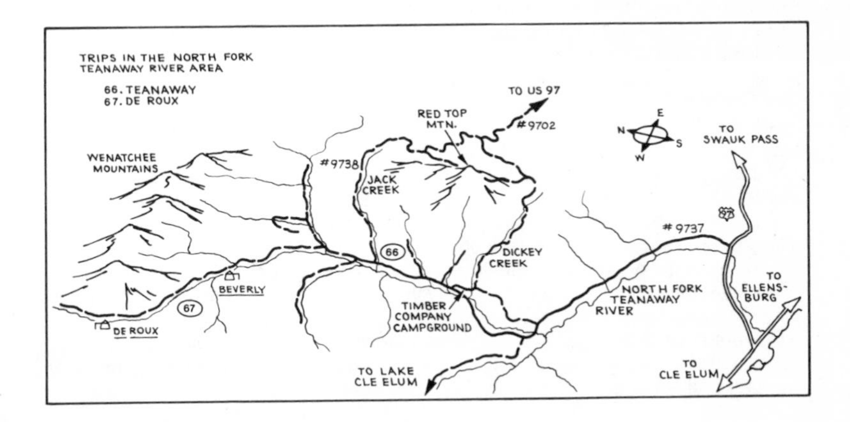

Fireweed

goats and—in the spring—for more waterfalls.

Drive to the end of the North Fork Teanaway Road No. 9737, about 22 miles from the junction with Highway 97. Parking spots and picnic tables below the falls at the road end.

The trail starts to the right of a series of falls (each short side trip to the river's edge brings a different view). And then makes its way sharply upstream to a junction with the Lake Ingalls trail in a long .5 mile.

Bear ahead now on an ancient mining road to a unmarked point in about .25 mile, where the main trail turns sharply to the right and climbs to a higher level on the slope.

You can continue ahead here on a soggy, unkept and unmarked path along the old road through a series of meadow pockets crowded with wet-rooted flowers.

Or—and just as interesting—follow the well-kept trail uphill across drier slopes and different flowers. This one has its soggy patches too.

Or go in on the dry trail and then return on the old, sloppy trail.

The trail starts climbing out of the valley in less than 2 miles in an open area where miners—and sometimes hikers—camp. Look up at diggings on the slopes.

Flowers here grow in all sorts of environments. Some bloom wildly on bone-dry slopes. Others literally explode in soggy places. And you'll find all of them—one after the other and some even side-by-side—along this path.

BEVERLY CREEK TRAIL

Gnarled alpine larch, hundreds of years old, in an open subalpine basin on upper Beverly Creek. A 2-mile hike.

Turn right off the river road onto Spur Road No. 112 just south of the Beverly Campground. Find the trail at the end of a logging spur in less than 2 miles.

Trail climbs to timberline in about 1.5 miles. Some of stunted larch and Douglas fir, big at the base but much shorter than their lower-valley counterparts, may be as much as 600 years old. Trail continues over the crest of the Wenatchee mountain ridge into Ingalls Creek. The route, a cattle driveway to alpine pastures, is also used to reach Mount Stuart.

DE ROUX CREEK TRAIL

A pleasant walk through open timber along a busy stream to series of small waterfalls.

Watch for a spur road to the west just north of the DeRoux Campground. Follow the spur downhill, past several primitive camp spots, driving as far as you can.

Find the trail off fire-road around the bottom edge of the clear-cut. Trail fords the river and follows the north side of the creek.

A series of waterfalls in 1.5 miles. For views, climb a very steep trail of less than .5 mile to the ridge above the Middle Fork. Watch for spur-trail sign. Main trail continues about 3.5 miles to Gallagher Head Lake in meadows between Hawkins Mountain and Esmeralda Peaks.

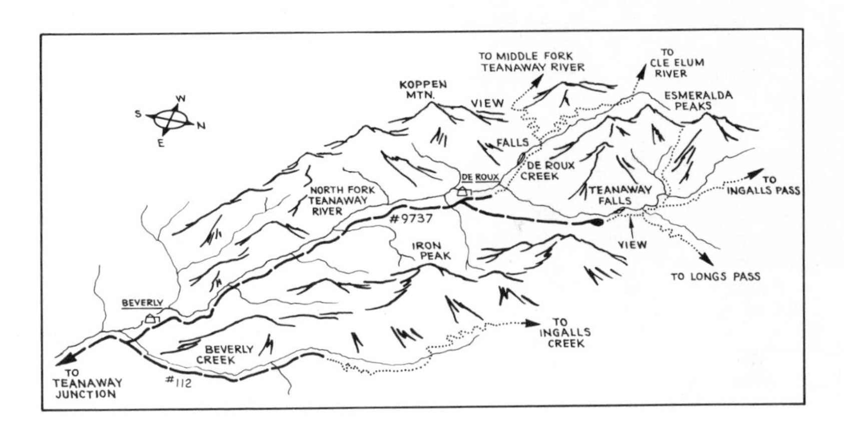

EE TANEUM (tay'num)

Ridge trails, high meadows, and lookout views from an area not as heavily used as most.

But there is no one simple way to reach this area. Residents of Cle Elum and Ellensburg take a half-dozen different routes on as many different roads.

For one route from Cle Elum, turn off I-90 from Seattle at the first Cle Elum exit. As you drop down into town, turn right on Fourth Street, crossing back under the freeway. At the edge of town, turn right at a T-intersection and follow Road No. 3350 as it winds first west and then uphill to the top of the ridge and the complex of roads there. Not for trailers.

Or, continue past Cle Elum on I-90 toward Ellensburg turning off at Thorp Interchange 93 bearing right and then sharply right again on a county road that heads back northwesterly, parallel with the freeway, before heading westward up Taneum Canyon to Taneum Campground on Road No. 33.

CAMPGROUNDS

Taneum—12 campsites, 16 picnic units in open timber area on Taneum Creek, 11 miles from I-90. Leave Thorp on Road No. 33. Some sites oriented to the river. Pit toilets. Piped water. Federal fee.

Tamarack Spring—3 sites in a corral near a boxed spring. Pit toilet. On Road No. 3120.

Quartz Spring—3 sites in wooded area just below Quartz Mountain. Pit toilets. Water. At end of Road No. 3100.

Buck Meadow—Primitive site near creek. Pit toilets.

Undeveloped camping spots available along most roads in the Gnat Flat–to–Quartz Mountain area.

68 TANEUM CREEK

"A WHITE WOMAN'S GRAVE"

A grave heaped with rock and surrounded by a wooden fence marks a tragedy of the pioneer past.

Find the grave about 75 yards from the road east of the Tamarack Spring Campground, just across the cattleguard. On Road No. 3120.

A woman who died in childbirth in the mid-1880s, while traveling with her family through the mountains by wagon train, was buried here. A marking states simply that it is "A White Woman's Grave."

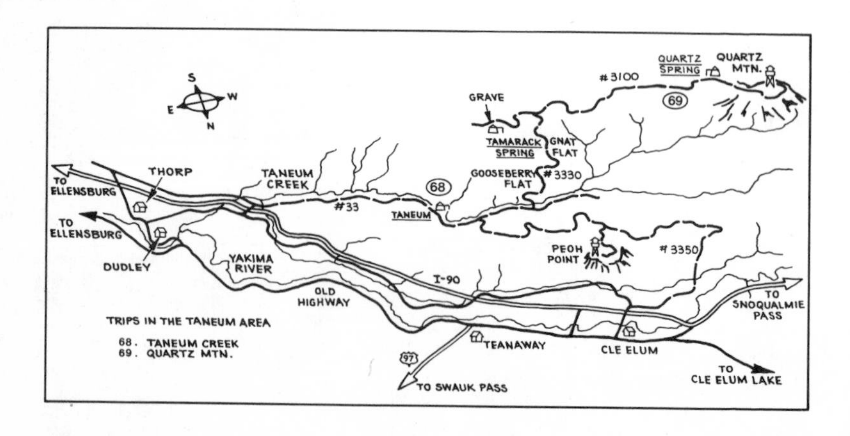

GNAT AND GOOSEBERRY FLATS

In early July, meadows of hyacinths, wild onion, and larkspur beneath glimpses of Rainier, Adams, and Stuart.

From Taneum Campground, drive west on Road No. 33, turning south in about 2.5 miles on Road No. 3330. Views and meadows mix as the road climbs first through Gooseberry and then Gnat Flats.

Continue to Quartz Mountain on Roads No. 3120 and 3100.

PEOH POINT

Airplane views of Cle Elum from a lookout 2,000 feet above the city and only 2 air-miles away.

Either drive south from Cle Elum on Road No. 3350 (see above) or west from Taneum Campground on Roads No. 33 and 119 to 3350. Atop the ridge, proceed north on a very narrow and rough road to the lookout. Or—better yet—turn eastward on 3350, taking a better developed Logging Road No. 114 to the north in a little more than .5 mile at a 4-way intersection.

Excellent views not only of Cle Elum but of the Yakima River valley, Lake Cle Elum, and the Cle Elum River drainage. To drive to Cle Elum, take Road No. 3350 downhill, following signs.

"A white woman's grave" on Taneum River Road

Dutch Miller Peaks from Quartz Mountain

69 QUARTZ MOUNTAIN

Drive through high meadows to ridge trails and awesome mountain views.

From Taneum Campground (see above), continue west on Road No. 33, turning south on No. 3330 in about 2.5 miles. Follow signs to the former lookout site at the end of Road No. 3100. Total distance 18 miles.

QUARTZ MOUNTAIN VIEWPOINT

Peaks spread from Mount Adams to Glacier during the day. At sunset, watch elk on lower meadows and at night, stars so thick you can't believe it.

If snow blocks the steep road to the bench where the tower used to be, park in a meadow and hike up.

From edge of the bench see Rainier, Stuart, and the Cascades, in addition to Adams and Glacier. A small, open meadow just north of the tower site provides an ideal spot for star- and elk-watching.

PEACHES RIDGE

A very nice name for a very nice place.

Watch for a trail off the last sharp turn on the road to Quartz Mountain lookout site. Drop down the Manastash Ridge trail to Peaches Ridge trail junction in about .5 mile.

With Mount Rainier over your left shoulder, walk out high meadows with views down the Yakima River valley and glimpses of the red barns near Ellensburg. Walk a mile or more. Trail drops into heavier timber the farther it goes.

TANEUM LAKE

A level trail leads to a small, pretty mountain lake nestled in timber. Three-quarters of a mile.

Watch for trail sign and small parking spot on north side of the road about 3 miles east of Quartz Mountain Lookout.

A primitive camping spot near the trail at the lake. Trails also loop the lake. Watch for blue anemone and clematis. No trail bikes or horses.

FROST MOUNTAIN

Hike 1.5 miles through timbered hills for views of Rainier, Cle Elum Lake, and the Stuart Range with deer and elk added in the evening and morning.

Find lookout sign on the north side of Road No. 3100 about 1.5 miles west of the junction with No. 3120.

Follow a steep path to the first bench above the road, then a trail that alternately crosses flat meadows and climbs steep slopes to the lookout at 5,740 feet. Tower is manned during the fire season.

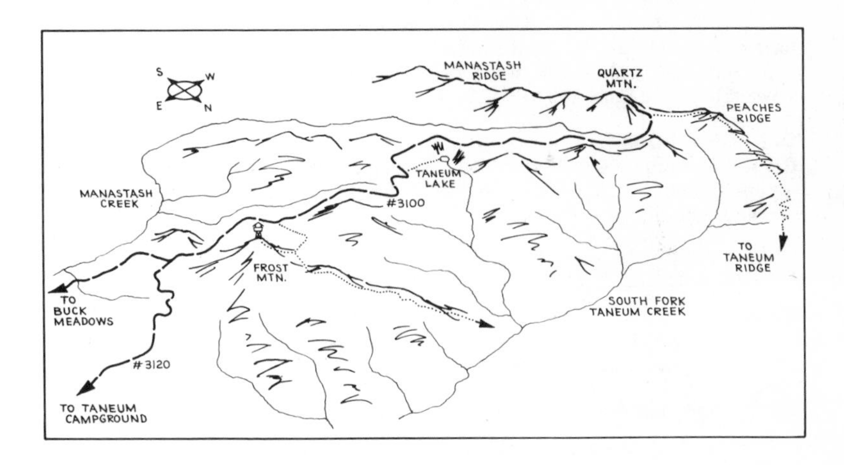

FF STAMPEDE PASS

A thousand acres of huckleberries and mile-squares of logged-off private land, criss-crossed by powerlines and construction roads, topped with a weather station.

Take the Kachess Lake–Stampede Pass turnoff on I-90 (Exit No. 62) about 2 miles beyond the end of Keechelus Lake. Turn right on Road No. 54. In 5 miles, turn left at Lizard Lake on Road No. 2190A, following the yellow targets to the weather station complex.

West end of the Green River Road is blocked by City of Tacoma watershed gates.

The **weather station,** the only one in the state atop the Cascade crest, keeps tabs 24 hours a day on shifting mountain weather, supplying information to other weather stations and passing airplanes.

The station's crew, snowbound in winter, welcomes visitors anytime. Equipment, which those on duty are glad to explain, ranges from a special scale for weighing the amount of moisture in wood—part of a procedure for rating forest fire danger—to exotic electronic gear for receiving and transmitting information on winds, temperatures, pressures, humidity, etc.

From a former lookout site nearby, find views of Lake Kachess, Mount Rainier, Mount Daniel, and the Yakima River and Cedar River valleys.

The concrete pads below the lookout site were once used as missile-test launching pads by Boeing.

PACIFIC CREST TRAIL

Hike north or south along the Pacific Crest rail for continuing new views of both the eastern and western slopes of the Cascades.

Find trail to the north near Lizard Lake at Stampede Pass (see above). Trail winds toward Dandy Pass in less than 2 miles.

To hike south, pick up trail at the weather station, hiking out ridges for continuing views. Snowshoe Butte in 5 miles.

CAMPGROUNDS

Crystal Springs—20 units stretched out along the Yakima River. Turn right at Stampede Pass turnoff. Most near the river. Timbered area closer to I-90 than it seems. Some highway noise. Pit toilets.

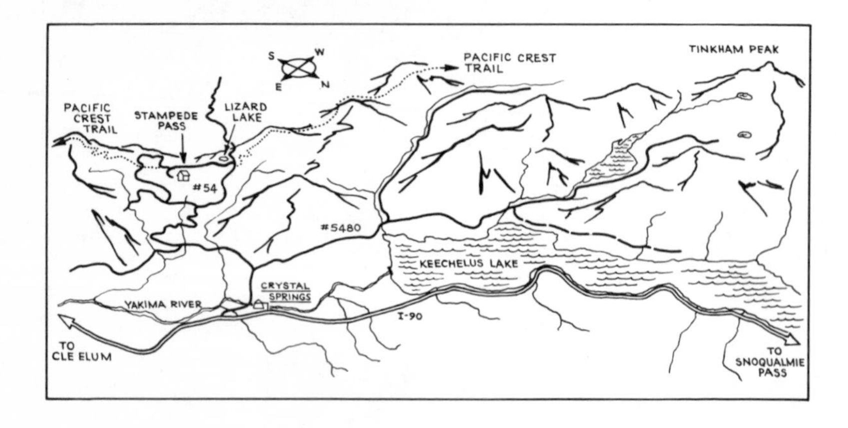

Weather station at Stampede Pass

GG KACHESS AND CLE ELUM LAKES

The two lakes are among the most heavily used recreation areas east of the Cascades. Both are within the Cle Elum Ranger District of Wenatchee National Forest. District headquarters are in Cle Elum.

To reach the lakes drive east from Seattle on I-90 over Snoqualmie Pass. Turn off to Kachess Lake at the Kachess Lake–Stampede Pass signs. To reach Cle Elum Lake, leave the freeway at Cle Elum or at the Salmon la Sac overpass 3 miles west of Cle Elum and follow signs through the mining towns of Roslyn and Ronald.

CAMPGROUNDS

Kachess—180 units, including 26 trailer-only sites. Located in a timbered peninsula between Kachess and Little Kachess Lakes. Some sites near the lakes, others on Gale Creek. Restrooms. Piped water. Swimming. Boat launching.

Wishpoosh—39 sites on Cle Elum Lake 10 miles north of Cle Elum. Boat-launch, picnic facility. Family sites. Toilets. Water.

Boating on Little Kachess Lake

Cle Elum River—17 tables in open timber near the Cle Elum River 15 miles from Cle Elum. Pit toilets.
Red Mountain—13 sites along the river. Pit toilets. Entrance road not recommended for trailers.
Owhi Camp—20 walk-in tent sites on Cooper Lake. All oriented to the lake. No motors on lake. Pit toilets.
Salmon la Sac—110 sites at the juncture of the Cle Elum and Cooper rivers. Most sites oriented to one of the rivers. A heavy-use area. Flush toilets. Piped water.
Fish Lake—10 sites near the Fish Lake Guard Station. Not recommended for trailers. Pit toilets.
Tucquala Meadows—9 sites along the river at the end of the road. Pit toilets.
Others—Undeveloped camping areas can be found all along the Cle Elum River from the lake to the end of the road at the trailhead to Hyas Lake. Tables have been placed in some areas. Most, however, consist simply of an open spot on a river bank.

70 KACHESS LAKE

Drive east from Seattle over Snoqualmie Pass on I-90. Turn off at the Stampede Pass–Kachess Lake sign and follow signs 5 miles to the Kachess Campground.

WATERFALLS AND BOX RIDGE VIEWS

Just 5 miles to views of the Cascades and out over Kachess Lake, with waterfalls along the way. Lots of color in the fall.

Take Road No. 4930 up Box Canyon Creek at the campground entrance junction.

Waterfalls to the right in Box Canyon Creek in the first mile. Watch for flashes of white water through the trees. Stop and explore on your own.

Views of Mount Margaret (5,500) over Box Canyon Creek, then over the lake before the road loops west again for views of Alta Mountain (6,144) and other Cascade peaks from about 3,900 feet.

LITTLE KACHESS TRAIL

An easy wooded walk above Little Kachess Lake, with a view of a small island in 2 miles.

Find trail at the upper end of Kachess Campground. If you camp, follow unmarked trails through camp and along the lakeshore to the trailhead. The trail continues to the end of the lake in about 5 miles, forking left up Mineral Creek less than a mile beyond the lake toward Cooper Pass.

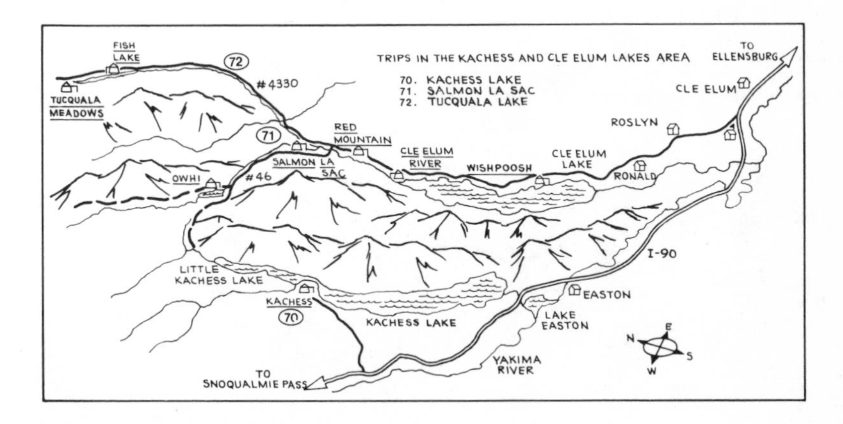

BIG TREE NATURE TRAIL

A .5-mile loop through an old-growth stand of Douglas fir, some measuring 7.5 feet in diameter. Fifteen signs describe the succession of plants in a forest and the interrelationship of plants, animals, insects, and humans in the evolution of forest life.

Trail begins at campground entrance. Watch for sign.

MUSHROOMS AND COLOR

Find both mushrooms and the brilliant reds of Douglas maple along Gale Creek Road No. 4948.

Turn left off Road No. 4930 (road to Box Ridge) in less than a mile from the "T" junction west of the campground.

Color in clear-cuts. Most mushrooms in old-growth timber. Search out your own.

At the road end, hike left up an old bulldozer trace to Swan Lake (below the track) and Rock Rabbit Lakes (at the end). Both in less than .5 mile. Both are fishing lakes, but still interesting spots to explore.

71 SALMON LA SAC

Drive east from Seattle over Snoqualmie Pass on I-90. Turn off at Salmon la Sac Interchange No. 80 or at Cle Elum. In Cle Elum follow signs to Roslyn and Ronald, old coal mining towns, and then on to Salmon la Sac, 19 miles from Cle Elum.

Salmon la Sac was named by Frenchmen who saw Indians netting salmon in rapids below the bridge in cedar bark (sack) baskets. Dams have long since ended the salmon runs.

COOPER PASS

An easy road to high views out of Salmon la Sac.

Turn west onto Road No. 46 off the Cle Elum River Road about a mile south of the Salmon la Sac Guard Station. Follow Road No. 4600 south of Cooper Lake to a pass with vistas over Kachess Lake and out to peaks of the Cascade crest.

(The road continues over the pass almost down to Kachess Lake. Conservationists hope it will never go any farther, but....)

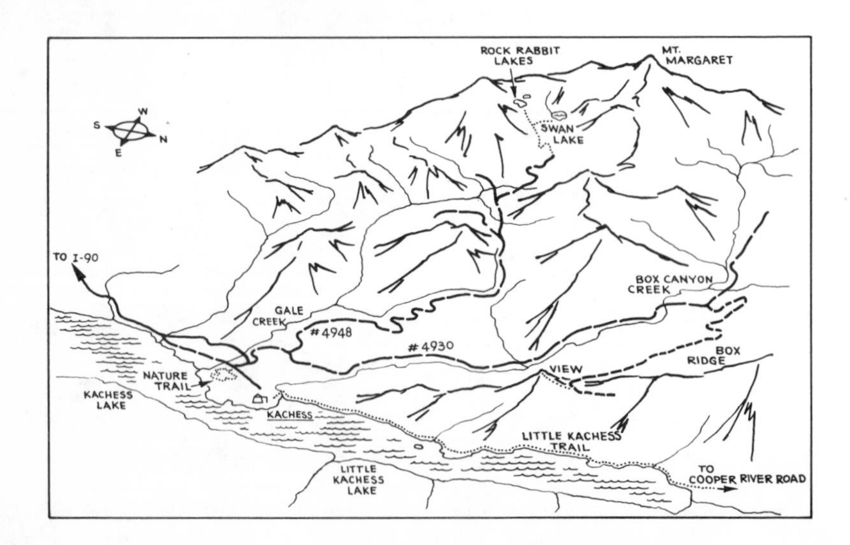

Dutch Miller Peaks from Cooper River Road

COOPER LAKE

A prime recreation area that's still in a state of flux. Recreationists feel strongly that it ought to be kept as the wild place it really is. But developers, loggers, and others have other ideas.

From Road No. 46 (see above) turn right onto road to Cooper Lake. Find Owhi Campground across the bridge to the left. A walk-in camp. No motors permitted on the lake.

PETE LAKE TRAIL

Snow-patched ridges circle a rock-filled lake that hints of all of the beauties to be found at lakes still farther on.

At the campground junction (see above), continue straight ahead uphill on Road No. 4616 to the end of the road. Trail leaves the road-end, crosses a clear-cut, and then drops downhill into lovely forest to join the old Cooper Lake–Pete Lake trail. Follow the old trail uphill to the lake. An easy and pleasant walk, 2.5 miles.

Viewpoints at the lake near the outlet and from rocky ridges above the trail on the way

Cooper Lake

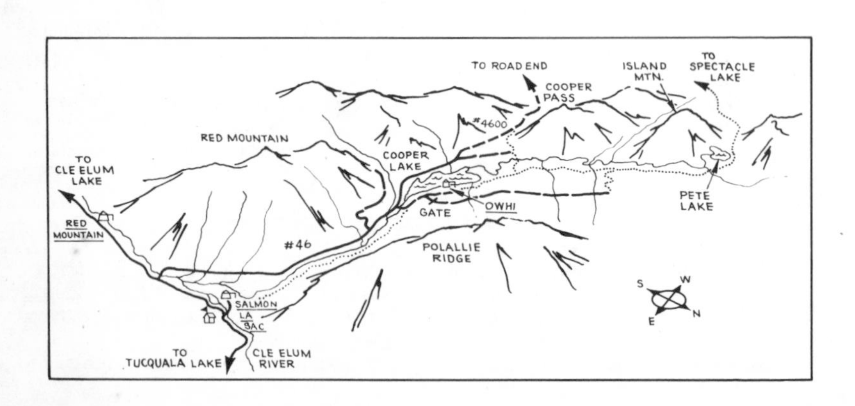
TO ROAD END
COOPER PASS
ISLAND MTN.
TO SPECTACLE LAKE
#4600
RED MOUNTAIN
COOPER LAKE
TO CLE ELUM LAKE
PETE LAKE
GATE
OWHI
RED MOUNTAIN
#46
POLALLIE RIDGE
SALMON LA SAC
TO TUCQUALA LAKE
CLE ELUM RIVER
S
W
E
N

to a shelter. Lots of picnic and camping spots. Paths continue on to Spectacle and Escondido Lakes.

If Road No. 4616 is gated, it's 4 miles to Pete Lake up the Cooper Lake trail. This road poses all the classic questions about the use of public money for logging roads. If you paid for the road, should it be left open for your use? Or did you want to subsidize its use for logging only? Or should it be "put to bed"—scarified and seeded—as federal law provides?

THORP MOUNTAIN

Follow a trail up across a lush meadow (if you can get there before the sheep do) to a vista-strewn ridge and on to a lookout with more views still.

Turn east off the Cle Elum River Road onto French Cabin Creek Road No. 4308 just beyond Cle Elum Lake. In 4.8 miles turn right onto Spur No. 120. Trailhead, uphill on the right, in 2 miles.

The trail tops the ridge in a shady saddle in about 1.25 miles and joins the Kachess trail that climbs from near Easton to Cooper Pass.

Before you turn right and head for the lookout, take time to walk to the top of the rock outcrop to the north for a quick "whoops!" straight down onto Thorp Lake (not for uncontrolled children) and across at the lookout—another 1.5 miles by trail but only a crow's caw by air.

COOPER RIVER TRAIL

Walk 4 miles, generally downhill, along the Cooper River from Cooper Lake to the Salmon la Sac Campground.

Find the trail on the north side of the river off the road to the Owhi Campground on Cooper Lake. A good walk home after a visit to the lake or the pass.

72 TUCQUALA LAKE

Some still call this area "Fish Lake." But the beautiful place deserves its Indian name of Tucquala.

From Seattle, drive over Snoqualmie Pass on I-90, turning off either at Salmon la Sac Interchange or at Cle Elum. From Cle Elum follow signs to Roslyn and past Salmon la Sac, about 29 miles to meadows at 3,400 feet.

HYAS LAKE

An extremely popular 1.5-mile walk for two very simple reasons: it's easy and it's scenic.

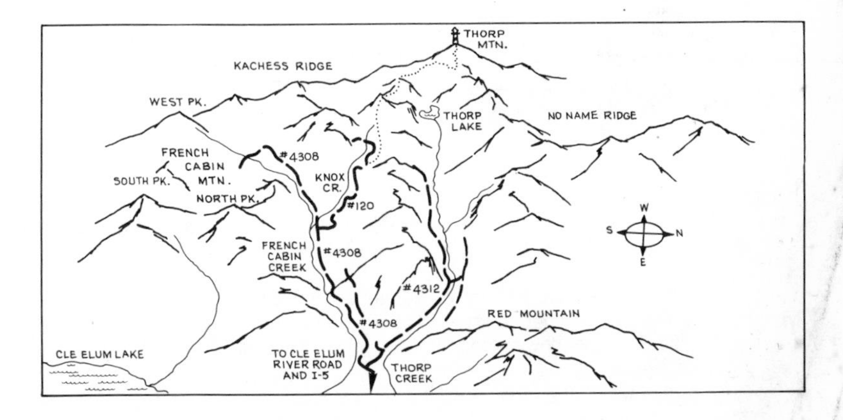

Tacquala (Fish) Lake

Drive to the end of the Cle Elum River Road No. 4330, about 2 miles beyond the Fish Lake Guard Station. Parking area and campground at the end of the road.

Trail wanders through timber and along the edge of an occasional meadow to a pretty lake nested below Cathedral Rock and Mount Daniel. Camp spots in timber just before the trail reaches the lake. Other campsites along the lake and at the upper end.

Best views from open slopes at the upper end of the lake. Trail continues on to Deception Pass, a steady climb of another 2 miles from the upper end of the lake.

TUCQUALA LAKE

A long string of water, bordered by flower meadows, that flows like a river in spots.

Drive 10.1 miles beyond the Salmon la Sac Guard Station. Formal camping spots at the southern end of the lake.

A beautiful place to explore by canoe. Paddle from the lower end of the lake up the deep riverlike channel to wider shallows in about 2 miles. Or explore the flat, marshy lower end of the lake. Meadows along the east side of the lake bloom full of shooting stars in the spring.

Uplake views of Cathedral Rock.

SQUAW LAKE TRAIL

Big peaks and bigger lakes overawe this alpine gem. But a walk of slightly more than 2 miles leads from a beautiful valley to an equally beautiful lake surrounded by its own worthwhile peaks.

Drive almost to the end of the Cle Elum River Road No. 4330, finding the trailhead off the west side of the road beyond Tucquala (Fish) Lake. A spur road leads to the river.

The trail climbs some 1,500 feet through trees in long switchbacks to the top of the ridge and then right (north) along the side of the ridge—with valley views—to a wooded, subalpine lake tucked into the base of a rocky cliff.

The trail continues north to the Crest trail below Cathedral Rock in another 2 miles.

PADDY-GO-EASY PASS

You can almost hear the old miner belaboring his mule to "go easy" up this persistent trail over the crest of the Wenatchee Mountains. From 3,400 to 6,100 feet in 3 miles (it just seems like 10).

Find the trail off a short parking spur about a mile beyond the small Forest Service cabin on Tucquala Lake.

It's nice to reach the top—views here from both sides of the ridge at 6,100 feet. But a struggle only part way will yield vistas worth the effort.

If you get to the top, hike a little farther—find a spur trail to the right—to small Sprite Lake, set like a diamond amid the rocks.

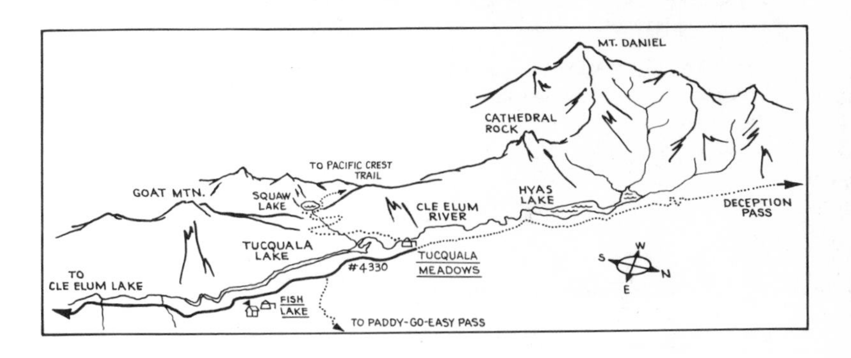

OBTAINING INFORMATION AND MAPS

Information on the condition of roads and trails can be obtained at the following headquarter and district offices of the U.S. Forest Service and National Park Service.

Maps can be obtained at ranger stations or by writing headquarter offices.

WENATCHEE NATIONAL FOREST

Headquarters, P.O. Box 811, Wenatchee, Wash. 98801.
Lake Wenatchee Ranger Station, Star Route, Leavenworth, Wash. 98826.
Leavenworth Ranger Station, Leavenworth, Wash. 98826.
Entiat Ranger Station, Entiat, Wash. 98822.
Chelan Ranger Station, Chelan, Wash. 98816.

OKANOGAN NATIONAL FOREST

Headquarters, Box 950, Okanogan, Wash. 98840.

MOUNT BAKER—SNOQUALMIE NATIONAL FOREST

Headquarters, 1601 2nd Ave., Seattle, Wash. 98101.
Baker River Ranger Station, Concrete, Wash. 98237.
Darrington Ranger Station, Darrington, Wash. 98241.
Skykomish Ranger Station, Skykomish, Wash. 98288.
North Bend Ranger Station, North Bend, Wash. 98045.

NORTH CASCADES NATIONAL PARK

Headquarters, 311 State Street, Sedro Woolley, Wash. 98284.

READING SUGGESTIONS

Readers may find the following books helpful in gaining a fuller understanding of the outdoors.

Trees, Flowers

Trees, Shrubs and Flowers to Know in Washington, C.P. Lyon, J.M. Dent and Sons, Ltd. Vancouver, B.C., Canada; 1956.

101 Wildflowers of Olympic National Park, Grant and Wenonah Sharpe. University of Washington Press. Seattle; 1957.

Vascular Plants of the Pacific Northwest, Hitchcock, Cronquist, Owenby and Thompson. 5 vols. University of Washington Press. Seattle; 1959.

Northwest Trees, Stephen F. Arno and Ramona P. Hammerly. The Mountaineers. Seattle; 1977.

Plants and Animals of the Pacific Northwest, Eugene N. Kozloff. University of Washington Press. Seattle; 1976.

Wild Plants of the San Juan Islands, Scott Atkinson and Fred Sharpe. The Mountaineers. Seattle; 1985.

Seashore

The Edge of the Sea, Rachel Carson. Houghton Mifflin and Co. Boston; 1955.

The Olympic Seashore, Ruth Kirk. Olympic Natural History Association. Port Angeles, Wash.; 1962.

Between Pacific Tides, Edward Rickets and Jack Calvin. Stanford University Press. Palo Alto, Calif.; 1948.

Animals of the Seashore, Muriel Guberlet. Binfords and Mort. Portland, Ore.; 1936.

Seaweeds at Ebbtide, Muriel Guberlet. University of Washington Press. Seattle; 1956.

Common Seaweeds of the Pacific Coast, J. Robert Waaland. Pacific Search Press. Seattle; 1977.

Living Shores of the Pacific Northwest, Lynwood Smith and Bernard Nist. Pacific Search Press. Seattle; 1976.

Nature Guides

A Field Guide to the Cascades and Olympics, Stephen R. Whitney. The Mountaineers. Seattle, 1983.

A Field Guide to Western Birds, Roger Tory Peterson. Houghton Mifflin Company. Boston.

A Field Guide to the Mammals, William H. Burt and Richard P. Grossenheider. Houghton Mifflin Company. Boston.

A Field Guide to Animal Tracks, Olaus J. Murie. Houghton Mifflin Company. Boston.

A Field Guide to the Ferns, Boughton Cobb. Houghton Mifflin Company. Boston.

A Field Book of Nature Activities and Conservation, William Hillcourt. Putnam and Sons. New York; 1961.

Insects, Ross E. Hutchins. Prentice-Hall, Inc. Englewood Cliffs, N.J.; 1966.

Butterflies Afield in the Pacific Northwest, William Neill and Douglas Hepburn. Pacific Search Press. Seattle; 1976.

Little Mammals of the Pacific Northwest, Ellen Kritzman. Pacific Search Press. Seattle; 1976.

The Audubon Society Field Guide to North American Birds: Western Region Guide, M.F.D. Udvardy. Alfred A. Knopf; 1977.

Geology

Scenic Geology of the Pacific Northwest, Leonard C. Ekman. Binfords and Mort. Portland, Ore.; 1962.

Principles of Geology, James Gilluly, A.C. Waters and A.O. Woodford. W.H. Freeman and Co., San Francisco; 1951.
Mountain Flowers, Harvey Manning. The Mountaineers. Seattle; 1979.
Origin of Cascade Landscapes, J. Hoover Mackin and Allen S. Cares. Div. Mines and Geology Ind. Circ. No. 41, Washington State Department of Conservation; 1965.
Routes and Rocks, Hiker's Guide to the North Cascades from Glacier Peak to Lake Chelan, D.F. Crowder and R.W. Tabor. The Mountaineers. Seattle; 1965. (Out of print)
Elements of Geology, James H. Zumberge. John Wiley and Sons, Inc. New York; 1959.
Fire and Ice, Stephen L. Harris. The Mountaineers and Pacific Search Press. Seattle; 1976.
Cascadia: The Geologic Evolution of the Pacific Northwest, Bates Mckee. McGraw-Hill Book Company; 1972.

Mushrooms

The Savory Wild Mushroom, Margaret McKenny. University of Washington Press. Seattle; 1962.
Mushroom Hunter's Field Guide, Alexander H. Smith. University of Michigan Press. Ann Arbor, Mich.; 1958.

Wilderness Travel

Mountaineering, The Freedom of the Hills, 4th ed. Ed Peters, ed. The Mountaineers. Seattle; 1982.
Going Light with Backpack or Burro, David Brower, ed. The Sierra Club. San Francisco; 1958.
Backpacking: One Step at a Time, Harvey Manning. Vintage Books. New York; 1984.

Conservation

Wild Cascades: Forgotten Parkland, Harvey Manning. The Sierra Club. San Francisco; 1965.
My Wilderness: The Pacific West, William O. Douglas. Doubleday and Company, Inc. Garden City, N.Y.; 1960.
A Sand County Almanac, Aldo Leopold. Oxford University Press. New York; 1949.
Steep Trails, John Muir. Houghton Mifflin Company. New York; 1918.

Guides

Cascade Alpine Guide: Climbing and High Routes; Columbia River to Stevens Pass (1973), *Stevens Pass to Rainy Pass* (1977), Fred Beckey. The Mountaineers. Seattle.
The Alpine Lakes, Ed Cooper, Bob Gunning and Brock Evans. The Mountaineers. Seattle; 1971. (Out of print)
100 Hikes in the North Cascades, Ira Spring and Harvey Manning. The Mountaineers. Seattle; 1985.
100 Hikes in the Alpine Lakes, Vicky Spring, Ira Spring, and Harvey Manning. The Mountaineers. Seattle; 1985.
San Juan Islands Afoot and Afloat, Marge Mueller. The Mountaineers. Seattle; 1979.

INDEX